THE POLITICS OF STREET CRIME

STREET CRIME

Criminal Process and
Cultural Obsession

THE POLITICS OF STREET CRIME

Criminal Process and Cultural Obsession

STUART A. SCHEINGOLD

Temple University Press

PHILADELPHIA

Temple University Press, Philadelphia 19122
Copyright © 1991 by Stuart A. Scheingold. All rights reserved
Published 1991
Printed in the United States of America

The paper used in this publication meets the minimum requirements
of American National Standard for Information Sciences—Permanence
of Paper for Printed Library Materials, ANSI Z39.48-1984

Library of Congress Cataloging-in-Publication Data
Scheingold, Stuart A.
The politics of street crime : criminal process and cultural obsession /
Stuart A. Scheingold.
    p. cm.
    Includes bibliographical references and index.
    ISBN 0-87722-825-6
    1. Criminal justice, Administration of—United States. 2. Crime—
United States. 3. Criminal justice, Administration of—United States—
Case studies. 4. Crime—United States—Case studies.
I. Title.
HV9950.S34   1991
364.973—dc20   90-48153

For Heinz Pol and Victor Bernstein
who
each in his own uniquely disputatious way
nurtured the concerns
that lie beneath the surface of this book

Contents

Contents

Tables and Figures

Preface

Americans are obsessed with street crime. Our politicians continually campaign against street crime, but if they were somehow successful in ridding our streets of crime, it would continue to flourish in our imaginations. We profess a fear and abhorence of street crime and street criminals, but we seek them out, albeit vicariously, in virtually all forms of popular culture. Street crime is big business in television, film, books, and the theater—not to speak of its contribution to journalism.

How is this obsession to be explained? And what difference does it make to politics and policy that Americans are hooked on street crime? My answer to the first question is that our obsession is only partially due to the extraordinarily high levels of street crime that have plagued this country for more than a quarter of a century. At least as important are a variety of anxieties that are themselves culturally constructed—meaning, therefore, that our obsession with crime has a life of its own. The consequences of this obsession are corrupting. It poisons and trivializes our politics, particularly our national politics, and focuses policy on scapegoats rather than on solutions—once again more destructively at the national level.

My own fascination with these matters, which is what this book is all about, goes back a long way. Having addressed them in one book, *The Politics of Law and Order,* I was struck by how little directly relevant primary research was available. The result was a book rooted primarily in indirect and circumstantial evidence. Accordingly, I sought and received support from the Law and Social Science Program of the National Science Foundation to generate directly relevant data. In effect, I ended up treating the findings of *The Politics of Law and Order* as hypotheses for the research presented in this book.

What struck me initially as a terrific idea had a decidedly seamy side. If my hypotheses were borne out by the new data, then there would be little reason to publish another book. Conversely, if the new findings cast substantial doubt on my hypotheses, *The Politics of Law and Order* would be discredited. While this no-win scenario presents the alternative outcomes too starkly, it is suggestive of a more fundamental problem that subliminally delayed progress on this manuscript. The idea of refining and reevaluating ideas and problems that I had already worked through was not a particularly inviting challenge.

At this point, I was trebly blessed—although the first of these blessings was very well disguised. The reviews of *The Politics of Law and Order* were generally favorable, but Alan Hunt took me sharply to task for writing a book that was myopically American. At first, I was genuinely puzzled by this review, since my explicit focus was on the United States. But Hunt was not suggesting that I should have done a comparative study but rather that I take account of research and researchers who were working on analogous problems, especially in the United Kingdom. Just as I began to sense what he had in mind, my colleague Lance Bennett directed my attention to a wonderfully insightful and evocative book on the politics of law and order in the United Kingdom, *Policing the Crime* by Stuart Hall, Chas Critcher, Tony Jefferson, John Clarke, and Brian Roberts. This book suggested ways of rethinking my enterprise so as to link the politics of law and order to the cultural values and material conditions of contemporary American life. And then in 1986 and 1987, I spent six months sabbatical leave in London, working primarily on another project. With David Nelken as my tutor, I was put directly in touch with the exciting work of the British school of criminology. Thus, while in one sense my sabbatical clearly delayed this book, the chances are that there would have been no book at all without this interlude. Certainly, it would have been a different and considerably narrower study.

As to the book itself, I do not claim to have fully or conclusively illuminated the political significance of America's obsession with street crime. I do, however, hope that I have made a strong case for taking this issue seriously. It has until now gotten relatively little systematic attention—probably because it lies in something of a scholar's limbo. While of residual concern to criminologists, sociologists, and political scientists, the cultural meaning of street crime and the interplay among culture, politics, and social conditions are not of central concern to any of these disciplines.

Perhaps it is another kind of myopia that leads me to believe that we cannot understand American criminal justice policy or the politics in which it is embroiled without understanding more about the nature and extent of our obsession with street crime. I do, however, hope that this book establishes that there is such an obsession, that it is a meaningful force influencing politics and policy, and that its influence depends less on the incidence of street crime than on the broader conditions of American life.

At best this book can be only a beginning. It is, after all, essentially a single case study that covers a little more than fifteen years in a single pseudonymous community, "Cedar City," the urban center of "Park County." I apologize to the reader for concealing the identity of my research site. My suspicion is that none of my respondents would have cared one way or the other, but that was not the case with the Human Subjects Review Committee at the University of Washington. To get my research under way, I was prepared to promise them almost anything. The result was a written agreement with each of my respondents to keep both their identities and that of the research site secret.

I close this book with some rather bold and sweeping generalizations, which are offered as no more than plausible extrapolations. There may well be other ways of interpreting my findings, and additional research will probably yield findings that directly call into question what I have to say. If this book leads to such research, I will consider it a resounding success.

Given the length of time that I have been working on this project, a full acknowledgment of all my debts would read like the telephone directory of a sizable city. Even the abbreviated accounting that I provide may tend to obscure how important each of those persons listed has been to the enterprise. Of course, there would have been no enterprise without the support of the Law and Social Science Program of the National Science

Foundation (grant no. SES8208832). Additional financial support at a crucial point was provided by the Graduate Research Fund at the University of Washington. Don McCrone, chair of the Political Science Department at the University of Washington, managed to find me a research assistant when I needed one desperately.

Lynne Gressett was associated with this project from the outset and was coauthor of earlier papers. She supervised the collection of quantitative data and was responsible for the statistical analysis of those data. At the end of the project, Bart Salisbury took over for her and was patient and resourceful as we worked through alternative forms of data analysis and presentation. Betsy Norton was immensely enterprising in gathering and organizing much of the library research. I am also indebted to Will Dean, John Gibson, and Anthony Zinicola for their research assistance.

Among my colleagues at the University of Washington, David Hodge helped me get an empirical purchase on the political geography of law and order populism; Peter May and Michael McCann were *always* there when I needed them—as I frequently did. Ezra Stotland and Hubert Locke shared their wisdom about the police in general and the research site in particular. Malcolm Feeley and Herb Jacob provided me with critiques of the entire manuscript. At various points along the way, I benefited from the help of Dan Lev, David Nelken, Milt Heumann, Wes Skogan, Terence Halliday, David Greenberg, and Marlie Wasserman. David Boerner played a singular role that only he and I can fully appreciate. Of course, my heaviest debt is to the judges, prosecutors, police officers, defense attorneys, and political leaders who provided patient and thoughtful access to the real world of criminal process.

At Temple University Press, Jane Cullen has been encouraging and responsive, and Mary Capouya has managed the production process in a thoughtful, efficient, and reassuring way.

Writing books does not seem to come more easily with experience. This one surely was a struggle. Through it all, Lee was my rock and my inspiration. Thank you, my love.

Seattle
1 July 1990

THE POLITICS OF STREET CRIME
STREET CRIME
Criminal Process and Cultural Obsession

1

Street Crime, Criminology, and the State

For almost three decades street crime has been a volatile, persistent, and intractable issue in American politics. Yet the significance of all this sound and fury remains unclear. At first glance, the problem seems to be primarily criminological. We have failed to keep street crime within acceptable limits despite what appear to be very favorable circumstances. In the struggle against street crime, there seems to be a veritable army of trained professionals backed by committed political leaders and an aroused public pitted against people who are for the most part marginalized Americans without much talent or training.

Upon closer examination, this first impression turns out to be profoundly misleading. To begin with, the institutions of criminal process are unable on their own to cope with street crime, which is rooted in problems beyond the reach of the police and the criminal courts. More to the point, the mystery of this Sisyphean struggle leads beyond criminology and criminal process to our cultural understandings of street crime and our political responses to it.

Put simply, the central thesis of this book is that the political will to tackle the problem of street crime is more apparent than real. For all of its attention to street crime, the political process tends to divert and to dilute rather than to mobilize purposeful political energy. This is not primarily a matter of manipulation and deception, although they do play a prominent role. More fundamentally, our responses follow a path of least resistance through a complex tangle of criminological uncertainty, social cleavage, cultural truths, and political prudence. All these issues will be explored here in Chapter 1, their net effect is to lead us to diagnose and treat the problem of street crime in the punitive terms associated with the cops and robbers images of popular fiction. Before considering these criminological and political matters, an introductory look at the research site is in order.

The Setting

At its empirical core, this is a case study of the politics, police, and criminal courts of "Cedar City," a medium-sized urban center in the western United States. Cedar City is the largest city in "Park County"—a metropolitan area with a population of slightly more than one million during the period from 1964 to 1980 covered by this inquiry. Cedar City prides itself on its "livability"—beautiful vistas, easy access to superb four-season recreational opportunities, and a good selection of urban amenities. Despite all of these attributes, Cedar City has had its share of urban problems that are directly relevant to criminal process.

Beginning in the mid-1960s, street crime in Cedar City became a salient political issue with a distinctly punitive edge to it, just as it did elsewhere in the United States. Another problem was the area's volatile economy, which was especially unstable during these years. Through most of the 1960s business boomed, but at the end of the decade a severe slump struck the city's dominant corporate employer. This slump continued into the mid-1970s and resulted in fiscal problems for the city, the county, and the state as well as a loss of population and skilled professionals. The corporation did not rebound until the late 1970s, and by then the national economic downturn had had a serious impact on the area's other major industry, forest products. Thus, for most of the period of this study Cedar City and Park County were suffering severe economic distress—with resultant pressures on public services and on the sense of civic well-being. At one point, billboards began to appear with the following message: "Will the last person to leave Cedar City please turn off the lights."

The traditionally placid politics of the region were disrupted by this economic volatility as well as by the social volatility that characterized urban America in the 1960s and early 1970s. During the prosperous years, the machine-style politics of the city, county, and state underwent significant reform, which began at the state level and filtered down to Park County and Cedar City. The most notable event was the exposure of a large-scale payoff system centered in the Cedar City Police Department but also implicating the Park County prosecutor, who files Cedar City felony cases in the county superior courts. The reform impulse was, however, broader than the payoff scandal and led to a significant turnover of elected officials at all levels of government as well as to a more open political style. By and large, these reformers were liberals—inclined to take a softer line on street crime.

Running counter to these liberal tendencies were the public-order anxieties that gripped Cedar City and many other American cities in the late 1960s and early 1970s. The large university, which provides identity to a major section of the city, was the center of protest activities that polarized the public, engaged the city police, and culminated in one of the federal government's celebrated conspiracy trials. The trial added fuel to the fires of protest, which were already burning brightly. In addition, the black community, while comprising just under 10 percent of the city's population and relatively prosperous, was politically mobilized on racial issues during this period. Street crime was a third factor in the public-order package and another symbol for expression of dissatisfaction with the "permissive" orientation of the liberal reformers.

While attempts to politicize street crime and public order were largely unsuccessful, a significant amount of political energy was generated. Indeed, a superficial survey of events could lead to the conclusion that street crime was effectively politicized in Cedar City. There is no doubt that the liberal reformers of the 1960s put under increasing pressure in the 1970s and that policy did move rightward during that period. On the other hand, liberal policies had considerable staying power within the agencies of criminal process.

In all these ways, Cedar City seems more typical than special. It is true that the tensions in Cedar City were rather moderate compared with the more stratified and strife-ridden cities of the East and the upper Midwest. It is, moreover, likely that these differences might explain variations in politicization from place to place. But on the basis of evidence and argument to be presented in Chapter 2, it seems reasonable to believe that urban centers in general are heavily influenced by the same moderating forces operative in Cedar City but generally missing from national politics, where cultural stereotypes and symbolic politics promote the politicization of street crime.

Conceptions of Crime

Generally speaking, there are two contrasting ways of thinking about street crime. Structural explanations focus on social disorganization with its roots in hierarchy, deprivation, coercion, and alienation. The alternative view associates street crime with individual pathologies—be they moral, emotional, or genetic. From a structural point of view, street crime is *determined* by the material conditions of the society, whereas those who think in terms of individual pathology see street crime as *volitional*—a matter of personal choice. There are a number of ways in which this dichotomy is false and misleading. Surely, a fair reading of criminological findings indicates that street crime is attributable to an interdependent web of social forces and individual characteristics.

Nonetheless, as I argue, dichotomous understandings tend to dominate political and even criminological discourse, and in the political arena there is a marked tendency to privilege volitional explanations of street crime. These two tendencies to simplify the complex reality of street crime can be explained by a combination of instrumental and expressive factors, which will be explored in this chapter.

Ostensibly the controversies among political leaders, criminal-process professionals, and criminologists and within the general public have to do with the causes of and the most effective responses to street crime. But even if the available criminological research were more convincing and less equivocal than it is, the public controversy would not be stilled, because the search for causes and effective policies is only part of the story. In the first place, and speaking in strictly *instrumental* terms, criminological validity may not be decisive. Empirical findings may lead in policy directions that are unwelcome because they are too costly, threaten vested interests, or are beyond the reach of existing institutions.

More fundamentally, there are *expressive* reasons for public controversy over street crime transcending its ostensible purposes of identifying causes and fashioning effective responses. Problem solving is not necessarily the primary objective of public policy. As Lance Bennett puts it, "Policies become means of affirming the larger images of the world on which they are based. In most policy areas it is more acceptable to suffer failure based on correct theories than it would be to achieve success at the price of sacrificing social values."[1] What is true of policy in general is likely to be particularly true of crime control policies. As its core, controversy over street crime comes down to competing visions of the good society and of human nature. Volitional criminology is anchored in Lockean and Hobbesian premises, while structural criminology can be traced to Rousseau and Marx—thus suggesting why volitional criminology tends to be privileged in American political discourse. Moreover, in an imperfect world from which crime cannot be purged, we must necessarily settle for the solace of "failure based on correct theories"—or, as Murray Edelman has put it, on "words that succeed and policies that fail."[2] Accordingly, an understanding of the society's approach to street crime is at least as much a reflection of its political culture and its institutional capabilities as of the current state of criminological knowledge.

The focus of this book is, therefore, on political culture and on the institutions of criminal process rather than on street crime's causes, consequences, or cures. By and large, the institutional issues are fairly straightforward, requiring relatively little in the way of introductory explanation. The institutional emphasis will be on the relative autonomy of the criminal process and on the insulation from politics thereby accorded to the policies pursued by the police and the criminal courts. Political culture is a more elusive idea, both in its own right and in terms of its applicability and relevance to criminal process. This chapter, then, will be devoted to developing a frame of reference for exploring the political culture of criminal process.

At the heart of this frame of reference are the competing conceptions of street crime—as rooted in social and individual pathologies, respectively. As I have already suggested, Americans are, generally speaking, much more willing to attribute street crime to individual pathology than to structural problems.

Indeed, this tendency is so marked, and so resistant to counterargument, that its critics sometimes characterize it as "false consciousness" generated by a conspiracy between political elites and the media.[3] Certainly, it is often in the interests of established elites to divert attention from structural problems by attributing street crime to individual pathology. It is similarly beyond doubt that the public tends to harbor an exaggerated view of the incidence and character of street crime—a view that reflects misleading media reporting and opportunistic political campaigning.[4] But this does not establish a conspiracy and, more important, it fails to convey either the ingrained aversion to structural explanations of street crime or the cultural and institutional staying power of volitional explanations.

The attractions of volitional explanations of street crime are rooted in a complex web of social values and material circumstances. Most generally, the preference for volitional explanations is integrally linked to an understandable concern with personal security and social order.[5] Insofar as crime is understood as a matter of individual pathology, our culture provides easy, reassuring, and morally satisfying responses—what I have referred to elsewhere as *the myth of crime and punishment*. According to this way of thinking, punishment is an effective remedy against crime and also expresses society's condemnation of predatory victimization.[6] Structural explanations refocus attention from individual criminals to the criminogenic features of the prevailing social order—ordinarily identified with extreme inequality.[7] Thus, we are all seen as responsible in some measure and expected to accept far-reaching, open-ended, and redistributive changes in the social order. In short, structural interpretations lead in more contingent directions and call upon more generous impulses rooted in distant and elusive ideals of social justice. All of this must be considered in more detail, but even if these premises are taken for the moment as givens, another question remains.

How are we to explain substantial variations in the political salience of street crime and in the expressive modes of politicization? Concern about crime tends to vary from time to time and place to place, and that concern is expressed in punitive, reformative, or transformative ways. While it might seem that these variations would be tied somehow to the incidence and the character of crime, that is not necessarily the case. The politicization of street crime seems to be related at least as much to broader social problems as to crime per se. Thus, Hall and his associates attribute the politicization of "mugging" in England in the 1970s to economic and cultural polarization, which led to the scapegoating of black immigrants who became the primary target of the antimugging campaign.[8] Similarly, the politics of law and order in the United States in the late 1960s and early 1970s seems to have been inextricably tied to the racial and antiwar turmoil of the period.[9]

Insofar as crime, thus, becomes a condensation symbol expressing a variety of public anxieties about seemingly intractable structural problems, there is a temptation to criminalize, or at least stigmatize, behaviors stemming from these problems—welfare dependency, political dissidence, drug abuse, educational deficiencies, long-term unemployment, and the rest. In short, there is a tendency to blame the victims, who are thus doubly victimized—first by the structural problems and next by the response of organized society to those problems.

The repressive implications are clear but exaggerated. As has already been suggested, public policy controversies over street crime have to do with mobilizing support by diverting attention from structural problems. In other words, politicization is about authority as well as crime control, and Douglas Hay has taught us that consistently punitive policies are not necessarily required to maintain authority.[10] Repression is, in any case, attenuated by the partial autonomy of criminal process, which is sustained by institutional practices and legal values. This is not to suggest that policy is immune from the repressive context of politicization. The agencies of public policy are both implicated in, and resistant to, the repressive political culture of criminal process, and the work of this chapter is to lay the basis for an exploration of this complex and contingent relationship.[11]

Criminological Discourse

It might seem that the distinction between structural and individual explanations of crime is unequivocally dichotomous. After all, a structural perspective suggests that criminals are victims of circumstance captured by forces beyond their control, while individual conceptions of criminality focus on personal deficiency and choice. The findings of criminological inquiry are, however, far too rich to sustain the illusion of mutually exclusive causal explanations rooted in an either–or choice between social and individual pathologies. Indeed, the only unequivocal, if still provisional, truth revealed by criminological theory and research is that there are both individual and structural sources of crime.[12] Further complicating the picture, and generally acknowledged by criminologists, is the influence of culture, which shapes the way individual personalities understand and react to their material circumstances.

Nonetheless, dichotomous interpretations dominate political *and* criminological discourse. In the 1988 presidential election, for example, the Bush campaign drew heavily and successfully on the imagery of individual pathology, perhaps of inborn criminality, to discredit prison-furlough programs. Given the symbolic shortcuts that dominate political discourse, it stands to reason that criminological complexity would be screened out. But even the work of criminologists, who acknowledge a confounding complexity and incorporate it into their analyses, is permeated with partisan advocacy of one or the other of the two perspectives. Two cases in point, which will be considered below, are Elliot Currie's *Confronting Crime*[13] and James Q. Wilson and Richard J. Herrnstein's *Crime and Human Nature*.[14] In comparing these two studies, the objective is to explore and explain the tension between the complexity of criminological findings and the persistent simplification of criminological advocacy.

Criminological Complexity

Wilson and Herrnstein's extended inquiry into the impact of human nature on crime is clearly rooted in a volitional conception of criminality. As they see things, some people are more likely to *choose* to abide by the law while others are more inclined to violate the law.[15] Moreover, these choices are driven by "constitutional" factors—that is, "factors usually present at or soon after birth, whose behavioral consequences appear gradually during the child's development."[16] The authors conclude that existing research clearly establishes a correlation between criminality and the constitutional factors of gender, age, intelligence, and personality.

At first glance, this conclusion would seem to put Wilson and Herrnstein unequivocally in the camp of those who locate the sources of criminality in the individual, a position with which Wilson has long been associated.[17] For example, in considering what they see as rather weak evidence of a relationship between unemployment and criminality, Wilson and Herrnstein are inclined to look to constitutional factors—for example, to "people who are intensely present-oriented and thus find looking for a job unattractive but stealing a purse irresistible."[18] Some people, they seem to say, have criminality engrained in their identity.

Closer examination suggests, however, that they take a more ambiguous position. Note, in the first place, that Wilson and Herrnstein do not make a causal, but only a correlational, claim. "Certain human features that are indisputably biological—an individual's anatomical configuration—are correlated with criminality. We do not argue that these anatomic features cause crime, only that they are correlated with criminal behavior."[19] Thus, research indicates that men with the XYY chromosome configuration are slightly more likely to have criminal records than those with the normal XY configuration.[20] But Wilson and Herrnstein's point is that biological factors of this sort only generate predispositions. Whether those predispositions lead to criminality depends, they say, on developmental factors, principally the family and the schools, and on the social context, including such factors as labor markets, culture, and the media. With respect to labor markets, they even go so far as to acknowledge that the shortage of better jobs in the inner city, clearly a structural factor, may lead people out of the work force and into criminal activity. In short, Wilson and Herrnstein "believe that criminal behavior, like all human behavior, results from a complex interaction of genetic and environmental factors."[21]

Currie's more structural analysis in *Confronting Crime* identifies inequality as the source of criminality. "The evidence for a strong association between inequality and crime is overwhelming. Denying it requires what we might politely describe as a highly selective interpretation of the facts."[22] A variety of evidentiary sources is deployed by Currie. He begins with "rough figures" that identify some U.S. cities with particularly high rates of violent crime. He finds that these cities are distinguished primarily by high poverty rates and high concentrations of blacks. Currie reports that this same convergence of crime, race, and poverty emerges in Marvin Wolfgang's seminal research on youth crime in Philadelphia as well as in other research on violent offenders in the United States, the United Kingdom, and Denmark.[23] More generally, Currie reports that cross-national comparisons of the United States, with its great discrepancies of wealth, with egalitarian nations like Japan, Holland, and Sweden indicate that crime and inequality covary directly with one another.[24]

But Currie goes well beyond a strictly structural criminology. Most broadly, Currie notes that material inequality is going to be more problematic in materialistic cultures, especially when the traditional social bonds are tenuous. "Supports of community and kinship can inhibit violence even where there is little money and few material goods."[25] Conversely, "enforced separation of people from these communal supports in the name of economic growth can be among the worst forms of impoverishment of all."[26]

Currie also acknowledges an association between criminality and such clearly nonstructural factors as race and IQ. Race, according to Currie, is relevant in its own right. "On balance . . . the evidence suggests that in the United States the effects of class and race on criminal violence in the United States are inextricably intertwined—but that race does have an independent effect."[27] So, too, with IQ. "The Philadelphia study found that several characteristics of youth's lives—school performance, IQ, and how often they had moved—were also related to delinquency."[28] By including IQ, arguably a constitutional factor, Currie seems to be edging still closer to Wilson and Herrnstein.

Criminological Advocacy

While it is, thus, possible to identify common ground between volitional and structural criminology, the convergence is more apparent than real. Each discourse clings to its own premises even as it incorporates the confounding complexity of criminological theory and research. In part, this dialogue of the deaf can be attributed to research findings that are scattered, suspect, and explain relatively little of the variance. But empirical shortcomings are only the beginning. At the heart of the matter are divergent policy preferences rooted in contrasting visions of the good society. It is therefore no exaggeration to say that there is a conscious determination to talk past one another. To do otherwise would be to betray strongly held values.

Consider, to begin with, the core issue, inequality. Wilson and Herrnstein acknowledge the convincing evidence that inequality correlates with homicide. On the other hand, they deny that there is any evidence that inequality correlates with "property crime" or with "the overall crime rate."[29] Currie reads the research record differently. He makes sweeping claims about the impact of inequality on crime, attributing lower crime rates in countries like Japan and Holland to a narrowing of the gap between rich and poor.[30] A careful analysis of Currie's presentation reveals, however, that these cross-national findings are drawn, as Wilson and Herrnstein claim, exclusively from studies of homicide. But Currie is able to link inequality with crime more broadly through delinquency research in the United States, the United Kingdom, and Denmark.[31] Wilson and Herrnstein simply ignore the work on delinquency, which lends credence to Currie's inequality thesis.

Still more revealing of the partisan character of criminological advocacy is the unemployment issue. While there is sharp empirical disagreement on whether unemployment correlates with crime, there is consensus that unemployment is best seen as a symptom of a deeper social malaise. There is even agreement that the malaise has to do with labor markets and attitudes toward work. But this common ground is interpreted in predictably different ways. Currie sees a causal link between structural failure and crime.

> Whether work can avert crime, in short, depends on whether it is part of a larger process through which the young are gradually integrated into a productive and valued role in a larger community. Similarly, whether unemployment leads to crime depends heavily on whether it is a temporary interruption of a longer and more hopeful trajectory into that kind of role, or represents a permanent condition of economic marginality that *virtually assures* a sense of purposelessness, alienation, and deprivation.[32]

Wilson and Herrnstein, after reviewing a bewildering array of provisional theories and inconclusive empirical research, look to choice rather than structure to explain the connections between labor market and crime.

> Within a block or two, one can encounter people who value work and people who do not; thieves who steal regularly and systematically and thieves who steal occasionally and casually, even while employed. But for reasons having to do with some combination of cultural and objective conditions, it seems clear that a significant fraction of young men in many inner-city areas *assign* a low, perhaps even negative, value to success achieved through legitimate employment.[33]

In spite of the inclusion of "objective conditions," there is an unmistakably volitional inflection to the conclusions drawn by Wilson and Herrnstein.

Of course, these conflicting interpretations are driven by altogether different visions of the good society and lead in divergent policy directions. Wilson and Herrnstein believe in a world of individual choice and personal responsibility, and for them the goal of policy is to encourage people to choose law-abiding behavior—principally by appealing to their consciences and their senses of justice. Currie concedes that there are pathological individuals—that "wicked people exist" and that "human beings have destructive and predatory impulses against which others must be protected."[34] He argues, however, that for policymakers these generalizations are really beside the point, because they

> cannot help us understand why crime is so much worse at some times or places than others. Why are people in St. Louis so much more "prone to crime" than those in Stockholm or, for that matter, Milwaukee? Why are people in Houston not only far more likely to kill each other than people in London or Zurich, but also much more likely to do so today than they were twenty-five years ago?[35]

Thus, Wilson and Herrnstein return relentlessly to criminality as the consequence of *flawed individuals* making the wrong choices. Currie, in contrast, sees a *flawed society* failing to offer adequate alternatives to crime.

For Wilson and Herrnstein, punishment becomes the essential tool for both correct choices and the right values. They want not only to reduce crime but also to transmit the moral message of personal responsibility to the entire society. Given this second objective, it is not sufficient to pursue a narrowly instrumental strategy that might, for example, reward noncriminal behavior through generous social programs.

As Wilson and Herrnstein see things, social programs undermine personal responsibility.[36] Their essential target is the collective conscience of the society, which, as they see it, can be reached by punishment but not by social welfare: "Conscience and justice (or equity) are not philosophical abstractions that clutter up the straight-forward business of finding a scientific explanation for criminality; they are a necessary part of the explanation itself."[37] More specifically, they argue for retributive punishment that fits the crime. And while there is an undeniable element of utilitarian general deterrence in their argument, the essential point is that equitable punishment has a deeper meaning for the society.

> Crime is held in check not only by the objective risk of punishment but by the subjective sense of wrongdoing. . . . Punishment as moral education almost certainly reduces more crime than punishment as deterrence. An internalized prohibition against offending is like an additional cost of crime, possibly strong enough to prevent its occurrence even when there is no risk of being caught and punished by society.[38]

Thus, Wilson and Herrnstein reject both "psychic determinism," which teaches "that every action is caused by the actor's circumstances," and a strictly utilitarian approach that employs behavior modification techniques to "provide the most cost-effective way of reducing crime."[39] Instead, they anchor their criminology in a moralistic individualism that, as an article of faith, shapes the inferences they draw from empirical findings.

For Currie, crime is much too fundamental a problem to be left to the symptomatic remedies available to the criminal justice system. If the problem is structural, so too must be the solution—namely, reducing inequality. Currie points to research that indicates, for example, "that higher AFDC payments had a clear and consistent negative effect on rates of homicide, burglarly, and rape."[40] But as with Wilson and Herrnstein, the instrumental and the moral messages reinforce one another. Thus, in commenting on the more generous welfare states of western Europe, Currie concludes: "What these figures represent is a historical commitment—often achieved through long and painful political struggle—to shift the moral balance of these societies toward concern for social solidarity and mutual support."[41] Individualism is, then, for Currie the problem rather than the solution: "In a society that values its people for what they can acquire rather than what they can contribute and that encourages predatory and manipulative behavior in the service of immediate gain as the guiding principle of economic life, we should not be altogether surprised if more explosive forms of the same ethos are expressed among the most deprived."[42]

Thus, the welfare state has been, according to Currie, an effective tool of crime control, because by "humanizing life under modern industrial capitalism" it succeeds in "lowering the level of interpersonal violence."[43]

The message of this section is not primarily that the empirical indeterminacy of criminological findings provides opportunities for advocacy to triumph over analysis. Nor is it that when criminologists turn to policy, they necessarily compromise their detachment and objectivity. While both of these generalizations are probably true, they actually conceal a deeper significance of the tendency of criminological advocacy to take priority over criminological complexity.

Criminological advocacy is not really about policymaking but about competing social visions. The questions raised by street crime go directly to the moral foundations of the social order. According to volitional criminology, criminal process is the guarantor of the social contract among autonomous and responsible individuals, who are equal before the law and provided with equal opportunities to make the most of their lives. The clear mission of criminal process is, therefore, to minimize deviance, which threatens public order and personal security and, thus, individual opportunities. Structural criminology sees street crime as a response to various kinds of social deprivations that bias the opportunities and limit the autonomy of individuals in the lower strata of society. Criminal process, according to this way of thinking, is best seen as a collection point for social pathologies and, therefore, as a kind of crude indicator of the need for concerted social action. Given what is at stake, it is neither surprising nor, in my judgment, a cause for concern that serious inquiry, even among professional criminologists, cannot be confined to the techniques and tactics of crime control.

The inextricable connection between criminology and ideology is, of course, even clearer in the political arena and in the policy processes. The dispute between structural and volitional criminologists over values and policy tends to be replicated among politicians and criminal process professionals—but with distinctive twists. Criminological controversy, however heated and however divergent its initial premises, is constrained by the standards of academic discourse. It is an ongoing and rather private colloquy, which is responsive to, if not determined by, empirical findings and well-constructed arguments with an exclusively criminological focus.

Real-world controversies among politicians and criminal process professionals are quite another matter. While the controversies are shaped by the same dichotomy between structure and volition, volitional approaches are consistently privileged in the political arena and, to a lesser extent, in criminal process. These outcomes are due, as I argue in the next section, to the cultural resonance of punitive values and to calculations of political interest, which, like the moral issues just discussed, transcend the practicalities of crime control and the empirical findings of criminological research.

The Cultural Resonance of Volitional Criminology

At first glance, the cultural resonance of volitional criminology seems pretty straightforward. Street crime evokes elemental concerns about personal safety that are widely, perhaps universally, shared—an insight that goes back at least as far as Hobbesian worries about a society in which life is "solitary, poor, nasty, brutish and short." It seems to follow, then, that a rising crime rate generates widespread fear, weakens social bonds, and awakens punitive impulses. These are, to continue along the Hobbesian path, the precursors of authoritarian politics.

Ralf Dahrendorf argues in his 1985 Hamlyn Lectures, *Law and Order*, that just such developments are under way these days in the United Kingdom and the United States.[44] We are, as he sees it, in the midst of dual crises. First, there is a breakdown of law and order, initiated by, but not confined to, increasing street crime. Second, he notes a drift toward authoritarian populism, which could lead ultimately in totalitarian directions. As Dahrendorf sees it, these two crises are causally linked: the decomposition of society, with its source in the failure to control crime, has led directly to a serious threat to democratic political institutions.

The available data suggest, however, that other forces are at work, and that the picture is much more complex and contingent than Dahrendorf suggests. While the punitive drift seems clear and indisputable, it is neither so universally shared nor so clearly linked to victimization as Dahrendorf's analysis implies. Stuart Hall's research on the mugging crisis in Britain in the late 1970s leads to a kind of reverse interpretation. "To put it simply, if paradoxically: 'mugging' for British readers *meant* 'general social crisis and rising crime' *first,* a particular kind of robbery occurring on the British streets second, and later."[45] In other words, a diffuse sense of social malaise was crystallized into a political crusade against mugging. Moreover, while there are clear signs of anxiety and frustration, it is less clear that society is coming apart at the seams as Dahrendorf believes. Finally, even if there is a crisis of public confidence with punitive and authoritarian overtones, that crisis is not, I argue, a direct consequence of objective social conditions but is instead attributable to how those conditions are interpreted.

Law and Order Solidarity

Dahrendorf believes that the current law and order crisis extends well beyond our failure to contain street crime. As he sees things, the crisis of public confidence, what he describes as a developing social anomie, stems from a broader breakdown of society's basic norms. "There are times when all predictability seems to fade from social life. Fears of a breakdown of law and order have to do with this nightmare. That such fears are present in many of the advanced societies of the free world, is beyond doubt."[46] He sees signs of this social decomposition in the growth of underground economies and organized crime; the development of "no-go" areas in cities where neither citizens nor even police feel safe; the routine disruption of social order for everything from political action through labor disputes to violence among fans at sporting events; and to the acceptance of a youth culture that flouts social as well as criminal norms.[47]

We have ample reasons, according to Dahrendorf, to fear this anomic situation in which "the social effectiveness and the cultural morality of norms tends towards zero."[48] First, the developing chaos of anomie robs us of the sense of physical security and of "cultural bonds" that are preconditions for purposeful and creative activity—the preconditions, that is, for positive freedom.[49] Second, as we are thus transformed by anomie into "a society of frightened or aggressive human beings," we fall prey to demagogues who promise order.

> The many are . . . more inclined to give their support to those who demand quick action for the re-establishment of law and order, and who seek extraordinary powers to do what they want. The political right can count on a volume of built-in support which the left seeks forever in vain. Put in straight political terms, the wobbly centre is at the end of the day more readily prepared to give its reluctant support to a leader of the right than to one of the left.[50]

Thus, Dahrendorf takes it as a given that a law and order crisis that extends beyond street crime will tend to privilege the punitive values of volitional criminology rather than the transformative values of structural criminology.

But why is this the case? Dahrendorf's own analysis, which offers a dual explanation for the breakdown of norms, suggests that a structural response would be at least as sensible as a punitive response. His primary argument is that anomie stems from impunity—the realization that violations of society's most fundamental rules will go unpunished. Impunity provides incentives to break rules, thus driving society toward the unpredictability, and ultimately the chaos, of anomie. But Dahrendorf also looks beyond this volitional explanation to the growth of an underclass that is effectively excluded from full citizenship. "Members of the 'underclass' are a reserve army for demonstrations and manifestations, including soccer violence, race riots, and running battles with the police."[51] Accordingly, he argues, albeit in a subsidiary fashion, that a meaningful response to anomie requires social justice as well as effective sanctions.

> All of a sudden, citizenship has become an exclusive rather than in [sic] inclusive concept. But of course those who are denied full citizenship rights by the very strength of these rights and their contradictions—by . . . poverty and unemployment actually resulting from the social state and the work society—do not go away. . . . But in the end, societies will either get to the root of the problem or run the risk of abandoning liberty in the search of [sic] unambiguous answers.[52]

It stands to reason, in other words, that insofar as full citizens appreciate and accept the plight of the underclass, they will be less likely to respond punitively to public order crises and more willing to face up to the structural reforms that will encourage widespread respect for our basic norms and rules.

It follows, then, from Dahrendorf's own analysis that the society's response to crime and other indexes of anomie depends at least in part on the social construction of those circumstances rather than on the circumstances themselves. Dahrendorf does not, however, pursue the logic of his own position. He wants us to take the breakdown of law and order and the development of anomie at face value. He thus illuminates only one part of the picture: the common stake that all citizens have in the minimum conditions of social order and their punitive and authoritarian reaction to a breakdown of that order. But anomie is as much a state of mind as a social condition, and the resonance of volitional criminology is neither so universal nor so value free as Dahrendorf's Hobbesian imagery suggests.

The Social Construction of Street Crime

Empirically, Dahrendorf portrays a society coming apart at the seams, and just this kind of "demographic collapse" has, according to Wesley Skogan, occurred in some neighborhoods in some cities.

After a while, their history of crime and disorder becomes the driving force in the population composition of areas deep in the cycle of decline. . . . As in large parts of Woodlawn (Chicago) and the South Bronx (New York City), such a high tolerance for risk is required to live in these places that the population drops precipitously. Disorder can continue to occur, but there is virtually no "community" remaining to define it as a problem.[53]

More broadly, however, the available research as well as readily observable daily life in urban areas suggests adaptations to crime and disorder that constrain but do not shatter the established social patterns of urban life. Consider the research conducted in Chicago, Philadelphia, and San Francisco by Skogan and Michael Maxfield:

> By far the most common risk-reduction strategy adopted by residents of these cities was to go out by car rather than walk at night: Almost 50% of those questioned indicated that they did this "most of the time." About one in four indicated that they frequently went out with other people and avoided certain places in their neighborhoods because of crime, and one in five usually "took something" (a euphemism we employed to grant anonymity to gun users) when they went out at night. . . . In all, 33% of our respondents reported doing two or more of these things most of the time, 27% one of them, and 40% none of them.[54]

This is not, to my way of thinking, indicative of the ominous image invoked by Dahrendorf of a drift into the Hobbesian war of each against all. It seems more suggestive of the adjustments city dwellers regularly make to the multiple burdens of urban life.

Consider also the way in which Dahrendorf includes among the social crises of a developing anomie "a youth culture that flouts social as well as criminal norms."[55] There are less threatening interpretations of youth subcultures—for example, as generationally driven efforts "to express *autonomy and difference* from parents"—as a kind of "last fling" prior to incorporation into the adult world.[56] If these ritual renunciations of prevailing values are to be perceived as crises of authority and threats to the social order, an explanation is called for.[57]

There are, moreover, confounding discontinuities between the social conditions and the punitive values that Dahrendorf packages together as anomie. As Samuel Walker has pointed out, the conditions of "normlessness" that Dahrendorf associates with anomie tend to be confined to neighborhoods inhabited by marginal groups in the society.

> Gang violence is directed primarily at other gangs and limited to their immediate neighborhoods, in only a few cities. Victims tend to be law-abiding people who live in these areas. For most Americans the risk of victimization continues to decline. . . . The real tragedy is that an acceptable quality of life is a privilege instead of a right today more than ever. Those who are at the bottom, the "underclass," are worse off; the rest of us are a little better off, both economically and in terms of our feeling safe from criminal victimization.[58]

Yet data collected by Arthur Stinchcombe and his research team indicate that the most punitive values in the United States are generated within the "rural hunting culture"—within a segment of the society that because of its distance from urban crime is both less fearful and less victimized.[59] Similarly, blacks, who are most victimized, are not the most fearful, and women and the elderly tend to be more fearful but not more punitive.[60] In sum, the segments of the society that are most likely to privilege volitional criminology are not necessarily those most burdened by the breakdown of law and order.

The minimum lesson to be learned from these findings is that the privileging of volitional criminology cannot be taken as the "natural" and direct consequence of a compelling and universally shared priority for public order. If blacks are more victimized but less punitive, it does not mean that personal safety is unimportant to them. It may, however, mean that they feel as threatened by punitive law enforcement as by street crime. Moreover, as Charles Silberman puts it: "Lower-class life involves an almost unbearable tension between . . . the desired adherence to the norms of the larger society and the insistent demands of life on the streets."[61] In other words, lower-class blacks may be more accepting of—or at least resigned to—conditions that middle-class whites and blacks perceive as threatening.

Conversely, whites may feel as threatened by changes in the prevailing values as by street crime. The flouting of conventional values can be, as Joseph Gusfield has demonstrated, deeply unsettling to groups whose identity and status are associated with those values: "Status discontents are likely to appear when the prestige accorded to persons and groups by prestige-givers is perceived as less than that which the person or group expects."[62] Lillian Rubin sees these broader and more diffuse anxieties at the core of the public's reaction to the trial of Bernhard Goetz, who gunned down four unarmed black teenagers in a New York City subway: "It is not justice that has been served, but our passions—historic passions about race, about the dangerous, alien 'other' that blackness embodies in the white American psyche; passions that have rent the nation in two in the past and that continue to foment divisions that grow wider and more dangerous with each decision."[63] Crime and punishment, in short, become symbols for a variety of insecurities associated with unsettling changes in American life.

To think of such problems as race, economic productivity, moral conflict, and poverty as street crime makes them *seem* much more familiar and much more manageable. This response is due to a powerful belief system, *the myth of crime and punishment*.[64] If the problem is street crime, we can readily identify the culprits and distance ourselves from them. They are unknown predators who seek out opportunities to prey upon us and disrupt our lives. This frightening image of street crime is compelling because in the myth of crime and punishment it is paired with the reassurance that punishment is an effective and virtuous response to crime.

In effect, the myth of crime and punishment is a simple morality play, a contest between good and evil, with the odds strongly in favor of good. Punishment provides a reliable mechanism of crime control and comes with a bracing and unequivocal moral imprimatur. "The moral case can be found, among other places, in the Old Testament with its prescription of an eye for an eye. In more practical terms, punishment is defended as a workable way of controlling crime through deterrence and incapacitation."[65]

The reduction, or reframing, of basic social problems as street crime is, then, precisely to justify recourse to punishment, which is seen as direct and effective because it liberates us from moral dilemmas.[66]

It is hard to see how any comparably consoling myth could be derived from either structural criminology or from the complexities of hard-core criminological discourse. Indeed, insofar as the stick of punishment is the objective, it is not only structural criminology that is marginalized. Also unwelcome are the nonpunitive forms of volitional criminology—the carrots of job training, drug rehabilitation, and other liberal measures. We do not want to hear that we are all responsible or that there is no quick fix. That would amount to giving up the consoling certainties of crime and punishment, the basic reason for reframing social problems as criminal problems.[67]

The threshold message of this section is that the punitive overtones of volitional criminology resonate intensely and insistently with contemporary culture in the United States. But these punitive predispositions are socially constructed and are not uniformly distributed within the society. The politics of criminal process is thus conducted within a fluid cultural context, which, since it is socially constructed, is responsive to political initiatives. The state is, in other words, both constrained by the prevailing culture and a powerful instrument for shaping it. As we see in the next section, the state has strong incentives for encouraging a volitional and, more specifically, a punitive interpretation of crime and anomie.

The Political Resonance of Volitional Criminology

To understand the political privileging of volitional criminology, it is necessary to look carefully at the responsibilities of the state. As Stuart Hall and Phil Scraton, drawing on Antonio Gramsci, have put it: "In addition to its role of regulating the economy, the state is also required to organize society, civil, moral and intellectual life around a series of 'fundamental historical tasks.' The state is the site and agency through which popular consent for these is won or lost."[68] In principle, the state could acquit the full range of its responsibilities by acknowledging criminological complexity. In practice, however, volitional criminology is likely to prove much more attractive than the structural alternative and, therefore, to dominate policy initiatives.

Generally speaking, volitional responses are simply less costly to the state. This is particularly true of the national government, which has minimal direct responsibility for the problems posed for public order by street crime—but primary responsibility for the ideological, economic, political, and social threats to the state. For local governments, which have primary responsibility for controlling street crime, the incentives to privilege volitional criminology are not nearly so strong. Accordingly, punitive values are likely to be more prominent in the largely symbolic national political arena than in the local political arena, which is more closely linked to operative policy. In other words, the politics of criminal process at the national level is more about authority than policy, while the converse is true at the local level.

Street Crime in National Politics

Structural interpretations of crime sorely tax the economic, political, and ideological resources of the state. Insofar as anomie is traced to material inequality, crime control becomes a matter of formulating redistributive economic policies and generating consent for them. In short, the premise of structural criminology is economic crisis, which the national government will be reluctant to recognize because the prescription for economic crisis is very risky business.

The only predictable things about structural change are that it will be controversial and divisive, and that generating consent will be an ideological as well as a more narrowly political challenge. In the first place, structural change will threaten the vested interests of the more affluent and influential elements of the society who will, by definition, be expected to bear a disproportionate share of the costs of redistribution and transformation. Structural change will also be technically difficult and unpredictable—fraught, no doubt, with mistakes and unintended consequences. Finally, structural change will pose ideological problems, since it is premised on collectivist and egalitarian values, which are at odds with the prevailing American ethos. In sum, structural interpretations of street crime call upon the "law-abiding" public to acknowledge that social pathologies are at the root of criminality, to take some responsibility for that criminality, and to pay the substantial costs of structural policies.

In contrast, volitional criminology discounts the economic causes of crime and thus puts less stress on the capabilities of the state. By identifying criminality with pathological individuals, volitional criminology stigmatizes criminals and validates punitive responses to them, and punishment is simply less costly across the board than structural transformation. "If black youth are thought of exclusively as 'muggers,' people will be less willing to consider the fact that they constitute the social group with the highest relative rate of unemployment."[69] And, of course, repressive policies imply fewer constraints on, and more prerogatives for, the state.

But it is the ideological as much as the repressive role of the state that is nurtured by volitional interpretations. To interpret crime in terms of individual pathology is, as argued in the last section, to provide a unifying image of victims against victimizers. The common stake in law and order is thus counterposed against special pleading on behalf of racial, class, and gender deprivations. As Stuart Hall puts it: "The complex centrality of crime gives 'crime as a public issue' a powerful mobilizing force—support can be rallied to a campaign against it, not by presenting it as an abstract issue, but as a tangible force which threatens the complexly balanced stabilities which represent the 'English [or American] way of life.'"[70] Criminal behavior is presented as a threat not only to our physical security but also to our sense of fair play. The criminal becomes someone who is trying to get something for nothing and thus makes a mockery of a reciprocal society in which we settle for what we have earned. Again, volitional criminology refocuses attention from structural problems that are a tremendous challenge for the state to individual pathology and the myth of crime and punishment.

Of course, volitional criminology mystifies the complex inequalities of social life. Both the victims and the victimizers of street crime are drawn disproportionately from the marginalized members of the society. Nor is it solely or even principally these marginal groups that pose a threat to social norms and legal rules. Except for street crime, with its grave risks and meager rewards, the established classes are at least as likely to violate social norms and legal rules. But while society's stake in law and order is not indivisible, the widespread belief that it is provides a hegemonic resource for the state, which is to that extent empowered to rally support for established authority and to deploy repressive policies.

The Local Level

The state is, however, something of a mystification itself, and therefore the repressive and, to a lesser extent, the ideological potential of volitional criminology are less imposing than the argument so far suggests. At the national level, where the most fundamental hegemonic responsibilities are borne, the appeals of volitional criminology are manifest. Crime control in the American federal system is, however, the business of local government and, in particular, of the agencies of criminal process, which are largely beyond the reach of Washington.[71] At the local level, the concerns are more instrumental, the complex realities of criminality are more insistent, and the myth of crime and punishment is more divisive. As a result, the state will be more willing and able to generate a climate for repression than actually to follow through on it.

At the heart of the matter are criminal-process professionals for whom the complexities of criminological discourse are truly meaningful. The daily grind of criminal process drives home the inadequacy of monocausal analyses and the illusion of easy answers—be they punitive or rehabilitative. Criminal process is also significantly insulated from the volitional preferences of the public. As a result, the marginalization of structural criminology proceeds in a more equivocal fashion.

With all that said, it remains true that criminal-process professionals are diverted from structure and complexity by two different kinds of forces. The institutional setting of criminal process is, in the first place, congenial to the individualistic values of volitional criminology. From arrest through disposition to incarceration, the essential question posed for the professionals is how to deal with an endless stream of individual defendants. Moreover, the legal values that are supposed to guide criminal-process professionals lead in equally individualistic directions.

The classic statement of the way legal values feed into criminal process was provided by Herbert Packer's analysis of the crime control and due process models.[72] The crime control model is driven by the threat that criminals pose to the social order and to social freedom and, therefore, tends to favor procedures that can accurately and efficiently sort out the criminals—those who are factually guilty. Conversely, the due process model is driven by the belief that the most serious threat to freedom is governmental power. From this starting point, factual accuracy and efficiency are less important than the rights of defendants, because these rights check repressive governmental institutions, which pose the greatest threat to freedom.

For Packer, these models are polarities within which legal professionals strike shifting balances.[73] At first glance, there might seem to be considerable consonance between the crime control–due process polarity identified by Packer and the volitional–structural polarity of criminological discourse. That consonance is, however, more apparent than real. It begins and ends with a superficial affinity between volitional criminology's obsession with punishing pathological individuals and the crime control model's preemptory treatment of suspects and defendants.

The more basic truth is that the values of both crime control and due process work against structural responses to crime. So long as the focus remains on the processing of individual cases, as it most decidedly does in both models, volitional criminology is ipso facto privileged. Irrespective of whether the emphasis is on protecting rights or on establishing guilt, criminal-process professionals are directed toward the fate of formally anonymous defendants and away from their broader social identities and circumstances.

This same volitional bias is built into the institutional structures of criminal process. It is, after all, only the individual who is subject to the agencies of criminal process. Criminal-process professionals who, for whatever reasons, are responsive to structural criminology are without institutional resources to promote structural solutions. Whether or not individual offenders are seen as symptoms of social pathology, it is the offenders and the threat they pose to society—most likely to others equally benighted—that the sentencing judge must respond to. Consider the example of a self-professed Marxist judge in Detroit.

I've gotten into situations where perhaps I've given some minimal time to a junky who's not assaultive, but he's got four or five previous arrests; he's been on probation; he violated probation. Obviously, if he has proven unresponsive to more sensible programs, I might give some sentence. I'll try to give him house time as opposed to prison time. . . . Then I'd put him on probation and add some probationary conditions, hoping to jolt him so he'll be more receptive toward treatment. But that's the persistent violator of property. The persistent violator of people, the person of violence, and so on, I put away. To protect society I'd put that person away.[74]

Thus, even if judges think of offenders as victims, the evidence that they are also victimizers cannot be ignored. The individualizing institutions of criminal process mean that professionals who may be persuaded by structural understandings of criminality are ultimately powerless to incorporate structural insights into criminal process. Structural responses are simply beyond the reach of judges or of any criminal justice professionals. Only legislative and executive agencies have the authority to make the kinds of redistributive decisions called for by structural understandings of criminality.

For reasons extrinsic to criminological discourse, politicians can be expected to follow the line of least resistance toward volitional, rather than structural, criminology. Structural responses to crime are more costly to the state in just about every way than are volitional responses. Structural measures entail redistributive and unpredictable policies, which divide the polity, because they require substantial commitments of resources and threaten vested interests. Volitional criminology, in contrast, discounts the economic causes of crime and validates punitive responses that are less costly and also unite the law-abiding majority against the criminal minority. Moreover, cracking down on crime, or at least promising to do so, leads in familiar directions and resonates well culturally.

But the picture is more complex than it might appear—due in large part to the significant tension between national and local institutions. At the national level, where structural responsibilities reside, volitional criminology has strong appeal in that it provides a unifying discourse and diverts attention from structural problems. Locally, the costs of volitional criminology are higher and its benefits less clear cut—thus making it considerably less attractive. Accordingly, the punitive message of volitional criminology is less compelling for those agencies of the state that have primary responsibility for dealing with street crime.

Moderation at the local level produces its own problematic. While there are countervailing forces that tend to moderate punitive policies, prison overcrowding is a clear indication that the politics of law and order has a significant impact on criminal process. Moreover, insofar as nonpunitive reforms have been undertaken, they follow a perilous path toward more sweeping and intrusive forms of social control. The variety of community-based programs for crime prevention and corrections, while intended as a beneficent alternative to hard-line policies, may "reproduce in the community the very same coercive features of the system they were designed to replace."[75]

> What is new is the scale of the operation and the technologies (drugs, surveillance and information gathering techniques) which facilitate the blurring and penetration [of the boundary between state and society]. . . . Systems of medicine, social work, education, welfare take on supervisory and judicial functions, while the penal apparatus itself becomes more influenced by medicine, education, psychology.[76]

In short, while the punitive tone of volitional criminology may be moderated at the local level, there is no discernible movement in structural directions. This is the message of the Cedar City experience, which is presented in the following chapters.

2

The Politicization of Street Crime

There are good reasons to believe that street crime has been a salient political issue in the United States since the mid-1960s. Survey data reveal increasing levels of public fear of crime as well as a persistent inclination to see crime as one of the country's most important political issues.[1] Street crime was also the primary focus of a national agency, the Law Enforcement Assistance Administration, which was created by Congress and actively functioned during the 1970s.

James Q. Wilson, one of the most influential commentators on the politicization of street crime, has argued that it can be traced to the dramatic increase in crime beginning in the 1960s. Thus, for Wilson, politicization attests to the vitality of pluralist democracy in the United States—that is, to political leaders responding to real public grievances.[2]

The experiences of Cedar City reveal a much more complex and problematic picture. There was surprisingly little politicization of street crime, although there was substantial politicization of *criminal process*. The payoff system mentioned in Chapter 1 was, for example, the key to the liberal reform movement that altered the character of city politics. The racial tensions stemming in part from allegations of racial bias in policing practices as well as in the hiring and promotion of police officers also had broad political ramifications. But street crime per se was only modestly and sporadically politicized despite a significant number of efforts to do so throughout the period.

The patterns of politicization in Cedar City also cast serious doubt on the reassuring consensual democratic pluralism that is

29

at the heart of Wilson's analysis. There was not much agreement among political leaders or within the general public on the politicization of street crime. Politicization campaigns were organized by the Cedar City Police Officers Guild and by small-business interests from the declining neighborhood of Crystal Valley, where some grass-roots support was to be found. Conversely, established business and media elites in the downtown core tended to play down the issue. Except for a brief period in the 1970s, the general public was unresponsive to law and order populism, and the most crime-ridden part of the city, the predominantly black central area, was clearly hostile. Thus, the political salience of street crime varied along class and race lines, while established elites worked effectively against politicization. In Cedar City there was neither consensus nor grass-roots democracy when it came to the politics of street crime.

Although it could be argued that these findings have to do with the particularities of Cedar City, there are good reasons to question Wilson's consensual democratic pluralist model of politicization and to pay more attention to the role of elites and to divisions within the public. The key distinction is not between Cedar City and other urban areas, but between the national level, where there is evidence of extensive politicization of street crime, and the local level with its limited politicization.

As suggested in Chapter 1, this distinction stems from the differing responsibilities for street crime at the two levels of government. At the local level, where politicians and criminal-process professionals must deal directly with street crime and with a divided public, politicization tends to create more problems than it resolves. At the national level, where the war on street crime is almost exclusively a symbolic activity uniting "us" against "them," politicization resonates very well with the public and is thus a tempting target of opportunity for politicians.

The temptations to politicize street crime have received a good deal of attention.[3] The Cedar City experience provides an understanding of politicization's drawbacks, which tend to make it the exception rather than the rule—at least at the local level. This leads to something of a paradox: In local politics, where the burdens of crime are the most concrete and where the primary responsibilities for policymaking reside, crime is less a political issue than it is in national politics, where crime is an abstraction and policy responsibilities are minimal.

Politicization

The politicization of street crime is a complex process and not at all easy to describe, let alone explain. Basically, to politicize crime is to put it on the political agenda. But which agenda? Political scientists tend to distinguish among different kinds of political agendas—corresponding roughly to how seriously the issue is taken by the polity. R. W. Cobb and C. D. Elder contrast the systemic and institutional agendas. The systemic agenda signifies a vague sense of public awareness—to "a general set of political controversies . . . falling within the range of legitimate concerns of the polity."[4] The institutional agenda, on the other hand, is composed of "a set of concrete, specific, items scheduled for active and serious consideration by a particular institutional decision-making body."[5]

This distinction between issues that preoccupy the public in a diffuse fashion and those that present concrete policy proposals is at the heart of the understanding of politicization to be employed in this chapter. To oversimplify, crime was fairly regularly on the systemic agenda in Cedar City politics during this period but seldom made it to the institutional agenda. Conversely, other criminal-process issues, such as corruption and racial bias, were seldom on the political agenda at all, but once politicized, they tended to be taken seriously.

To dichotomize in this fashion, however, is to miss some important variations or stages of politicization. In its most limited form, politicization is simply public awareness. Insofar as policy proposals are formulated, politicization reaches a second stage. Once these proposals are taken seriously, politicization has reached its penultimate stage. Finally, election of candidates campaigning on the proposals or acceptance of the proposals by governmental institutions signals the most advanced stage of politicization. Thus, politicization is separate from policy implementation, which may or may not be an objective.[6] In this chapter, our concern is solely with the limited politicization of street crime. Implementation is considered in Chapters 3 and 4, on the police and the criminal courts respectively.

Research on public policy at the national level reveals the barriers to politicization and also suggests that politicization is an interactive process involving both political leadership and public sentiments. John Kingdon argues, for example, that the political arena is generally well supplied with policy proposals but that only a few of them reach the political agenda.[7] While the public clearly is involved, there is substantial agreement among public policy analysts that political leaders have more to say about what is on the political agenda than does the general public.[8]

Kingdon makes a further distinction between agenda items and realistic alternatives. The former are primarily attributable to *elected* government officials, and the latter emerge out of the interplay of organized interest groups.[9] The election process forces political leaders to pay some attention to the public's mood and in this way imposes constraints on influential elites; for a number of reasons, however, these limits are rather modest.

The political leaders with whom Kingdon spoke do not look to public opinion polls to assess the national mood. Instead, they look to attentive publics with whom they are regularly in contact. Moreover, in their relationships with the general public, political leaders are at least as likely to exert influence as to be influenced.[10] Note that the media play a role in setting the agenda and in so doing contribute to the attenuation of the public's impact on the process. Kingdon tells us that what the media choose to report tends to be taken by political leaders as a reflection of the national mood. Kingdon goes on to argue that media coverage is frequently misleading—exaggerating, for example, the importance of social movements and thus conveying a sense of national mood that is not an accurate reflection of public concern. Of course, media attention may in and of itself reshape public sentiments in the manner of a self-fulfilling prophecy.[11]

There are data suggesting that Kingdon's interactive model is directly applicable to the politicization of street crime. Skogan and Maxfield's study of public reactions to crime reveals levels of fear that are much higher than would be suggested by the incidence of crime. "The substantial disparity between the two frequencies guarantees that direct personal victimization cannot account for much of the overall variation in levels of fear in the general population, although it certainly may be linked to the fears of those who were directly victimized."[12] Both political leaders and the media seem to contribute to this disparity. George Gerbner and Larry Gross argue that television leads the public to exaggerate the incidence and the severity of street crime.[13] Skogan and Maxfield put more emphasis on vicarious victimization: "Personal neighborhood comunication networks substantially magnify the apparent volume of violence. . . . Like media coverage of crime, the processes which lead victims' stories of their personal experience to 'get around' seem to accentuate the apparent volume of personal as opposed to property crime."[14] Either way, the public's fear of crime and thus the raw material of politicization is precariously rooted in erroneous impressions. This all adds up to an anxious and malleable public responsive to political leaders who wish to politicize crime.[15]

Politicization of street crime seems to follow an interactive course based on complex relationships among elected officials, influential elites, media messages, and public perceptions. It is most likely to occur when political leaders, in part taking their cues from the media, choose to play upon public anxieties that are themselves inflamed by media imagery and vicarious victimization rather than by crime as such. For these and other reasons, it would seem inappropriate to think of politicization of street crime as a self-generating public reaction to an increase in victimization, as Wilson's analysis suggests.

The findings presented in this chapter provide a more explicit empirical picture of the politicization. After analyzing the patterns of systemic and institutional politicization in the next section, the focus shifts to explanation. The section on public quiescence explores the rather lukewarm public reactions to street crime in Cedar City. The next examines the law and order coalition, spearheaded by the Cedar City Police Officers Guild and some small-business interests from the marginal neighborhood of Crystal Valley. Examination of the successful resistance by civic elites to the politicization of street crime follows. The concluding section considers both the generalizations and the qualifications flowing from Cedar City research.

Patterns of Politicization

Given the breadth of the politicization continuum, no single empirical indicator will suffice. At the low end, politicization has to do with public attitudes—a public that is increasingly preoccupied by and fearful of street crime. At the high end, politicization is expressed in public policy proposals such as those to limit plea bargaining, increase the severity of sentencing, and give the police more leeway. Somewhere in the middle of the continuum are political campaigns in which law and order values are salient. Analysis of politicization will, therefore, be drawn eclectically from two different sources.

In the absence of local public opinion data, newspaper reporting on crime served as one indicator of politicization. Content coding was used to trace variations in the frequency and character of crime reporting.[16] The guiding premise, consonant with the interactive understanding of politicization presented in the previous section, was that newspapers both reflect and influence the political ethos. Content coding also provided a systematic and comprehensive, if indirect, picture of politicization over the almost two decades covered by this research.[17]

Analysis of the frequency and the success of campaigning on crime provides a more direct, but rather episodic, indicator of politicization. A cursory reading of the electoral record could easily lead to the conclusion that street crime was a pervasively prominent political issue from 1964 to 1980. Early signs appeared in 1964 with candidates promising better streetlighting as a way to reduce crime[18] and with the establishment of an unofficial "police legislative committee" to introduce a police presence into electoral politics.[19] In 1967 law and order themes surfaced more explicitly—as exemplified by one City Council candidate who proposed the following program to "combat" crime, violence, and immorality:

C: communication between the police department and city hall
O: organization of crime control districts
M: mechanization of the police department for more efficiency
B: budgeting priorities on protection
A: awareness through a campaign to alert the public
T: timing . . . NOW.[20]

This militant note was to be struck frequently in subsequent years, and as late as 1979 the initiative process was employed in an effort to stiffen felony sentencing. Thus, one could argue that there was considerable politicization of street crime in the years between 1964 and 1980.

But a close look at the events of that period indicates that the politicization of street crime was weak and sporadic. Although attempts to politicize it were made throughout the years covered by the study, these attempts were relatively infrequent. Moreover, as often as not opposing candidates were able to finesse, rather than join, the issue, or the electorate failed to rally to the law and order cause. While law and order candidates were occasionally successful, they were never able to build on these victories. Candidates with other issues had more success and more staying power.

At any rate, content analysis of crime reporting and qualitative analysis of campaigning on crime provide two independent measures of politicization and thus serve as checks on one another. As it turns out, they yield matching patterns of politicization. At the same time, they reveal distinctive dimensions of the politicization process. Analysis of these patterns and dimensions is a prelude to the search for explanations later.

Crime Reporting

The content analysis of newspaper reporting of crime between 1964 and 1980 provides several different measures of politicization—each representing different points on the continuum between the systemic and institutional agendas. All articles on crime were tabulated and then broken down so as to distinguish:

1. *Reports of local crime from accounts of crime elsewhere in the country.* For example, a story about murder in Cedar City was coded differently from a murder in Chicago.
2. *Straight crime reporting from articles that raise policy issues.* For example, an article reporting an increase in burglary rates was coded differently from an article reporting that the police department had developed a new program for tracking burglary patterns.
3. *Among policy articles in order to identify those challenging or supporting current practices.* For example, an article defending established police patrol practices would be coded differently from one advocating increased foot patrol.
4. *Among punitive, due process, and/or managerial values promoted by the policy articles.* For example, articles that advocated

tougher sentencing would be coded differently from articles advocating extension of the Miranda rule or more judges to reduce case backloads, respectively.[21]

Local crime was distinguished from crime elsewhere in the country on the assumption that a local focus is suggestive of immediate concern—although still very much at the systemic, or low, end of the politicization continuum. To separate out policy articles is, of course, to move toward the institutional, or high, end of the continuum. Institutional tendencies are further revealed by looking, respectively, at the intensity of the conflict and the values at stake in the policy debate. The four distinctions are indicative of ascending levels of politicization—that is, movement from the systemic toward the institutional agenda.[22]

According to these data, there was considerable variation between systemic and institutional politicization. Figure 2.1 reveals that basic crime reporting, the weakest indicator of public concern, peaked most prominently in 1970 with significant but lesser elevations in 1965–1966, 1972, and 1976–1978. Conversely, according to Figure 2.2, the highest concentration of institutional or policy-relevant reporting occurred in the 1975–1978 period, during which the articles tended to be increasingly critical and, according to Figure 2.3, increasingly punitive. Thus, the first finding is that the heightening of vague public concerns occurs more frequently than does policy-relevant politicization. Systemic politicization of street crime is, according to the data, more volatile than institutional politicization.

More curious are the variations in the frequency of local and nonlocal crime reporting. While local crime reports outnumbered crime reports from elsewhere in the country with some consistency, Figure 2.1 reveals that the year-to-year changes tended to run in opposite directions (Pearson's $r = -.295$), with a clear and puzzling convergence reaching its peak in 1977, when the number of local articles actually dipped below reports from around the nation. We are thus presented with an anomaly. During the 1975–1978 period, when politicization was becoming the most policy relevant or institutional, the vague and distant messages of crime elsewhere were becoming disproportionately more prominent in local news reporting.

With respect to institutional politicization itself, further in-

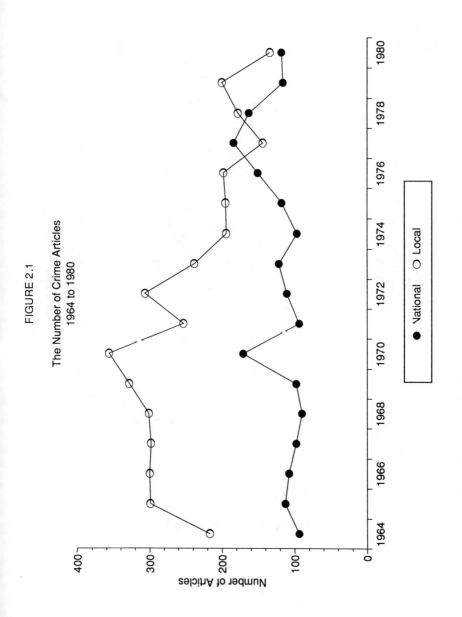

FIGURE 2.1

The Number of Crime Articles
1964 to 1980

● National   ○ Local

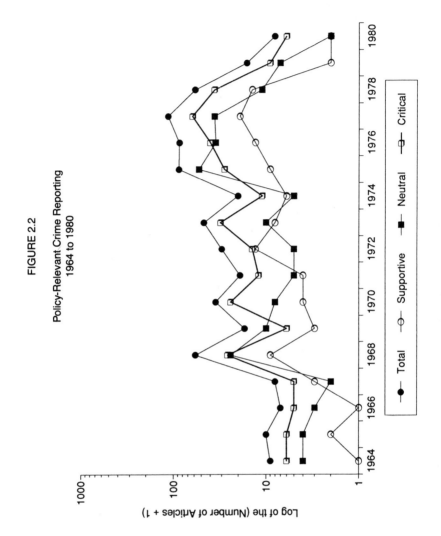

FIGURE 2.2

Policy-Relevant Crime Reporting
1964 to 1980

triguing patterns emerge from the data. There are striking corre-
spondences among the policy-relevant indicators. The period
from 1975 through 1978 stands out as one during which policy
issues were discussed frequently and somewhat critically (Figure
2.2), with punitive and managerial themes ascendant (Figure

FIGURE 2.3

Policy-Controversy Crime Reporting
1964 to 1980

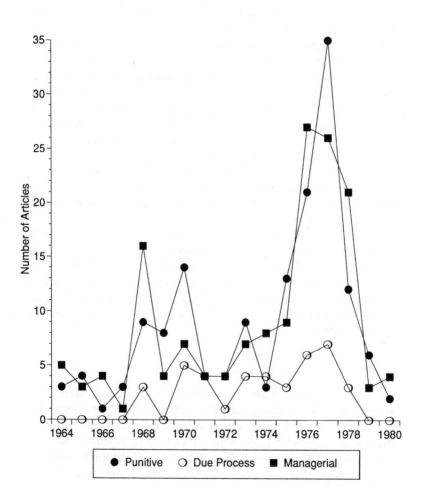

2.3). Some qualifications to these generalizations are, however, in order. There is a modest peaking of policy in the 1968–1970 period—again with punitive, managerial, and critical tendencies. Moreover, even when policy advocacy was most punitive and most critical, other positions continued to be prominently represented.

Three generalizations emerge from these findings. First, there were clear and readily identifiable periods of politicization. Second, it was much easier to get crime on the vague systemic agenda than on the more concrete institutional agenda. In only four of the seventeen years covered by this study were there distinctively high levels of institutional politicization of crime. Third, when politicization occurred, its tone was distinctly critical and punitive—although not exclusively so.

These findings also raise some interesting questions. How is the relatively modest degree of politicization to be explained? After all, during a seventeen-year period when law and order seemed to figure prominently in the political ethos, institutional politicization was essentially confined to the four years from 1975 through 1978. And what is it about that particular period that explains the heightened politicization of street crime? Is there, moreover, any significance to the disproportionate shift from local to nonlocal crime reporting during the four years when politicization peaked?

But before addressing these questions, it is necessary to look at the companion indicator of politicization, campaigning on crime. As has already been suggested, this second indicator provides a rough test of how accurately crime reporting portrays the patterns of politicization. In addition, analysis of campaigning on crime puts us immediately in touch with concrete aspects of politicization.

Campaigning on Crime

There were essentially two avenues to the politicization of street crime. Candidates for public office did sometimes make street crime a campaign issue, and the results of such efforts are presented in Table 2.1. A more direct way to advance law and order values was to formulate policy proposals in the legislature or in the form of initiatives and revenue bonds presented to the

TABLE 2.1
Record of Candidates Endorsed by Law and Order Groups,
1964 to 1980

Year	Race	Total	Wins	Losses
1964	Mayoral	1	0	1
1967	City Council	3	1	2
1970	Prosecuting Attorney	1	0	1
1972	Superior Court	2	0	2
1973	Superior Court	2	2	0
	City Council	4	3	1
1974	Prosecuting Attorney	1	0	1
1975	City Council	5	3	2
1976	Superior Court	9	6	3
1977	Mayoral	1	0	1
	City Council	1	0	1
1978	State Supreme Court	1	0	1
	Court of Appeals	3	2	1
	Prosecuting Attorney	1	1	0
	City Council	1	0	1
1979	City Council	2	1	1
		38	19	19

electorate, as shown in Table 2.2. The issue was usually joined more clearly in the latter than the former, because candidates were frequently evasive. Still, in both instances, crude balance sheets can be drawn up and embellished with narrative detail so as to reveal a nuanced picture of campaigning on crime.

Between 1964 and 1980, policy issues relating to crime arose 12 times—in other words, less than once a year. But these summary figures are misleading in a couple of ways. The proposals were not spread evenly over the period: 7 of 12 instances were concentrated in the four years from 1975 through 1978. Second, not all of the questions raised bore directly on street crime. Notice that Table 2.2 includes bond issues for funding of criminal justice facilities, initiatives connected to the legalization of gambling, the prohibition of pornography, restrictions on gays, and the decriminalization of marijuana, as well as a proposal to create an intermediate court of appeals. These marginal issues were included in the table because they were often attacked or defended in terms of their relationship to street crime—albeit in a partial

TABLE 2.2
Success of Politicization of Law and Order Policy Proposals,
1964 to 1980

Year	Policy Proposal	Proposal Passed	Successful Politicization of Issue
1964	Initiative: to allow local licensing of pinball, punch cards, and card games	No	Yes
1966	Initiative: to increase police hiring	No	No
1968	Legislation: creating a Court of Appeals	Yes	No
1970	Bond issue: including a detention and rehabilitation center	No	No
1974	Initiative: to legalize possession of small amounts of marijuana	No	Yes
1975	Initiative: mandatory capital punishment	Yes	Yes
1976	Initiative: antipornography	No	No
	Initiative: ban on speed traps	No	Yes
1977	Bond issue: new police precinct houses	Yes	Yes
	Bond issue: repair of public safety building	No	No
	Initiative: direct mayoral appointment of chief of police (without examination)	No	Yes
1978	Initiative: antigay	No	No
	Initiative: rollback of police shooting policy	Yes	Yes

and indirect fashion. As for hard-core street crime issues, there were only three: increased police hiring in 1966, capital punishment in 1975, and police shooting policy in 1978.

The advocates of law and order had a two-out-of-three success rate on the hard-core issues. The failure occurred in 1966, when there was insufficient support from the electorate to force the hiring of more police officers.[23] On the other hand, a 1975 initiative requiring capital punishment for those convicted of murder in the first degree passed by a 2-to-1 margin, and in 1978, an initiative was passed forcing the city council to relax restrictions on police shooting policy. On the marginal matters, the outcomes were more evenly divided.

The same spotty pattern of activity and mixed rate of success applies to candidates who campaigned on crime. The tabulation presented in Table 2.1 is based on candidates endorsed by groups associated with the law and order issues. On average, law and order campaigning tended to be concentrated in the period between 1975 and 1978, with law and order candidates successful about 50 percent of the time.

Clearly, the most avid proponents of politicization would be disappointed by the numbers in these two tables. Nonetheless, these figures probably exaggerate the extent to which street crime was politicized. Looking beneath the balance sheet to the specifics of campaigning on crime suggests that the politicization of crime was both ephemeral and idiosyncratic. It was ephemeral in that it was largely confined to a brief period in the latter part of the 1970s, and idiosyncratic in that it seemed to be based heavily on personality and contingent circumstances.

Consider first the entry of rank-and-file police officers into electoral politics. While several tried for office, the records of three presidents of the Cedar City Police Officers Guild are most instructive, given the pivotal role of the guild in efforts to politicize street crime. When Mark Victor stepped down as guild president and was elected to the City Council in 1969, it looked as if police candidates might prosper in electoral politics. Victor was the driving force behind the guild's political action committee, and he quickly became a person of influence on the council and in city politics more generally. His reelection to the council in 1973 emboldened him to enter the mayoral race in 1977, but he failed even to secure enough votes in the primary to make the run-off election. After failing in an attempt to get back on the council in 1978, Victor left politics and entered private business.

Only at the end of the period did two other guild presidents try their hands at politics, and their records are also revealing. Donald Martin was twice unsuccessful in efforts to gain a seat on the City Council—despite support from business and trade union groups, as well as the guild and others associated with law and order values. In contrast, Wayne Michaels was elected to the state legislature in 1980. However, his own view was that his childhood roots in the legislative district and his fiscal conservatism accounted more for his success than his image as a police officer. He also claimed that he was much less dependent on the work of fellow police officers than Martin was. In any case, election to the legislature did not require a citywide constituency and thus is not a particularly good indicator of the politicization of street crime in Cedar City.

The record of Park County prosecutorial races is also revealing. Table 2.1 indicates that on two of three occasions, law and order candidates lost, and that the single law and order victory occurred in 1978, during the peak period of politicization. While these issues will be taken up in more detail in Chapter 4, which focuses on the criminal courts, a brief overview should be helpful here.

The 1970 law and order campaign of the machine incumbent, Dana Phillips, was largely irrelevant in a primary won by reformer Whitney Steele. The basic issue was the police payoff system, which cast a shadow over the prosecutor's office. Steele went on to win the general election in a close race against his Democratic rival. Four years later, this same Democrat tried to close the gap with a law and order campaign, but Steele won handily. That campaign was, nonetheless, a learning experience for Steele. He sensed a shift in the public mood, changed his policies, and began to build a moderate law and order image—in part because he anticipated running for governor. Thus, the 1978 law and order victory of Jeffrey Griffin, a key Steele aide, would seem to be indicative of an earlier change in the political climate—providing further confirmation of the years from 1975 to 1978 as a period of heightened politicization.

But even this high point of politicization cannot be taken at face value. Consider the signal event of that period: the electoral defeat of two liberal incumbent judges in 1976. Both judges had been targeted by a coalition of law and order groups led by the Cedar City Police Officers Guild, which had also handpicked the successful challengers. Defeat of two incumbent judges was taken by both friends and foes as an unequivocal sign of politicization.

In retrospect, however, there may have been less there than met the eye. In the first place, only two of five judges targeted by the law and order coalition were defeated. Moreover, these two chose to make the election into a plebicite on the liberal reforms that they favored, thus contributing to politicization. Finally, there seems to have been an undercurrent of anti-Semitism against the two, both of whom had clearly Jewish names. In any case, there was no Superior Court follow-up, and, indeed, one of the defeated incumbents was subsequently appointed to the State Court of Appeals, where he sat until his retirement with the man who had defeated his liberal colleague in the 1976 election.

The other notable successes of politicization were the two initiative campaigns already mentioned. In 1975, the electorate responded enthusiastically and positively to a capital punishment proposal. And, in 1978, the police guild led a successful fight against restrictions that the City Council had placed on police use of firearms. Both of these victories are certainly indicative of successful politicization. The capital punishment issue was pretty straightforward and suggested that in 1975 the Cedar City electorate was in tune with the punitive values of the broader American public, 60 percent of whom were favorably disposed toward capital punishment for those convicted of murder.[24]

The initiative on police shooting policy is even more suggestive of effective politicization. Police shootings had been an issue in Cedar City at least since 1971, when a young black man was shot while allegedly placing a bomb outside a postal substation. Although a divided coroner's jury held that there were grounds for pressing charges against the police officer who had fired the fatal shots, the prosecutor's office took no action. Through the years, there were other instances of questionable police shootings— usually involving blacks—and a variety of relevant proposals emerged for setting up review boards, for the exclusion of hollow-point bullets, and the like. It was not, however, until 1977 that City Council acted. The council's ordinance restricted the use of deadly force to situations in which police officers were defending themselves or others in imminent danger or apprehending an armed or violent suspect. Donald Martin, guild president at the time, organized the initiative campaign that successfully and significantly relaxed these restrictions—thus directly rebuking the City Council.

But once again, there is a hollow quality to these victories. Martin was unable to parlay his instrumental role in the initiative campaign into a seat on the City Council even though his opponent, a minority woman, supported the council's more restrictive ordinance. Moreover, the 1979 initiative campaign to compel judges to give prison sentences under certain circumstances did not merely fail to gain voter approval, it could not even attract enough signatures to get on the ballot. The initiative campaigns thus provide yet another instance of episodic politicization with little or no generative momentum.

The crime reporting and the campaign data present consistent and puzzling pictures of the politicization of street crime. The clearest common chord is the concentration of politicization in the period from 1975–1978. Roughly two-thirds of the endorsements occurred during these years, as did 12 of the 19 victories by law and order endorsees. This was also the period of peak activity with respect to initiatives and referenda. Another common chord is the equivocal quality of politicization. That is to say, only in that period did crime reporting take on a clear policy cast—and even then the focus seemed to shift toward distant nonlocal matters.

Yet it would be an overreaction to dismiss street crime altogether as a salient issue. There was, of course, at least the one four-year period in which street crime was fairly successfully politicized—albeit with mixed results. More broadly, even though campaigning on street crime was seldom successful, the tone of political discourse did shift in a distinctly law and order direction during the seventeen years covered in this research. Consider, for example, the increasing level of controversy in crime reporting. Moreover, even candidates who did not campaign on crime were generally careful not to appear unconcerned or soft on the issue. Consequently, due process proposals and candidates became relatively rare in the later 1970s and did not fare very well. Street crime, therefore, is seen best as a latent, rather than a manifest, issue that cast a significant shadow across the political arena.

But however these patterns of politicization are characterized, they pose two broad questions to be considered in the remainder of this chapter. How is the relatively limited politicization of the 1964–1980 period to be explained? What is it about the 1975–1978 period that led to disproportionate politicization during those four years?

Public Quiescence

A major obstacle to politicization of street crime was widespread public apathy on the issue. Interviews with Cedar City political leaders revealed very little grass-roots pressure on street crime. As we shall see, prominent politicians seemed virtually oblivious to the issue or inflected it in ways that were not consistent with a sense of public urgency. Of course, the politicization data indicate that the public was not apathetic all the time. There were intervals from the late 1960s to the late 1970s when the public was sufficiently responsive to make campaigning on crime a viable option. Moreover, as we see below, there were also constituencies in Cedar City that were more or less continuously preoccupied with crime. The objective here is to explore and explain the modest and uneven levels of public concern about street crime.

It has already been suggested that the general rule of public apathy on street crime and the exceptions to it can be best understood by thinking about street crime as a latent rather than a manifest public concern. While the public seems to have a real and continuing fear of street crime, this fear is normally politically dormant. Accordingly, there was relatively little pressure on candidates to campaign on crime and usually relatively little response to those who did. This seems to be the basic message of the Cedar City interviews that are considered here.

But to think of public concerns about street crime as latent raises two further questions. Why is it that, during a period when the public's fear of crime was increasing rather steadily, street crime turned out to be such an ephemeral issue? And what about the exceptions to the general rule—the occasions when the public was sufficiently aroused to put street crime on the institutional or the systemic agenda? These two questions are considered below.

Street Crime as a Latent Concern

Street crime was sufficiently beside the point that it was difficult to get political leaders to address it directly in interviews. Consider, for example, the parallel patterns of response of two members of the City Council when asked to talk about the issue. There was an inclination to confuse street crime with the "tolerance policy"—that is, with the police payoff scandal that rocked the city in the late 1960s.

Frances Norton: The concern is always up here, I think the tolerance policy hit us.

> John Coleman: It was always a challenge to the Chief of Police to keep organized crime out of Cedar City.

Once the focus on street crime was finally established, there was a tendency to personalize the issue rather than to think in terms of constituency pressures.

> Frances Norton: The worst thing that happened was the other night. I had been out to a meeting. I came home and still had not hung my coat up. I was sitting there with my coat on talking to my husband about midnight, and somebody tries to break into the house.
> John Coleman: He [the police chief] probably gave me [his place of business] more than average attention . . . not to the point of patronage.

Finally, when pressed, both council members made pro forma declarations lacking in conviction and hardly suggestive of an inclination to politicize street crime.

> Frances Norton: I am not insensitive to it. I want to put it that way. We did have our law and justice issues that we got into.
> John Coleman: I have a great burden for the people who get robbed, who are mugged, storekeepers.

While this precise pattern was not repeated by other respondents, the low salience of street crime was consistently confirmed in a variety of ways.

Consider the rather oblique path another member of the council took to making street crime an issue in his unsuccessful mayoral bid. The issue emerged from a kind of random search for targets of opportunity. One staff member who participated in the process described it as follows:

> One issue was bad checks. He wanted to make it a crime to knowingly—because of business men not being able to get enforcement against bad check writers—write more than three bad checks or something like that. And he ran into a wall, so he didn't get anywhere with that. . . . And of course he made a lot of noise about community crime prevention

programs. . . . We came up with something new every two or three days. I spent a lot of time doing basically PR work. A lot of my job was just thinking up ideas and coming up with press releases. This was maybe nine months or a year before the election and just trying to get his name in the paper as much as possible. So you would see those things—like zoo do. That's where you'd sell the elephant dung [for commercial purposes].

Presumably "zoo do" had less to contribute to a coherent campaign image than crime. But when asked what led the candidate to campaign on crime, the staffer expressed considerable doubt.

I don't know why. Probably because he was a liberal and wanted to bolster his conservative support. . . . He takes positions for consciously political reasons quite a lot. . . . I think he was looking for ways to get a portion of the vote that responds. *Even though it's small*, there is that portion of the vote. And I think he was looking for ways to get it [italics added].

In other words, crime was not chosen because it was perceived as an issue of major public concern, but because it served as a conservative litmus test and might provide access to a small segment of the electorate.

Even Mark Victor, the first police guild activist to seek public office, tended to steer clear of street crime as a priority issue. It is hardly surprising, therefore, that his relationships with erstwhile associates on the guild tended to be rather cool.

Mark did help us a lot because he came from us and he had another viewpoint in his vote. However, the presidents who followed him in my estimation had ego problems, and they thought it was beneath them to go to Mr. Victor. They thought Mr. Victor should come to them. So there really was not a close tie with Victor's office. . . . So a lot of members are bitter about Victor, and he blames the guild.

It would thus appear that Victor continued to identify with and speak on behalf of law and order values. But he also seemed to have kept the guild at arm's length in an effort to broaden his base of support. This once again is suggestive of the political marginality of street crime.

The most notable exception to this rule was George Walker, a long-time council member who represented the predominantly black area of the city. By the time of our interview in 1983, Walker felt less pressure, but he could clearly recall when street crime was a priority problem for his constituents.

> They don't hammer away on it anymore; they have almost given up on the fact that it's going to get any better. . . . Nobody basically jumps on me anymore. . . . At this time it doesn't come up any more than any other issue, like land use. . . . There was a time that was the primary thing that came up in the early years. From the time I came on the council [1967] until we got out past the police corruption to the latter part of the West administration [1977]. It's gotten back to where it's just another issue like everything else now. It's not because the crime is dropping off, it's because we've sort of woke up to living in the period we are in.

Because there was a high level of concern about street crime among blacks, Walker came to the council determined to take on justice issues, but not as a law and order advocate. Instead, he saw himself as a "buffer between the police and the black community, which were increasingly at each other's throat." He was, in short, less concerned with politicizing street crime than with politicizing the racial bias of policing.

The conclusion to be drawn from these comments is that street crime was consistently a *manifest issue* for only small portions of the public. This simple truth was driven home to candidates who tried unsuccessfully to build citywide law and order constituencies. For the broader public, street crime seems to have been a latent issue—perhaps a real and continuing fear but one that came to the surface only occasionally.[25]

The Social Construction of Victimization

It is tempting, but inadequate, to explain these patterns of public response to street crime in terms of victimization. It seems to follow, for example, that blacks are preoccupied with street crime because they tend to be disproportionately victimized. Moreover, the core of the law and order constituency seems to have been drawn from Crystal Valley, which, as Table 2.3 indicates, was another relatively high-crime area of Cedar City. But the Cedar City data as well as research elsewhere suggest that victimization is not so good a predictor of politicization as race and other socioeconomic variables.

Recall the national surveys mentioned in Chapter 1, which regularly revealed revealed discontinuities between victimization and reactions to it. Blacks were, for example, more victimized, more fearful, but less punitive. Women, in contrast, were less victimized, more frightened, and less punitive. Finally, the most punitive group in the American society comprised rural white males, who were less victimized and less fearful.[26] Thus, victimization provides neither a necessary nor a sufficient explanation for the kind of punitive politicization of crime associated with the politics of law and order.

Cedar City findings are compatible with these national patterns. If victimization had been the key to public arousal, then there would have been a close association between the crime rate and crime reporting in the 1960s and 1970s, but this is not the case. Figure 2.4 indicates that, as the local crime rate was rising, local crime reporting tended to decline (Pearson's $r = -.408$). If anything, it was national crime reporting that increased as the local crime rate went up (Pearson's $r = .263$).[27] The least tendentious interpretation of these data would suggest that crime reporting and the public sentiments associated with it seemed to have lives of their own in Cedar City—quite distinct from the actual incidence of crime. But it could also be argued that crime reporting in Cedar City diverted attention from local crime to national crime.

Still more revealing are the patterns of politicization in two key Cedar City neighborhoods. Table 2.3 indicates that both Crystal Valley and the Central Area are relatively high crime areas, but Table 2.4 reveals that the two neighborhoods are polar opposites on politicization issues. Crystal Valley, the less victimized of the two, supported initiatives that, respectively, brought a return to capital punishment and relaxed the city council's restrictions on police shooting policy. The more heavily victimized Central Area, in contrast, rejected the two initiatives. These data thus

TABLE 2.3
Incidence of Crime and Demographic Changes,
1970 and 1980

		1970			1980		
		Crystal Valley	Central Area	Cedar City (Other)	Crystal Valley	Central Area	Cedar City (Other)
Selected street crimes							
Burglary	No.	924	840	13,006	612	682	12,486
	%	3.64	5.84	2.65	2.54	4.97	2.74
Robbery	No.	96	185	1,703	166	139	1,948
	%	0.38	1.29	0.35	0.69	1.01	0.43
Aggravated	No.	52	104	798	146	240	1,987
assault	%	0.20	0.72	0.16	0.61	1.75	0.44
Selected demographic indicators							
Population		25,369	14,380	491,082	24,108	13,726	456,012
Percent change					−5.00	−4.30	−7.14
Black population		3,353	11,259	23,256	5,509	9,378	31,868
Percent black		13.22	78.30	4.74	22.85	68.32	6.99
Percent population below poverty line		7.90	16.50	5.59	10.00	21.00	5.99

Notes: The percentages for street crimes are derived by dividing the number of crimes by the population figures as presented here. There are some discontinuities between the socioeconomic and the crime data, which are derived from different sources and are based on different ways of dividing up the city.

1. Socioeconomic data are based on two core neighborhoods of the Crystal Valley (Numbers 68 and 69) and Central Area (Numbers 61 and 62) portions of the city derived from a neighborhood reworking of the census tract data from the 1980 U.S. Census. *Neighborhood Statistics Program, Cedar City.*
2. Crime data were collected by the police and reported by census tract. These data have been aggregated for the whole of Crystal Valley (Tracts 94, 100, and 104) and the Central Area (Tracts 77, 78, 79, and 80). Cedar City Police Department, *Annual Report, 1979* (Cedar City, 1980).
3. Mean incidence of reported crime for 121 census tracts.

FIGURE 2.4

Local Crime Rates and the Number of National and Local Crime Articles*
1964 to 1980

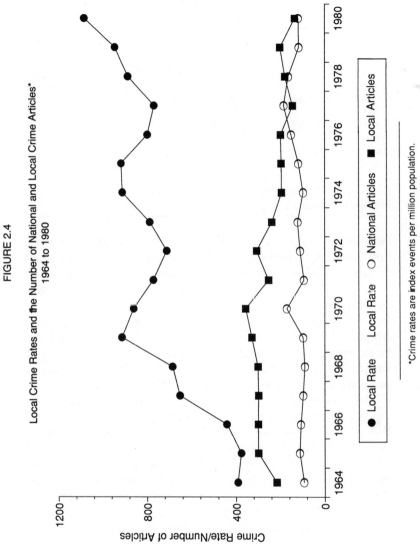

● Local Rate ☐ Local Rate ○ National Articles ■ Local Articles

*Crime rates are index events per million population.

TABLE 2.4
Selected Initiatives

		Result for Crystal Valley		Result for Central Area	
		Yes	No	Yes	No
Capital Punishment	Number	3,477	1,796	721	1,285
No. 316 (1975)	Percent	66	34	36	64
Police Shooting Policy	Number	2,867	2,311	704	1,909
No. 15 (1978)	Percent	55	45	27	73
Anti–School Busing	Number	2,808	2,234	799	1,730
No. 350 (1978)	Percent	56	44	32	68

Source: Post-election printout provided by Park County Records and Elections Division.

indicate that it is not victimization per se but how that victimization is construed that determines the course of politicization.

Table 2.3 helps us understand why street crime was construed differently in the two neighborhoods. The explanation is relatively simple for the Central Area. Law and order proposals forced a choice between controlling the police and controlling crime, and the predominantly black Central Area was apparently more worried about racial bias in criminal process than about street crime. Certainly, this was the view of black political leaders, as we see in the section on containing politicization below.

The reverse seems to have been true in Crystal Valley, although the picture seems a good deal more complex. Crystal Valley in the 1970s was a neighborhood in transition with a poverty rate that was rising faster than the citywide average and an increasing influx of blacks, whose numbers doubled during the 1970s. In all probability the residents of Crystal Valley associated increasing crime and economic decline with the growing black presence in their neighborhood. Thus, law and order values drew sustenance from racial hostility and social crisis.

Table 2.4 further underscores the salience of race by revealing the consonance between the outcomes of the law and order initiatives and the initiative to overturn Cedar City's school busing program. Blacks are sensitive to the racial overtones of law and order values and wary of policies that empower the police and move the criminal courts in punitive directions.

We have begun the process of explaining the modest extent of politicization in Cedar City during the high-crime years of the late 1960s and 1970s. The Crystal Valley and Central Area data suggest that the "natural constituency" for politicization, those people most victimized, was divided. More specifically, blacks were diverted from law and order populism by their fears of racial bias in the criminal process and by the antiblack overtones of the law and order ethos. Conversely, for most of the residents of Cedar City most of the time, street crime was at best a latent rather than a manifest issue. The average person in Cedar City just did not seem to think about street crime in political terms.

While this second finding adds to our understanding of the weakness of the politicization impulse, it begs the underlying question, which is considered in the rest of the chapter. How are we to account for political quiescence on an issue about which there seem to be such strong feelings? The interactive model of politicization presented at the outset of this chapter suggests that political leaders both shape and reflect public attitudes. If so, given latent public concerns about crime, there is reason to believe that committed elites could have effectively mounted a symbolic crusade on behalf of law and order values.[28] In Cedar City, however, the established elites were opposed to politicization, while the leaders of the law and order campaign were relatively weak and marginalized.

The Law and Order Coalition

The politicization campaign was led by the police guild and some small-business interests in Crystal Valley. Occasionally, it was possible for them to work effectively on behalf of law and order values. In general, however, the law and order coalition, with limited resources, was simply no match for the established civic elites, who worked with the leadership of the black community to neutralize efforts to politicize street crime.

The Cedar City Police Guild

The guild's interest in politics was fueled during the 1970s by two different kinds of frustrations. The rank and file felt that they were not getting their fair share when it came to pay and working conditions. More generally, they felt that their status was under assault from a number of quarters. The bitterness on these two fronts, which is detailed in Chapter 3, allowed the new guild leadership to gain significant support from the membership for political action directed at enhancing police prestige and improving wages and working conditions.

On the other hand, guild leaders had to contend with both apathy and resistance from the rank and file. In part, the problem was the free-rider tendency that plagues most organizations. Another problem was rooted in priorities. Although there is no reason to doubt the membership's acceptance of law and order values, only on the bread-and-butter issues directly related to wages and working conditions was consistent politicization of the rank and file possible. Finally, Cedar City police officers harbored the typical police distaste for politics and politicians and thus were reluctant to get involved in political action.

Politics tends to be a dirty word for police officers in Cedar City, as elsewhere. This basic distrust of politics is rooted in the firmly held belief that politics poses a dual threat to police professionalism. Politicians are seen as outsiders intent on pandering to the public or doing favors for the influential. As one guild official put it: "Policemen tend to be fairly cynical individuals in one regard. That is politics. They are absolutely convinced that bad politicians get elected no matter what you do. They feel that it is generally a waste of time to become involved in the political process." This congenital inclination of elected officials to curry favor is believed at the very least to interfere with even-handed law enforcement and, in the worst-case scenario, to deteriorate into full-scale corruption. Second, politicians are perceived as amateurs who, leaving aside their questionable probity, simply do not understand law enforcement.

Cedar City police officers were particularly sensitive to the links between politics and corruption because of the widespread police payoff system that was exposed toward the end of the 1960s. None of the respondents denied that corruption was pervasive, but they traced it, as well as its prejudicial exposure, to perfidious politicians who had introduced a "tolerance policy"— that is, a policy of selective enforcement of vice laws. In other words, politicians without the courage to live by their own vice laws, whether for personal profit or campaign support, planted the seeds of corruption. Then, in an effort to escape personal responsibility for the inevitable consequences of their own policy, they made the police department a scapegoat to be torn apart by the subsequent grand jury investigation. To add insult to injury, the police were convinced that politicians, most notably Park County Prosecuting Attorney Phillips, were directly implicated in the payoff system and yet were escaping largely unscathed.

It was during this period that the guild's first unfortunate foray into politics took place. The guild leadership, without consulting the membership, broke with a tradition of electoral neutrality to support, of all people, incumbent prosecutor Phillips when he ran for reelection in 1970. Needless to say, the rank-and-file guild members felt further compromised by this unilateral decision, which openly linked the department to a politician directly associated with the tolerance policy who seemed to be evading responsibility for its corrupting consequences.[29] This episode further soured rank-and-file police officers on politics.

A residual political cynicism, therefore, dogged the reform elements that took over the guild in the wake of the corruption scandal. Moreover, the members' distrust of politicians extended to their own leaders, who they feared were using guild office as a stepping stone. Of course, Mark Victor, a prime mover in the efforts to politicize police grievances, did capitalize on his high visibility to gain election to the City Council, but as we have already seen, Victor's subsequent relations with the guild were apparently not very smooth.

In addition, guild politics, like politics in general, was hardly pure, and sometimes it was deemed necessary to work with organizations that were suspect. "We had organizations come to us that we didn't necessarily agree with their philosophy and what they did, but they came to us for their own reasons, and if the situation fit we'd work with them." Thus, the guild allied with the ACLU in fighting against mandatory polygraph testing and apparently had at least tangential relations with radical-right organizations. As one guild activist put it:

> While I viewed our position as a moderate to conservative effort, I met with some people that were so damned far out, right-wing conservative, they scared me more than the left-

wing liberal type people. God they were scary. . . . I want nothing to do with these kinds of people. They were some really scary people, vigilante types almost.

What was true of organizations was also true of candidates.

If you have Candidate One who has such a strong political base, and. . . it's obvious from the backing he has or the money behind his campaign, . . . [that] he is going to win this election hands down—as opposed to his opponent, Candidate Two, who may be a highly motivated, extremely honest, desirable candidate, one that you might personally favor. But this is a key position . . . you know for a fact that he won't win. You probably as a responsible group will actually go for Candidate One, however reluctantly, because at least you'll have the door open to that candidate.

Even if the members accept that kind of logic and the endorsements that flow from it, it does not follow that they will have much enthusiasm or that they will participate actively.

Of course, there were rank-and-file members who were sympathetic to the objectives and methods of the guild. But even among these loyalists it was difficult to generate the kind of energy necessary for effective campaigning. A certain amount of political activity was possible without much participation by the rank and file. Ad hoc endorsements of candidates, for example, made very modest demands on organizational resources. Consider the guild's Saturday screening sessions, in which candidates were questioned by a membership committee. Obviously, a relatively small group of politically committed members could bear this burden.

While endorsements were the easiest way to go, what the candidates really looked for were campaign workers who would assemble and distribute lawn signs, collect money, ring doorbells, and otherwise carry the message to the voters. "You don't really have to do very much for each candidate to have that open door because they appreciate so much whatever they get. They need that free labor. We have the potential. A thousand members. If only a few were active, we'd be heroes." But the membership was difficult to activate.

Like most people, police officers are reluctant to devote their free time to political work. Thus, it was particularly difficult to sustain political activity over an extended period of time—as was required, for example, to carry out a plan for continuous monitoring of judges: "Not when it's an everyday thing. It was another job. Another piece of paper to be filled out. And they do that all day long." It was also difficult to turn out election workers on behalf of candidates espousing law and order values, even when these candidates were guild members. And unlike fire fighters, who, according to the police, have time to assemble signs and stuff envelopes on duty, only off-duty time was available to the guild's Political Action Committee.

Adding to the reluctance of police officers to campaign actively was their embarrassment at having to approach strangers. The irony did not escape guild activists. "Now here is an officer who deals with strangers all day long. Knock on the door and give a thirty-second spiel. It really embarrasses them. They don't want to be confronted. They don't want to be asked hard questions. They don't want to be embarrassed. And they're not in control. On the street they're in control. It's a whole new world." As a result, the "vast majority" of police officers would rather give money than canvass a neighborhood. And while some could be enlisted, even with those "you have to ask each one individually. You have to lead them by the hand. You have to organize the project and lay it all out for them. It's a tremendous job with a lot of disappointments."

Crystal Valley Activism

More than any other researcher, James Q. Wilson has provided insight into the populist sentiments that have given rise to the politics of law and order. As Wilson sees it, order maintenance is distinct from but intimately related to crime control:

A stable neighborhood of families who care for their homes, mind each other's children, and confidently frown on unwarranted intruders can change in a few years, or even a few months, to an inhospitable and frightening jungle. A piece of property is abandoned, weeds grow up, a window is smashed. Adults stop scolding rowdy children; the children, emboldened, become more rowdy. Families move out, unmarried adults move in. Teenagers gather in front of the corner store. The merchant asks them to move; they refuse. Fights occur. Litter accumulates. People start drinking in front of the grocery; in time, an inebriate slumps to the sidewalk and is allowed to sleep it off. Pedestrians are approached by panhandlers.

At this point it is not inevitable that serious crime will flourish or violent attacks on strangers will occur. But many residents will think that crime, especially violent crime, is on the rise, and they will modify their behavior accordingly.[30]

Irrespective of the empirical validity of Wilson's claim, a setting in which the public feels itself threatened by a diffuse and synergistic combination of disorder and crime is conducive to a politics of law and order.

This certainly seems to have been the case in Crystal Valley. The police guild found its organized support primarily in troubled residential–commercial neighborhoods. The analysis of one guild activist reads like a paraphrase of Wilson.

People in the Crystal Valley . . . were literally being put out of business. The whole area was undergoing a transformation, but it was accelerated by the fact that several neighborhood groups . . . literally ran in packs out there and the Park County judges as a group simply adopted release policies that you put them in jail and within a matter of hours they're back on the street, even for very serious crimes. . . . And the sentencing of those people and particularly their early release . . . led community leaders such as Betty Sawyer, who was a real estate agent in that area and candidly whose livelihood, now this is my opinion . . . if the area is allowed to go to pot, the property values drop and the business just isn't there.

In other words, small-business persons, whose economic interests and social status were directly threatened, took the lead in mobilizing locals to support and participate in a variety of law and order programs.

For the most part, the law and order activism involved seemingly ad hoc efforts organized for particular purposes—for exam-

ple, the Redwood Merchant Patrol, a Guardian Angels–like un-
dertaking to reassure shoppers during the Christmas season;[31]
Help Eliminate Lawless Protesting (HELP), apparently put together by a maverick downtown businessman with the covert
help of dissident police officers with the objective of unleashing
the police against anti–Vietnam war protesters;[32] Family and
Friends of Missing Persons and Victims of Violent Crimes, which
supported the 1975 capital punishment initiative accepted by the
electorate;[33] and the Civic Builders, who campaigned unsuccessfully against two council members who had not been sufficiently sympathetic to the Cedar City Police Department.[34]

Amid this welter of ephemeral activity, only the business persons of the Crystal Valley seem to have provided the police guild
with a reasonably constant ally. Sometimes presenting themselves as the Crystal Business Club and at other times as the
Crystal Valley Chamber of Commerce, this group got under way
in 1969. At that time, its president, Sheldon Plumber, addressed
the public safety committee of the Cedar City Council and complained about rising crime in general and the recent murder of a
local grocer in particular. Plumber warned the council that a
recent community meeting had talked of vigilante action and
complained about council restrictions on the police and about the
sentencing practices of judges. More specifically, he asked that
restrictions be lifted on a police practice of photographing juve-
niles: "Why cannot police be trusted to use their own judgment?
We have here a classic example of concern for criminal sensibilities over the welfare of society."[35] Plumber also voiced his
opposition to lenient sentencing practices: "It is a form of madness to turn loose a criminal with two or three previous convictions (on the tenth or twentieth offense) after a short confine-
ment. . . . We must fairly face the failure of our present parole and
rehabilitation practices."[36]

Five years later, these same Crystal Valley business persons
repeated their objections to rehabilitation and, under the aegis of
Chamber of Commerce president Betty Sawyer, organized a
"courtwatchers" program to monitor the sentencing practices of
Park County Superior Court judges. As a columnist for the *Cedar
City Tribune* put it, "Some groups or individuals have been con-
tent to gripe about the crime situation but the Crystal Valley
Chamber decided to do something about it."[37] The courtwatchers

established an insistent presence, although there is no way to know how much impact they had on sentencing practices—an issue discussed in Chapter 4. Subsequently the Crystal Valley Chamber joined with several other law and order groups to put together a Courtwatch Coalition, which together with the police guild played a leading role in the successful effort to unseat two liberal judges.[38]

The essential conclusion here is that the law and order coalition was not very strong. Neither guild leadership nor Crystal Valley business persons had significant financial capabilities or ready access to the mass media. Both groups were heavily dependent on the enthusiasm and commitment of volunteers who could rise to the occasion only from time to time. Crystal Valley court-watchers did, for example, establish a meaningful presence in Park Country courtrooms toward the end of the 1970s. The guild rank and file was now and then mobilized, most notably in successful efforts to relax restrictions on the use of firearms by the police and to unseat the two liberal judges who had shown little sympathy or respect for the police. But these volunteers could not be counted upon to provide the strong and consistent support required for effective politicization.

Containing Politicization

The intrinsic limitations of the law and order coalition stood in stark contrast to the formidable opposition to politicization. The core of this opposition was composed of local government offi-cials, corporate executives, and leading professionals, who had strong incentives for promoting a salubrious image of downtown Cedar City. They were joined by the leaders and community groups representing Central Area blacks, who, of course, had other reasons for rejecting the politics of law and order. Under the circumstances, it is hardly surprising that opponents usually had sufficient political clout to divert, co-opt or simply defeat the politicization of street crime.

Established Elites

For three distinct reasons, established elites resisted efforts to politicize street crime. It was conventional practice in Cedar City to avoid highly charged electoral campaigns. As attorney Austin Sedley, who worked in both the City Council and the mayor's office during the 1970s, put it:

> This is such a conservative city in a certain way. . . . Politicians don't attack each other directly, and when they do, they get in trouble. You're only supposed to talk about yourself and perhaps the issues—but no *ad hominem* at all. And you're not supposed to be incendiary. And if you are, the *Cedar City Tribune* just gets after you. So campaigns are low-key.

Second, the downtown elites were civic boosters with a promotional program of their own. To portray Cedar City as crime-ridden was hardly consistent with their program or with efforts to woo shoppers from suburban malls and conventions from other cities. Third, street crime was a racially divisive issue, and once blacks became an electoral force, the politicization of street crime became an increasingly risky strategy.

Accordingly, the established elites put most of their energies into their own long-term Campaign for Civic Excellence, in which crime took a back seat to a variety of civic improvements. The campaign began in 1966 and proposed a series of bond issues in 1968 and again in 1970 for such amenities as mass transit, a new stadium, parks and recreation, low-income housing, improved sewage systems, and highways. The 1970 bonds did include funding for construction of crime-related facilities—albeit with a rehabilitative, rather than a law and order, bias.[39]

There were both positive and negative ways in which the established elites refocused attention and energy away from the politicization of street crime to the Campaign for Civic Excellence. On the one hand, the elite supported a Community Crime Prevention Council (CCPC), which created twenty-two community councils throughout the city. On the other hand, they withheld support from candidates who were inclined to politicize crime. As attorney Austin Sedley saw things:

> It's a lot easier to go out there and positively be an advocate for the neighborhoods, and in connection with that you can certainly advocate a community crime prevention program. That's great and they have had a lot of support. But to charge

that somebody is soft on crime is not a nice thing to say about somebody, and it's probably not true. So I think it has to do with the nature of politics in this town.

Thus, the Community Crime Prevention Council, while not particularly successful, did provide a noncontroversial alternative to more radical law and order proposals to empower the police and constrain the judges. The council's tensions with the police department were in part the result of the CCPC's refusal to adopt a hard line on crime.[40] As for candidates intent on politicizing street crime, they were unable to get the endorsement of the established elite's Good Government League. More informally, the liberal judicial incumbents in the 1976 election were admonished to evade rather than respond to law and order charges, and the conservatives who defeated them were not readily accepted into the establishment, as we see in Chapter 4.

The newspaper data reported earlier also shed some light on the containment of crime as a political issue. As politicization reached its peak in the period from 1975 to 1978, the proportion of local crime reporting diminished to the point where it actually fell beneath reports of crime elsewhere in the country. There is no way of knowing whether this was intentional, but the diversion of public attention from the immediate street crime problems of Cedar City was surely consistent with the depoliticization objectives of the established elites.

Central Area Blacks

The street crime concerns of Central Area blacks were expressed in the priority given to public safety issues by George Walker, the black member of the City Council. Community groups also regularly spoke out on criminal justice issues. But black distrust of the police put them at odds with the law and order coalition. For them police reform was the necessary precondition to effective police service and thus took initial precedence over crime control as such.

Consequently, the black community was seriously out of step with politicized whites on the street crime issue. Street crime did not become a significantly salient issue in Cedar City until roughly 1975, but according to Walker it was the "primary thing" for blacks beginning in the late 1960s and had petered out by the late 1970s. Thus, just as the rest of the community was turning on to street crime, blacks seemed to be turning off.

More specifically, black leaders opposed the capital punishment initiative at the expressive core of the politicization campaign.[41] And throughout the period, blacks complained about the police, who were, of course, the spiritual and organizational leaders of the law and order coalition. As early as 1969, the Negro Voters League met with the mayor and asked him to replace the chief of police.[42]

Blacks were also among the earliest proponents of citizen participation in the struggle against crime.[43] Accordingly, they supported or initiated proposals for giving the community a voice in police disciplinary proceedings dealing with excessive force and other harassment of citizens.[44]

As it turned out, black concerns with fairness and citizen participation were much more influential than the law and order objectives associated with the politicization of crime, except perhaps in the 1975–1978 period, because, in part, Walker and some other black leaders were willing to play a mediating role consistent with the concerns of the established elites. In addition, due to their dependence on black votes, the two mayors who governed the city throughout the 1970s became increasingly responsive to the complaints of Cedar City blacks about the behavior and composition of the police department. A more detailed account follows in Chapter 3; suffice it to say here that law and order values were subordinated to the racial concerns of the black community.

The balance of political power in Cedar City clearly ran against politicization. The law and order coalition, working on its own, was seldom strong enough or sufficiently savvy to mobilize latent public fears of crime. Nor was the coalition in a position to reach out to blacks or gain the acceptance of established elites. Blacks, although genuinely concerned about street crime, felt themselves threatened by the policies and values of the law and order coalition—especially the pro-police and pro–capital punishment proposals. Established elites were loath to portray Cedar City as a crime-ravaged city and preferred the kind of low-key approach to crime control that precluded politicization.

The sporadic success of efforts to politicize street crime in Cedar City can be traced to two major obstacles. Support for politicization among the general public seems to have been fragmented, lukewarm, and latent. Second, there seems to have been a tacit agreement among community leaders not to exploit latent opportunities.

It might seem that these findings are idiosyncratic, telling us more about the peculiarities of Cedar City than about the politicization of street crime. Certainly, each setting is special, and it is important to be sensitive to the particularities of Cedar City. But both the empirical record and the logic of politicization suggest that Cedar City experiences reveal important generalizations about the politicization of street crime in the United States.

Perhaps the central finding of the Cedar City research is that street crime was not a particularly promising target of opportunity for local political entrepreneurs. The rate of success was poor both for individual candidates who campaigned on street crime and for other kinds of electoral efforts on behalf of law and order values. Still, crime was effectively politicized from time to time, thus raising questions about how and why politicization does occur.

There are some indications that the occasional politicization of street crime was directly linked to social disorganization. The two areas of the city most responsive to politicization, the Central Area and Crystal Valley, were, after all, high-crime areas where people were most likely to feel the effects of street crime. Beyond crime as such, the areas were also characterized by low income, unemployment, and other indexes of poverty.

The ostensible implication of tracing politicization to victimization and poverty is that there is a direct and unproblematic linkage between material conditions and politicization. Accordingly, it might reasonably be inferred that the low levels of politicization in Cedar City were due to its acceptably safe streets and relatively prosperous circumstances. This inference would be, however, at best a misleading oversimplification.

On closer examination, the Cedar City findings indicate that the relationship between material conditions and politicization are complex and contingent. Recall that Figure 2.4 reveals a very weak relationship between the crime rate and press coverage of crime. More concretely, Figure 2.5 indicates that the 1975–1978 period of peak politicization was not characterized by corresponding elevations in the crime rate. Figures for murder and burglary were not particularly high during those four years,

Figure 2.5

Cedar City Crime Profile
1970-1979

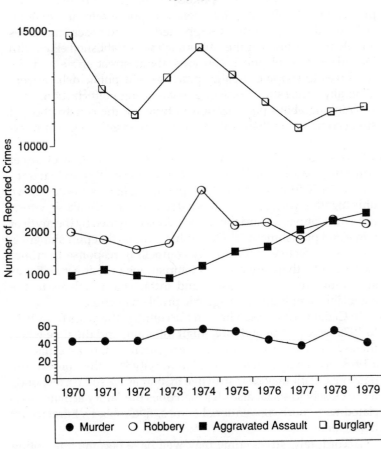

Source: Cedar City Police Department, <u>Annual Report</u>, 1979 (Cedar City, 1980).

although robbery rates did increase somewhat and assault figures were significantly higher. In other words, criminal victimization as such does not seem to provide an adequate explanation for the aberrant levels of politicization during that period.

The alternative argument is that politicization is dependent on an indeterminate variety of material conditions and on how these conditions are construed. Thus, while poverty and victimization seemed to work together to influence politicization, race was a cross-cutting factor, leading to sharply contrasting ways of expressing street crime as a political issue. The priority for the predominantly black Central Area was police reform, while racially divided Crystal Valley supported law and order candidates and their program. For the city as a whole, established elites with incentives to cool public concerns about street crime and the resources to shape campaign practices and public debate were generally successful at resisting or co-opting politicization.

Thinking about politicization in terms of the construction of street crime rather than as its direct reflection also suggests an explanation for the relatively effective politicization of the 1975–1978 period. As I argue elsewhere, the politicization of street crime may be associated with perceptions of social crisis that transcend street crime as such. "The politics of law and order thrive only together with a more extended sense of social malaise, which drives the public toward the consolations provided by the myth of crime and punishment."[45] Our culture tells us that punishment is a simple, effective, and morally compelling response to crime. Accordingly, there are obvious temptations to redirect anxieties stemming from more elusive and intractable problems to the ostensibly simple and manageable problem of crime.

In Cedar City, as elsewhere in the country, the years from 1975 to 1978 were a time of double-digit inflation, and the time when the explosive issue of school desegregation and, more explicitly, a 1978 antibusing initiative divided the city.[46] In this context, the data on assault may be instructive insofar as assault corresponds more closely to social disorder than does predatory activity associated with more conventional crimes, like robbery, burglary, or homicide.

Accordingly, street crime may well have become a tempting condensation symbol during this period. Given the moral dilemmas of busing, the technical complexities of inflation, and the pervasiveness of urban disorder, the attractions of a relatively straightforward problem like street crime may have been sufficient to undermine the moderating influences of established elites. If so, high crime may have been a necessary, but hardly a sufficient, precondition to politicization—thus helping explain the long time lag between increased street crime in the 1960s and politicization in the late 1970s.

The best available data for putting Cedar City in context come from a major research project on governmental responses to crime in ten cities between 1948 and 1978.[47] The research findings reveal striking similarities between the patterns of politicization uncovered in Cedar City and those to be found elsewhere in the United States, suggesting that the lessons of Cedar City are more generally applicable. At the same time, this research suggests that by national standards the level of politicization in Cedar City was relatively, *but not uniquely,* low—thus providing some insight into the circumstances that promote moderation in the politics of street crime. Both the Cedar City variations and its more typical tendencies help to explain when, why, and to what extent street crime is likely to become politically salient.

The overall patterns of politicization discovered in the ten cities studied in the governmental responses to crime project are virtually identical to those found in Cedar City. That is to say, politicization emerged rather belatedly, tended to be sporadic, and was concentrated in the years between 1974 and 1978. (See Table 2.5.) Herbert Jacob, one of the principal investigators for the project, put it this way:

> From the middle 1960s—when official crime rates were rising most markedly—the political agendas of cities were crowded with issues. . . . Crime thus had stiff competition from other issues. . . . Only during the last period (1974–1978) did crime reach the number one position; budget and tax problems and the economy continued to rank near the top.[48]

Jacob's findings are also consistent with the idea of crime as a condensation symbol. He points out that, while crime was just one issue among many, its salience "may have been related to the public's attention to school desegregation, race relations, and civil disorders, matters that some persons linked to crime."[49]

TABLE 2.5
Salience of the Crime Issue in Local Elections,
1948 to 1978

City	1948–1962	1962–1978	1974–1978	1948–1978
Atlanta (N = 4)	1.00	3.50	5.00	3.25
Boston (N = 4)	5.50	4.00	4.00	4.75
Houston (N = 7	1.50	1.00	5.50	2.57
Indianapolis (N = 7)	3.57	2.67	6.00	3.57
Minneapolis (N = 7)	3.50	4.33	3.50	3.86
Newark (N = 3)	3.00	5.00	6.00	4.67
Oakland (N = 5)	1.50	1.00	4.00	1.80
Philadelphia (N = 5)	1.67	1.00	6.00	2.40
Phoenix (N = 8)	4.50	2.00	3.50	3.63
San Jose (N = 4)	1.00	1.00	4.00	1.75
Ten cities (N = 54)	2.87	2.61	4.62	3.20

Note: N = number of mayoral incumbencies.
Source: Herbert Jacob, Robert L. Lineberry, with Anne M. Heinz, Janice A. Beecher, Jack Moran, and Duanne H. Swank, *Governmental Responses to Crime: Crime on Urban Agendas* (Washington, D.C.: National Institute of Justice, 1982), p. 32.
Key: 1 = crime was not a salient election issue at all.
    7 = crime was a very salient election issue.

With all that said, the governmental responses to crime research suggests a more moderate level of politicization in Cedar City than elsewhere in the country. It seems unlikely, for example, that the salience of street crime in Cedar City ever reached the levels of Indianapolis, Newark, and Philadelphia. Nor does crime seem to have intruded into the politics of Cedar City as consistently as it did in Boston and Minneapolis. Conversely, other middle-sized western cities, Phoenix, Oakland, and San Jose, reveal a moderation comparable to Cedar City's. In short, the moderation of politicization in Cedar City seems to distinguish it from about two-thirds of the ten cities in the governmental responses to crime project.

There is, however, another way of looking at this. An examiniation of Table 2.5 indicates that moderation is the rule rather than the exception. Most of the time in most places, the politicization of crime was not very intense, and the Cedar City findings help us explain the underlying strength of the forces of moderation. Yet, given the right combination of circumstances, intense politicization did develop in a number of cities—although not in Cedar City, which therefore provides some insight into the conditions likely to contain politicization. Cedar City teaches us something about the basic tendencies that promote moderation and also about the special circumstances that reinforce moderation when it is under pressure.

3

Policy, Politics, and the Police

In principle, it might seem that a law and order political climate would reinforce an already strong police commitment to a punitive version of volitional criminology. At the heart of this kind of thinking are the traditionally punitive police subculture and the assumption of a political alliance between the police and law and order elements within the public. That was certainly my view several years ago when I wrote: "It . . . seems likely, as long as the politics of law-and-order continue to predominate, that the political arena will be receptive to rank-and-file demands for a more punitive policy posture."[1] In practice, things have not worked out this way, and the politics of law and order has flourished along with significant moderation and reform of police practices.

There have been two distinct lines of reform: an initial move from the punitive style of *traditional* policing to the legalistic style of *professional* policing and a more recent move to a consensual style associated with *community* policing. Although the ultimate shape and staying power of these reforms is uncertain, they do represent shifts that run counter to the punitive implications of the politics of law and order. The point is not so much that major transformations have taken place but rather that tendencies have developed in unanticipated directions—toward nonpunitive forms of volitional criminology.

This chapter attempts to show how and why the punitive influences of the politics of law and order were undercut by a variety of competing forces.

73

From Traditional to Professional Policing

Punitive values are powerfully embedded in traditional policing practices. According to a rich and persuasive body of research, police have preferred to think of themselves as crime
fighters for whom coercive force serves both instrumental and
expressive purposes. On the one hand, the baton and the gun
are simple "tools of trade," as Jonathan Rubenstein has put it:
"The use of force is not a philosophical issue for a policeman. It is
not a question of should or whether, but when and how much."[2]
On the other hand, the expressive use of force is a matter of self-
respect and "public education." According to Albert Reiss:
"There are strong subcultural beliefs that the officer who ignores
challenges from citizens loses the respect of the citizenry and
makes it difficult for officers to work in the precinct. No challenge
to authority, therefore, can go unmet until there is acquiescence
to it."[3] These punitive values carry over to sentencing and lead to
a strong police commitment to incarceration as a way to deter
and incapacitate criminals. There is, accordingly, considerable
hostility toward judges and criminal justice professionals who
engage in permissive sentencing practices,—thus accounting for
the Cedar City Police Guild's determined campaign against two
liberal judges. Permissive sentencing practices are seen as incon-
sistent with crime control and public order. At a more personal
level, permissive practices are taken as a gratuitous repudiation
of the work of arresting officers, who are repeatedly burdened
and threatened by this recycling of felons.

There is a strong discretionary as well as a punitive side to
traditional policing. In organizational terms, traditional American policing has been both decentralized and discretionary. De-
centralization stemmed from machine politics and the intimate
relationships between police precincts and the ward bosses who
serviced the machine's constituents.[4] Discretionary authority for
patrol officers is, in part, a functional imperative of street-level
bureaucracy.[5] But it also reflects an acceptance of a territorial
view of policing. As Rubenstein put it: "The police are organized
to control the streets and the successful patrolman is an informal
specialist in street use. He combines his knowledge of local behavior with his conception of how the public streets are used to
analyze and perform many of his routine obligations."[6] The net

effect is to give individual patrol officers a significant measure of autonomy. Even for rank-and-file officers who are not punitively inclined, the autonomy afforded by traditional policing has obvious attractions.

But traditional policing has been under significant pressure from a number of directions over at least the last thirty years. The good-government reformers who fought with considerable success against machine politics have also worked to remove policing from partisan politics and to "professionalize" both law enforcement and departmental administration. In law enforcement, professionalization means uniform, nonpartisan policing—"without fear or favor," as one of my respondents put it. Administratively speaking, professionalism has been associated with the development of a centralized organization staffed by police managers who seek control over street-level policing.[7] Generally speaking, professionalization has been more attractive to police managers than to rank-and-file officers.

Chiefs of police generally are chosen by, are responsible to, and serve at the pleasure of the incumbent political administration. With their jobs on the line, police chiefs want to minimize the chances that individual patrol officers will misbehave in politically damaging ways. Traditional policing maximizes discretion and, accordingly, the opportunities for politically embarrassing misbehavior. Traditional policing has been associated with corruption, which, once uncovered, is at best awkward for political leaders and virtually certain to cost a police chief his job. More recently, punitive misbehavior at the expense of newly empowered minority communities has been a politically sensitive issue. Of course, it is not only job security that leads police managers away from traditional and toward professional policing. Police managers, like managers in business or other government agencies, are attracted to centralization insofar as it seems to maximize power and control and minimize uncertainty and unwelcome surprises. In sum, police managers reject traditional policing because it attenuates managerial control and can create political problems.[8]

For rank-and-file officers the incentives run in the opposite direction, and the years since the 1960s have called for painful adjustments. While rank-and-file officers do welcome nonpartisan law enforcement, they do not like the way in which centralized administrative control impinges on their discretion—a discretion they believe they are entitled to as "professionals." In addition to the assertion of managerial prerogatives, the autonomy of patrol officers has been further eroded by decisions of the Warren Court, which put restrictions on a number of police activities—most notably on investigation and interrogation practices. Finally, the police came under close political scrutiny as a result of street conflicts stemming from the civil rights and anti-war movements of the late 1960s and early 1970s. Thus, it is not surprising that rank-and-file officers have taken the lead in trying to politicize their image as crime fighters who should be reinvested with the discretionary authority of traditional policing.[9]

While rank-and-file politicization has become overt and aggressive in Cedar City and elsewhere, it has been only sporadically successful. The rank and file is, in the first place, significantly and increasingly divided along ideological and color lines as a result of changing patterns of police recruitment, which are bringing in significant number of minorities and women and are also raising educational levels.[10] And politicization itself is a controversial issue, at least insofar as it extends beyond the bread-and-butter issues covered by the employment contract. Rank-and-file officers have discovered that their wages and working conditions are controlled by political decisions and have organized to increase their influence on these decisions. But the last chapter revealed that the politicization of broader issues of criminological ideology tends to be deeply suspect and a sometime thing.

The Advent of Community Policing

A second and more recent current of reform has been community policing. The initial impetus for community policing came from the Police Foundation, which encouraged police managers to develop a consensual alternative to the coercive practices of traditional policing, as well as to the detached and legalistic style of professional policing.[11] Since that time, community policing has become increasingly prominent in efforts to reform policing practices.[12]

At the heart of community policing is the notion that the police mission has as much to do with social service as with crime control. According to this way of thinking, a primary responsibility of the police is public order,—making neighborhoods both safer and more harmonious. As James Q. Wilson puts it: "When I speak of the concern for 'community,' I refer to a desire for the observance of standards of right and seemly conduct in the public places in which one lives and moves, those standards to be consistent with, and supportive of, the values and life styles of the particular individual."[13] Community policing calls upon street-level officers to develop close relationships with their neighborhoods by way of long-term assignment practices, increased emphasis on foot patrol, initiation of police-organized neighborhood activities, public safety programs in schools, and the like.[14] The police are also expected to work with and through local community organizations rather than claim a monopoly on public safety activities.[15] Finally, the police are expected to contribute directly to community building by engaging in a variety of problem-solving activities—intervening as neighborhood advocates with public agencies, landlords, and merchants.[16]

A crime control case is also made on behalf of community policing. First, it is argued that information is the most important tool of crime control and that a coercive approach to policing tends to cut the police off from their best source of information, the community.[17] Second, there is a growing belief that a well-ordered community is less vulnerable to crime.[18]

The shift toward community policing puts a good deal of pressure on both the traditional police subculture and the professional style of policing. Nonetheless, it seems to be gaining increasing acceptability among police managers and street-level officers alike. It is much too early to assess the long-term prospects of community policing or even to project what form it will finally take. Still, despite the fact that community policing calls upon managers and street-level officers to alter established practices and values, it provides some trade-offs that are increasingly attractive under current conditions.

The more interesting and complex trade-offs concern rank-and-file police officers, who are expected to subject themselves to community standards of behavior and to minimize coercive practices. William K. Muir's research is particularly helpful for understanding the street-level implications of the changes that must take place. Community policing calls for an approach rather like that of Jay Justice, one of the police officers who was part of Muir's Laconia study. Justice believed in the use of force:

"You can't do much when they don't fear the law, . . . when they are not afraid of anything." Coercion was essential to gaining control of individuals who were otherwise ungovernable.[19]

But Justice also had a broad conception of his responsibilities:

"Our job" as policemen is . . . to help individuals survive for the time being, to buy time "right now," to offset the despair of the moment. . . . Calming people was a big enough job to occupy a mortal. It meant, for example, that he had better learn a little insurance law to help families recover indemnity for malicious damage to their houses. It meant he had better apply a little knowledge of psychology so that he could get an old man hospitalized before the neighborhood kids taunted and drove him into desperate and destructive actions. In short, his job was to work his beat.[20]

Justice operated, as Muir put it, with a "sense of limited purpose. . . . He felt no responsibility for improving things totally. He held no utopian or perfectionist standards."[21]

Conversely, Muir's "enforcer," Frank Russo,

sounded a theme absent from Justice's discussion of coercion. Russo felt morally compelled to use force when laws and departmental regulations forbade it. . . . The law may have forbidden maximum force, but Russo perceived it to be an act of betrayal and cowardice to knuckle under to the law. His need for moral worth, his "pride" would eventually overcome his timidity; defiance of the laws and the regulations would be the hallmark of good police conduct.[22]

Clearly, there was an expressive quality to Russo's approach to force, whereas for Justice, the use of force was based on a narrowly circumscribed, instrumental calculation. Russo's more traditional view of coercion carried over to the police mission more generally:

Since crime-fighting was the only job which was morally legitimate under his one-dimensional scale of values, whenever
Russo acted in other capacities, he felt he was wasting his
time. Talking with victimized families was "public relations; it
couldn't be a bigger waste of time." Resolving family beefs
happily through patient talk was "bullshit" or dishonesty.
Writing a good report for police or social services was "secre-
tarial work."[23]

Russo, thus, saw himself exclusively as a crime fighter, and every
crime as a personal affront and an indication that he was failing at
his job. He had a more ambitious but a much narrower conception of policing. It was more ambitious in that his objective was to
root out crime, but it also reduced policing to the restrictive
dimensions of cops and robbers.

There are probably a variety of reasons that community policing seems to be gaining ground with rank-and-file officers, even
though it downgrades the importance of coercion and crime
control. At the heart of the matter is a kind of trade-off between
coercion and discretion. Community policing may constrain the
use of force, but it also shifts decision-making authority from the
central administration to the community level and then to patrol
officers who are vested with a good deal more responsibility.
George Kelling summarizes research on the response of officers
to the opportunities provided by community problem solving:
"Police officers enjoy operating with a holistic approach to their
work; they have the capacity to do it successfully; they can work
with citizens and other agencies to solve problems; and citizens
seem to appreciate working with police."[24] In a sense, then,
community policing allows street-level officers to regain some
of the ground lost as a result of professionalization. Community
policing also helps to resolve a contradiction of professionalization. One of the fruits of professionalization has been better-
educated and better-trained police departments. Generally
speaking, autonomy is one of the attractions of professionalization, but within police circles professionalization attempted to
mix an enhanced sense of personal efficacy with tighter and more
centralized control. Inevitably, these better-trained and better-
educated officers bridled at such constraints. It may also be that
these same changes provided police with skills and perspectives

that made coercion seem both less necessary and less appropriate.

Actually, it is the police managers, rather than rank-and-file officers, who have been more resistant to community policing. They are, of course, uneasy about relinquishing organizational control. Thus, it was fairly common in the early days of community policing for experiments in what was then called "team policing" to be undertaken with only grudging support from police managers, who were probably responding more to the incentives provided by Law Enforcement Assistance Administration funds than to the goals and principles of reform. As a result, the experiments tended to be poorly planned, carried out half-heartedly, and terminated as soon as the funding ran out, if not sooner.[25] If police managers are now beginning to see the light, it is probably due both to the realization that coercive practices were not sufficient and to the increasing resistance of newly empowered minority communities to police coercion. Community policing in effect enlists the community to help police managers avoid the kinds of excessive force that create serious political problems for the mayors, city managers, and city council members who are, in effect, the police chief's employers.

Rank-and-file officers as well as police managers thus have both negative and positive incentives for accepting community policing. On the negative side, community policing represents a kind of second-best alternative. For rank-and-file officers community policing is preferable to the rigidities of the professional model. For police managers, community policing offers a way of minimizing politically explosive confrontations between the police and the public—especially in black and minority urban neighborhoods. More positively, community policing amounts to a recognition by thoughtful and progressive elements within police departments that the police do a better job of maintaining order than of fighting crime, that their meager crime-fighting capabilities are further compromised by punitive policing, and that it is both possible and preferable to develop cooperative relationships between the police and the public(s).

The Cedar City findings presented below provide data for testing the general propositions offered above. In the next section, the focus is primarily on quantitative indicators that reveal the broad patterns of policy change and the key explanatory variables. Because these data do not go beyond the early 1980s, we can see only the precursors of community policing, which did not get a serious testing until the end of the decade. While the quantitative data provide a useful overview, the interviews on which the remainder of the chapter is based offer a more nuanced picture of the character of reform and a more persuasive confirmation of the explanations developed here.

Patterns of Policy Change

Two kinds of quantitative indicators are available for tracing patterns of police reform. *Arrest rates* provide a direct measure of police policy and of the currents of reform. *Variations in police funding* do not tell us so much about the police as about the priority given the police by political leaders. The search for variables to explain policy trends tends to confirm the emerging theme of this research. Neither the crime rate nor crime reporting was helpful, according to regression analysis, for explaining policy variations.[26] The politicization of street crime appears to be at most a marginal factor in policymaking.

On the other hand, changes in police leadership did help explain variations in arrest rates and in police funding. This outcome is consistent with Muir's work on the importance of police leadership as well as with the interview data presented below. The underlying message of these data extends, however, beyond leadership per se to the political forces that ultimately determine the appointment and tenure of chiefs of police. In any case, there were four distinctive regimes during the years covered by this research: Dewey Cheatham, 1964–1969; W. C. Brush, 1970–1973; Charlie Goodfellow, 1974–1977; and Richard Tracy, 1979–1982.[27]

Police Funding

Changes in the percentage of the budget going to the police are a good test of political commitment. The analysis is, however, complicated by a distinction between the city's total budget, which includes funds from outside sources, and the general fund budget, which includes only tax revenues raised by the city. The efforts of the city itself, revealed in the general fund trends in Figure 3.1, seemed to peak in the early 1970s and drop off there-

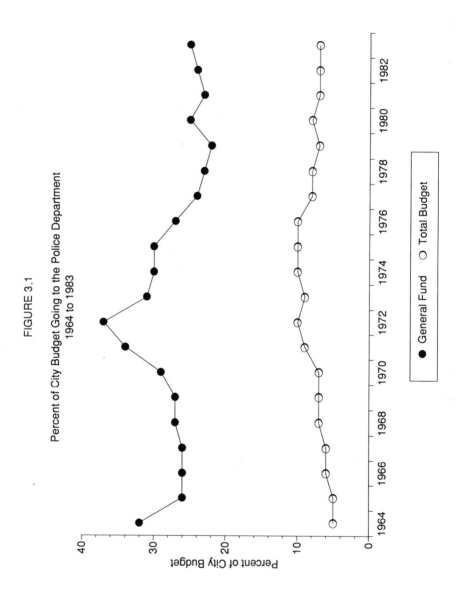

FIGURE 3.1

Percent of City Budget Going to the Police Department
1964 to 1983

● General Fund   ○ Total Budget

TABLE 3.1
Impact of Police Regime on Major Policy Indicators

Policy Indicator	Regime Averages[a]			
	Cheatham	Brush	Goodfellow	Tracy
Percent general fund to police	26.1	33.2	26.0	24.4
Percent total budget to police	6.3	9.4	8.9	6.9
UCR Part I Arrests[b]	4,060.0	1,965.5	6,975.5	8,289
Vice Arrests[b]	769.4	1,169.5	1,440.0	1,870.8
Efficiency[c]	4.13	1.72	6.77	7.91
Effectiveness[d]	0.36	0.18	0.27	0.26

Notes:
[a]Averages represent "Lagged Chief Regimes." The lagging is accomplished by advancing each chief's stay in office one year under the assumption that the impact of policies implemented will be delayed one year.
[b]Arrest figures are per year averages.
[c]Average number of arrests per sworn officer per year.
[d]Number of street crime arrests divided by reported street crimes.

after. In effect, Chief Brush stands out, and he did very well indeed. Table 3.1 indicates that Brush's mean annual share of the general fund budget, 33 percent, was better by roughly 6 to 9 percent on average than the other chiefs'.

At first glance, these findings are somewhat puzzling. As we shall see from the interview data, Brush was in almost continual conflict with the mayor and the City Council and was regularly criticized for his lack of political skills. The other chiefs got along very well with the political leaders of Cedar City. This was particularly true of Tracy. Why is it, then, that Tracy, the most politically savvy of the chiefs, did so poorly with city funding while Brush, who treated politicians with contempt, was funded most generously of all? It is likely that the reform mayor and City Council decided, in the wake of the payoff scandal, that the department had to be better funded. There was good reason to believe, as is evident below, that poor pay made police officers more receptive to the temptations of the payoff system. It is also probable that outside funding contributed to Brush's success, in that he was chief during the heyday of the federally funded

Law Enforcement Assistance Administration (LEAA). In short, Brush's personal influence was more apparent than real.

More generally, these budgetary figures suggest that corruption control was a more salient factor in police funding than the control of street crime. The basic flatness of the portion of the total budget going to the police (Figure 3.1) also suggests that outside funding, from the LEAA, for example, was less likely to be used to enhance the crime control effort than to maintain a settled political formula for dividing revenue among the various claimants on city funds. This thesis also gains in credibility from the interview data. In sum, the budget figures lend further weight to the conclusion that street crime was simply not a high political priority during this period.

Arrest Rates

Arrests are, admittedly, a controversial measure of police activity.[28] Police reformers and advocates of traditional policing are inclined to believe that there are better ways to spend police dollars than on arrests—that is, on a variety of proactive measures that would reduce the crime rate. Accordingly, it might be argued, as does one of the police managers quoted later, that judgments about police performance should be based on the crime rate rather than the arrest rate. But not many criminologists or police officers would claim that the police are really responsible for significant changes, whether up or down, in the crime rate.

Irrespective of these qualifications, variations in arrest rates may well be indicative of reform. The legalistic style of policing associated with professionalization would seem likely to generate more arrests than either traditional policing, which relies on informal coercion, or community policing, which stresses consensual forms of dispute resolution.[29] Variations in arrest rates might also be expected to provide some insight into police priorities insofar as there are inverse relationships among arrest rates for different types of crime. Thus, a department that decided to crack down on street crime might divert resources from the vice squad, thus leading to a decrease in vice arrests.

The arrest data can be further refined to provide meaningful, if crude, measures of police efficiency and effectiveness. Insofar as the police are able to increase the number of arrests per sworn officer, it could be said that they were becoming more efficient. Similarly, changes in police effectiveness can be inferred from an index based on the relationship between reported street crime and street crime arrests.[30]

The arrest data are once again particularly revealing as to the Brush tenure. Table 3.1 indicates that Brush's arrest record is weak. His department was the least effective in dealing with street crime, and his term was also characterized by the lowest arrest rates and lowest arrest efficiency rate. In other words, despite relatively generous funding, the department did not perform well according to the arrest indicators. Not only was Brush generously funded; he was also far and away the chief most popular with the rank and file, who regarded him as a tough law-and-order police officer. To be fair to Brush, it must be acknowledged that he took over a department that was deeply divided and demoralized by the corruption scandal. Still, the memories of the Brush era that follow, when combined with these disappointing performance figures, suggest that Chief Brush had more to offer rank-and-file officers than the citizens of Cedar City.

Conversely, the other chiefs look relatively good in terms of these quantitative indicators. Perhaps the only real surprise comes from Chief Cheatham's rankings. During the early years covered by this study, he presided over a corruption-ridden department, but nonetheless, his term stands out as the most effective at dealing with street crime—if only marginally more than Goodfellow's or Tracy's. On the other hand, Cheatham's arrest totals and efficiency are relatively low. The explanation for the low rate of vice arrests is clear enough given the payoff system. As for the other findings—high effectiveness, low efficiency, and low overall arrest rates—it seems most reasonable to attribute this to the traditional style of policing that prevailed during that period. Police officers remember the years before 1970 as the good old days when police could do just about whatever they pleased without legal or political scrutiny. Accordingly, it was probably somewhat easier to catch and convict criminals, and a good deal of police activity was handled informally—that is to say, without arrests.

Finally, we come to Chiefs Goodfellow and Tracy, who according to these arrest indicators fall between the other two and whose rankings are quite similar. Goodfellow was ever-so-slightly more effective, while Tracy was a bit more efficient and made more arrests. What can we say, then, about the direction of the department in the more recent period? First, while the department improved its street crime effectiveness from the low levels of the Brush era, it never did regain the level of effectiveness achieved under Chief Cheatham. This does not seem to have been for want of trying. On the contrary, the city appears to have gotten a good deal of work from its police officers in later years. The force was, after all, making markedly more arrests overall and per sworn officer. In all likelihood, the department has been less effective because of the constraints imposed by the shift away from traditional policing and because the city has not provided sufficient resources to keep pace with the crime rate.

These data further underscore the modest politicization of street crime in Cedar City. They also reveal a shift away from traditional policing after the departure of Chief Cheatham, who presided over a department that downplayed arrests in general but was the most effective at clearing street crimes.

While the department was better funded during Brush's term, the city got relatively little from its investment. Whether measured in terms of overall arrests, efficiency, or effectiveness, Brush's regime performed poorly. But there is reason to believe that the increased investment during Brush's term was for corruption control, not crime control. The objective was to improve the financial circumstances and thereby the professional quality and the morale of rank-and-file police officers, thus making them less vulnerable to corruption. In these terms, as we see in the next section, the investment did pay off.

The data do not reveal very marked differences between the Goodfellow and Tracy regimes—although Tracy's department did perform slightly better on most measures. That neither Goodfellow nor Tracy was able to reach the same level of effectiveness as was probably due to tight budgets imposed by the city and to constraints on police behavior stemming from three different sources. First, there were the due process restrictions of the Warren Court. Second, there was a local political climate that pushed the department away from traditional policing. Finally, there were reform elements within the department that were

uncomfortable with the expressive violence of traditional policing. Certainly, Cedar City police officers were inclined to explain
things this way.

More fundamentally, for our purposes, the resurgence of arrest rates during both Goodfellow's and Tracy's terms is indicative of a more professional—that is, a more legalistic—style of
policing. Only from the interview data do we get a glimpse of the
forces that would eventually drive Tracy beyond professional
style reform toward community policing.

The Resilience of Traditional Policing

Until at least the late 1960s, traditional policing was very well
entrenched in Cedar City. This was a decentralized police department organized around personal networks of influence, generally shielded from public scrutiny, committed to the values of
traditional policing, and distinctly resistant to racial equality. It
was also a corrupt department, with Chief Cheatham presiding
over an extensive payoff system. Exposure of that system led to a
significant change in local politics and thus paved the way for
police reform. But exposure also had a traumatic impact on the
morale and the organization of the department, thus reinforcing
internal resistance to reform.

This section on traditional policing traces a cycle that begins
with the "good old days," as several of my respondents thought
of the period prior to the exposure of the payoff system. This was
followed by the trauma of a grand jury investigation, which
exposed the payoff system and led to a purge of the department.
At about the same time, the outside world was encroaching on
the department in several other unwelcome ways. Finally we
take a look at the reconstruction of the department—cleansed of
corruption but clinging in important ways to the vestiges of
traditional policing.

The Good Old Days

What made the good old days so attractive to Cedar City police
officers was not the payoff system but the ethos that made the
payoff system possible—the freedom to work the streets as they
saw fit. "The beat man wasn't tied up to a radio. . . . They used to
have call boxes on the corners and they had to ring in every half

hour. They were more or less on their own out there. The only one who would come and really check on them was the sergeant. In a patrol car, you're, well, the radio runs you." There was also a strong sense of departmental solidarity. According to one old-timer, this was an era when you could count on "your sergeants and captains, lieutenants. Their feeling was of protecting their own men. I don't think you'd have that same backing today."

During this period the police were, in short, free to think of themselves as crime fighters working according to standards and values derived from the traditional police subculture. As one officer who became an influential police manager put it: "There are quite frankly people out there on the street who you can't even get their attention until you've whopped them one. Then you can talk, but up to that point there just isn't any communication." Patrol officers, thus, felt free to administer "curbside justice" without much concern about second-guessing by police managers or the courts.

There is good reason to believe that blacks were often victimized by curbside justice. Certainly, during the time that Cheatham was chief, the department had a reputation for harassing blacks and for making things difficult for black police officers. One of the minuscule number of black police officers did somehow manage to rise to the rank of sergeant, but it is said that his promotion to lieutenant was blocked by Cheatham. This officer was promoted only after bringing suit successfully against the chief.[31]

Clearly, this was a hostile environment for black police officers. Consider the following account of the police locker-room subculture during that period, as reported by a black officer.

> I'd come in any number of mornings and white officers would be standing two rows over talking about how they kicked a nigger's ass. . . . I can remember so vividly how some people arrested the prior night, and in particular the black female prostitutes, would be paraded up and down in front of the officers who were standing roll call. The remarks and the humiliation they obviously suffered. And there were white female prostitutes being arrested, and you never saw those unless they had black customers.

Or consider what this same black officer had to say about the
kind of differential patrol tactics that were taught in the police
academy.

> If you get a disturbance call in the central part of the city,
> which was at that time almost predominantly black, you go in
> and bat heads and kick asses. If you get a disturbance call, a
> loud party or whatever, in a predominantly white neighbor-
> hood, you casually cruise by, get the address off the door, go to
> a telephone, look up that address, call them and tell them you
> have some complaints about them disturbing the neighbor-
> hood, if they would please cooperate by lessening the noise.

A white officer described that era in an altogether compatible
way:

> There was a mystique about being a policeman. It was called
> the brotherhood in blue. And it had some good points and
> there were tremendous police personnel. At the same time
> there are those who would argue that there were also some
> constitutional principles violated; racism was endemic, if not
> epidemic; and that the abuses far outweighed the benefits.

But even officers who deplored departmental racism and were
unwilling to participate in the payoff system felt that the department was doing its crime-fighting job well.

> I would say those were good old days. We were addressing
> the crime problem, I thought. In the field, you were recog-
> nized for what you did, not by how many arrests you made or
> anything like that, but by legitimate criteria—whether or not
> there was a great deal of crime in your beat.

This claim tends to be supported by the data presented in the
preceding section indicating that during Chief Cheatham's administration the department was more effective against street
crime.

With respect to the payoff system itself, there was a feeling
that it was not all that bad. An officer who was untainted by the
payoff system and played a key administrative role in the Brush

regime claimed that the payoff system served an important public purpose.

> What those licensees that were making payoffs were doing was making sure there was no competition in their area of influence. And this was kind of by unofficial agreement between them and the vice squad. If competition sprang up they'd call their contact and say, "Hey, I'm paying for this license, where's my protection?" The vice squad would then raid the competing place. So it became a form of social control that has never been replaced.

While this officer was quick to add that the payoff system was an inappropriate and undesirable way to control vice activities, the fact remains that even officers who did not participate accepted the payoff system to some degree.

It would be wrong, however, to believe that there were no complaints about the good old days. The department was run in an arbitrary manner. "In the old days, the chief had a lot more prerogatives, you know. I mean he says: 'Resign or be fired.'" This was a department in which police officers were essentially without any rights and in which veteran officers were firmly entrenched within systems of informal authority. Perhaps most fundamentally, the pay was so poor that many officers felt compelled to choose between the payoff system and moonlighting.

> I wouldn't want to mislead you and give you the idea that the greatly decentralized, informal process was all beer and skittles. It wasn't. You want to get into the detectives. This was a campaign that people mounted and it used to be assumed that unless you had a very brown ring around your nose, you weren't going to make it. To some extent, from what I observed, that probably is pretty close to the truth. There were six hundred and some odd policemen, and who was going to notice one. . . . There were great drawbacks to the old system. . . . The pay scale was lousy. I took a $10 cut from being a grocery clerk to become a policeman.

The pre-exposure status quo was both attractive and problematic. The informalities of the old system were particularly hard on ambitious and able younger officers who were reluctant to compromise their integrity either for financial gain or for career advancement.

There was, therefore, a constituency, albeit modest, for reform. However, this constituency was undermined by the exposure of the payoff system, which tended to unite the department against all outsiders and against any threats to discretionary authority. It is ironic that the same event that paved the way for police reform also made its realization so much more difficult. In any event, the struggle over reform had very little, if anything, to do with matters of crime control.

External Scrutiny, Internal Demoralization

The exposure of the payoff system was the most traumatic of several developments that briefly shook the Cedar City Police Department loose from its traditional moorings. Suddenly, for example, the police were charged with being unresponsive to the community—in effect, to minorities—but that is not the way the rank and file saw things: "I'd have to say it's probably the opposite. They were probably responsive to the majority of the community, but that majority had changed." Consider also the social turmoil that brought the police into a continuing series of struggles in the streets against a variety of social movements that rejected conventional values and were committed to confrontational styles of political action. As one officer put it:

In the Korean War you didn't hear anybody say, "Get out, do this, do that." And you take '68, '69, and [the] seventies, the riots that were around here that affected a lot of policemen. . . . I remember I was out at the university in a group over there. Well, a bunch of students, you know, were playing games, so we had to march out. There was about fifty of us. Then you stand more or less looking at these students, and they're yelling and screaming and that stuff. OK. We're leaving. They start throwing rocks . . . and you can't turn back. And probably what broke up a lot of rioting here was up at the courthouse here when all those people were up to really raising cane. They finally said: "Go get 'em. Clean 'em up." And I think, you know, personally, that there were a lot of policemen with revenge, you know, after all this time taking all this abuse.

At the same time that their jobs were being made more difficult by an increasingly militant and divided society, the police were being subjected to unprecedented scrutiny and restrictions by the Warren Court. The contrast with the good old days was clear to the rank and file.

> Now, there were a lot fewer constraints on the way the job got handled then. The courts were a great deal less inclined to want to look into at great depth every claim that somebody has been roughly handled. The options an officer could exercise for achieving his objective were quite frankly rough. There were fewer people that wanted to review his every action and word and gesture at great length.

Officers also recall a sense of solidarity and homogeneity during that period. "The guys were closer. We were all basically the same kind of people. The big percentage of us came out of World War II and Korea." It was also seen as a time when the world was simpler: "The social problems, you know. Things have gotten more complex in the last twenty years." In other words, the grand jury investigation was loosely associated not just with the end of corruption but with the end of an era in which policing was long on prerogatives and short on constraints.

But, with all that said, the grand jury investigation was surely the heaviest blow suffered by the department. Police officers were exposed to public ridicule—"your children looking at you twice, that sort of thing." "Ordinary citizens out there could make innuendos, you know, 'Well, what are you doing around talking to me?' You know, 'You guys are crooks, we're not.' You know, this kind of stuff." The investigation had also divided the department. Those who played a role in exposing the corruption, *the most reform-minded members of the department,* were perceived not as conscientious police officers but as self-serving careerists who had staged a "palace revolt" to gain power and who were insensitive to the lives they were ruining. "I think there wasn't 10 percent of the department that respected any of them after that." Moreover, some of these pretenders were themselves implicated in the payoff system.

> They were going to get rid of Cheatham and his regime, and that backfired at that time also. George Wilson looked like he

was going to come in and be the interim chief. You know what I mean? He was supposed to be taking over. Well, then, boom, it showed he had some of the problems he was accusing other people of having. Wayne Cooper was the same way. He was gonna clean it up, but was using it.

Names had been tossed around and reputations soiled indiscrimately and perhaps maliciously.

One reason morale had been low is that you don't know, somebody would go and name you—whether you did anything or not. Then you'd be called over there. And I mean hire an attorney and everything and defend yourself. And you don't know what you're defending yourself against.

All of this added up to tremendous internal turmoil fueled by suspicions and recrimination.

Reasserting Autonomy, Rebuilding Solidarity

The long-term consequences of the grand jury's investigation of the payoff system can be traced along two different, albeit convergent, paths. On the one hand, the battered and demoralized rank and file regrouped around an increasingly militant and politically assertive police guild. More broadly, Mark West, a reform-oriented, liberal mayor, took office in 1969, and he was able to count on the support of a like-minded City Council and county prosecutor.

The point of convergence of these two lines of force was W. C. Brush, the outside chief of police brought in by the mayor to clean up the department and restore its morale. On both counts, Brush was impressively successful. No doubt the restoration of police morale can be attributed in part to an infusion of funds. In this way the city administration responded to the long-standing salary grievances. But while this may have been a necessary first step, it was not sufficient. Brush's own contribution was to become an uncompromising advocate of departmental independence from the political process. In so doing he effectively consolidated his own position but at the cost of both broader currents of reform and political accountability. Simply put, Chief Brush yielded to the militant rank and file's nostalgia for the good old days—thus reinforcing rather than challenging the values and practices of traditional policing.

By the time Mayor West appointed Chief Brush, the post-payoff purge had been pretty well completed by interim chiefs who were brought in from outside the state for that purpose. At the very least, the officers most heavily implicated in the payoff system were no longer in the department. There was also considerable agreement that the cronyism on which the payoff system had fed should be avoided in future. Chief Brush could thus count on something of a consensus among the remaining officers, who had borne the burden of divisiveness and loss of public confidence. They did not want to return to payoffs, and they favored a system that rewarded competence rather than influence. That was the good news.

The bad news for the new chief was that there were increasingly influential elements within the police guild that wanted the rank and file to go it alone. While the politicians and political interference were the immediate target of the guild, a militant and well-organized rank and file also represented a threat to the authority of the chief.

The rank and file believed that political interference had initially corrupted and ultimately destroyed the department. Accordingly, there was a simple solution to the department's problems. First, it was taken as a given that the department was basically sound, albeit divided. The divisions, like all the other problems, were attributed to political interference. Accordingly, the solution was simple: reassert the independence of the police department from the politicians. Politicians had passed vice laws and then decided to enforce them selectively. Politicians had also paid police officers so poorly that they felt compelled in order to support their families either to work a second job or to take advantage of the payoff system. Finally, a new group of politicians had used the grand jury investigation as a ploy to unseat the incumbents. Rank-and-file sentiments were expressed by one officer this way: "I'm convinced that it was started as a political football, as a political power play. . . . They didn't care who they destroyed or who they hurt to meet their ends, to get their political force into power." The grand jury investigation became, in effect, the last straw—one of a series of rank-and-file grievances that transformed a hitherto compliant rank and file.

As the same officer put it: "This is the time that the guild became the strongest it had ever been up to that time."[32]

The lesson drawn by those who took the lead in organizing the rank and file was that political influence was a precondition to adequate pay and decent working conditions. This was unequivocally clear with respect to wages, pension rights, and collective bargaining. These were matters for the legislature and hence led the guild into concerted political action with other police organizations around the state. According to one of the founding members of the guild's political action committee: "Police labor relations deal in the political arena itself. It's not merely economic, as in the private sector. If we want to get anything done, it has to be through the political processes. Our wages, our pensions, our procedures—everything either comes from the local, state, or federal political body." Politicization also seemed, to those guild members who organized the political action committee, to be a good way of ending the erosion of department independence and public confidence. "The demonstrations—officers were being charged with various violations and stuff, where you needed, you know, protection per se. And like I said, we had to go and influence the political system, because that's where all our wherewithal comes from. So the political action committee was formed." The police simply felt that they could not count on others and would have to look after their own interests.

This idea of taking the rank and file's case directly to the public was, of course, controversial. Insofar as the goal was to defend the department from politics and politicians, there was something of a paradox in resorting to political action. This paradox was not lost on the rank and file, who feared that the leaders who proposed a political strategy were likely to turn out no better than other politicians. At any rate, all of the unwelcome developments of the 1950s and 1960s were interpreted in essentially political terms.

From this viewpoint, Brush was clearly the right man in the right place at the right time. He was perceived to be a real police officer—not an administrator who had dallied briefly in the rank and file on his way to management.[33] He was a man who understood the plight of the street cop and was supportive of his officers. Consider the views of a guild activist.

Brush, I think, was a combination of two things. We felt for the first time we had a good veteran, experienced police administrator. A guy who had all the credentials, who had been a good street cop. . . . He had all the paper qualifications . . . and he was honest. . . . They made sure he was squeaky clean, supposedly, but he was also a professional. And he said (you know he came to many roll calls) and he'd say there are two things you got to know about me. If you make a mistake and you're doing your job, I'll back you to the hilt. If you deliberately mess up, I'll be the first one to see you go to jail. And that's all the guys wanted.

Even in the 1980s when I was doing this research—almost a decade after he was gone—he was still considered by some as an heroic figure.

Still more fundamentally, Chief Brush quickly demonstrated his uncompromising commitment to purging the police department of outside interference and, in particular, to establishing his—and, therefore, the department's—independence from politicians, including the mayor and the City Council, to whom he was ostensibly responsible. As one police officer put it:

The reason they liked Chief Brush, at least in my opinion, was that he had no hesitancy in telling the press to take a flying leap off a short bridge. . . . He did one thing that always seemed to be lacking around here and that was someone who would stand up to the politicians across the street. At the time that [he] was here, we were taking a real lambasting not just for the corruption issue but for insensitivity to minorities, everything someone wanted to pile on us. . . . The cops were on the bottom.

Whether this was a conscious strategy for gaining the confidence of his officers, reestablishing the morale of the department, and undercutting support for rank-and-file militants in the guild or simply a reflection of his own beliefs and commitments, it succeeded brilliantly.

What people don't understand is that we were going through the pressures outside—the courts, the grand jury, which is a big outside pressure, the riots, the university, the blacks. Terrible pressure on the men. Long hours. We had this terrible inner strife going on inside. It was like a big cancer. It was just eating the hell out of us. . . . It was a political thing stirring dishonesty, and there was backstabbing, and there were vendettas coming out from the people. God, you just didn't know where to turn. He sorted it out. He gave us back a little bit of a calm feeling within.

Indeed, one of his defenders claimed that whereas most departments take about ten years to come back from a major investigation, Chief Brush was able to cut recovery time in half.

Lurching toward Reform

Insofar as Mayor West's agenda was to heal departmental wounds, Chief Brush was clearly an unqualified success. But the strategy and public image that were successful within the department antagonized both Mayor West and the City Council, who saw their new chief as rigid and defensive. Brush's aggressive independence made for particularly conflictual relationships with the mayor, an assertive, politically ambitious, hands-on reformer. He was determined to gain control of all elements of the bureaucracy, including the police department. The mayor was also young and, according to his political advisors, interested in moving on to higher office.

West meddled, if you want to use that term, in almost every department. . . . [He] built a staff of about ten people, which was larger than any previous mayor, and the purpose was twofold. One was to know more about what was going on . . . and help the mayor to monitor the major decisions. . . . The second purpose of that staff was to permit the mayor to have a more active role in public and community relations. . . . He was a politician. I don't know whether he thought of running for governor then or thought when he might run for governor, but he sure saw himself as an elected official—mayor, governor, congressman, senator. That was how he viewed the world, so he was bound and determined to have high visibility as mayor.

The result was that the mayor and the chief of police ended locked in a struggle, ostensibly over three important issues of police *policy*. This section is organized around these policy conflicts, which concern illegal gambling, racial tensions, and law and justice planning.

For both sides, however, these policy disputes were symbols of a more fundamental conflict over *principles* bearing directly on the prospects for police reform. From Mayor West's point of view, the principle at stake was the political accountability of the police to elected officials and, therefore, to the public. Chief Brush and his department perceived themselves as advocates for police independence in the service of impartial law enforcement. These were, of course, principles with considerable salience, given the grand jury findings that had been the prelude to Mayor West's administration and the reconstruction of the police department.

But along with policy and principle, *power* was clearly at stake in these ongoing conflicts between the mayor and his hand-picked chief of police. These were two determined and ambitious men who were not only guarding their prerogatives but also their authority. Mayor West had put together a liberal, electoral coalition based on "the neighborhoods." He was, therefore, inclined to pursue what might be termed pluralistic policing policies that would be responsive to these constituencies. Conversely, the chief's authority within the department was rooted in his independence from any and all outside interference.

But however the conflict is defined—be it in terms of policy, principle, power, or some mix of the three—it raged throughout Mayor West's two terms in office. Chief Brush dominated the first act, defending his terrain with great success against the mayor's preferences and priorities. More than once, the department put the mayor on the defensive. Consider the example, mentioned by a well-informed outsider, of the vice squad's raid on a "Chinese after-hours gambling place five minutes after West left . . . in an effort to embarrass West."

The mayor was, however, finally able to force Chief Brush from office, and after that he occupied center stage in the second act—working through Chief Goodfellow, who was much more responsive to the mayor's initiatives in the three policy areas mentioned above. Goodfellow's primary qualification seems to have been his heavy debt to Mayor West. Goodfellow had served with no particular distinction and was elevated by Mayor West well beyond his level of competence.[34]

As a result, his term in office was clouded by charges of political interference, a return to corrupt practices, and general ineffectiveness. The data presented in Table 3.1 do not really bear out these charges. I am inclined to believe that a more professional police force did begin to emerge during Chief Goodfellow's term—perhaps in spite of him rather than because of him. It was not, however, until Chief Tracy was appointed by Mayor West's successor, Phillip Mercer, that these reforms were consolidated.

Illegal Gambling

The differences between Chief Brush and Mayor West over gambling concerned so-called recreational gambling, low stakes games that were apparently common within the mayor's Asian and black constituencies. In the words of a civic leader who was influential behind the scenes in decisions about the police:

> I really felt that West, be it good or bad, knew there was gambling in the Asian community. He felt that was an ethnic thing, and he wanted to keep it. There was gambling in the black community. There were after-hours places where you could go get booze and you could gamble. And I think Mark, be he right or wrong and be he involved or not, felt that was an ethnic thing and we shouldn't touch that.

Perhaps the mayor was just trying to make a virtue out of political expediency. But whatever the motivation, he was inclined to exclude recreational gambling from police vice activities.

To Chief Brush and to many members of the department, it was important that the laws against gambling be enforced uniformly. Recreational exemptions were seen as problematic, in part because of the difficulty of drawing a clear line between "recreational" gambling among friends and the threatening world of "professional" gambling. Payoff systems can, of course, be spawned in discretionary ambiguities between licit and illicit activities, but this was only the tip of the iceberg of police concerns. The threat was not so much that the police would be tempted as that they would be trapped in a system that they neither created nor controlled but for which they might once again be held responsible. They charged the mayor with granting exemptions to "back room" gambling in business establishments in the black and Asian communities that played significant roles in the mayor's electoral coalitions. In short, the police saw the mayor heading down the same slippery slope of political influence peddling that led to the payoff system and to what they saw as the scapegoating of the police department.

Once Brush was forced out, the department adopted a more relaxed policy on recreational gambling. The retreat from gambling arrests led the commander of the vice squad, a very well respected officer, to resign from the department. Another officer told me that the policy change under Goodfellow drove him out of vice work. "You just stopped working. . . . One of the reasons I left was because there was no challenge. There were certain things you didn't do. You could go out and arrest narcotics violators, but we didn't make any raids into Chinatown." Goodfellow acknowledged the change in policy. "I'm no bluenose. Brush was more vice-oriented than I am."[35] He denied, however, that the change would "open" the city or that the department would "overlook" any crimes.[36]

The mayor's advisers acknowledged that he was determined to shift law enforcement resources away from vice toward more serious crime. However, they dismissed departmental concerns about political interference as just another example of Chief Brush's irrational paranoia about any and all efforts to establish police accountability to the public. They pointed to covert police surveillance of anyone who was critical of the department— including two locally prominent television personalities with distinctly liberal political values.

While the conflict over illegal gambling raised serious questions about West's commitment to reform, the arrest data presented in Table 3.1 do not really support any of the concerns about Goodfellow's term. These data indicate that department productivity improved pretty much across the board while Goodfellow was chief. The biggest change came in the FBI's Uniform Crime Reports (UCR) Part I crimes, but vice productivity increased as well. Goodfellow's department was also more efficient and effective. The numbers suggest, therefore, that

Brush did not use his independence in ways that were conducive to the crime-fighting objectives of his most committed supporters. While the overall patterns do not lend credence to the charges against Mayor West, the interviews strongly indicate a determination to make gambling exceptions for influential campaign contributors, a practice that probably had more to do with electoral politics than with corruption.[37]

Racial Tensions

The complaints of Cedar City blacks about being policed by an overwhelmingly white department compromised by racism were the source of a second conflict. On these racial matters, Mayor West's case as a reformer is somewhat stronger. Again, this goes back to the electoral process. As one of the mayor's close advisers put it: "If it hadn't been for West's support in the black area, he wouldn't have been mayor." Even then progress was slow and the changes relatively modest. The mayor's case is, however, weakened by the two chiefs whom he appointed, particularly by Brush.

Although all of the mayor's advisers insisted that he had a strong commitment to reducing police harassment and to increasing police hiring of minorities, there is also general agreement that he chose a chief of police who was completely unresponsive to the racial problems of the police department. "Chief Brush didn't have much use for minorities," was the way one of the mayor's advisers put it. Nor, said another mayoral adviser, did Chief Brush's vision of the department "include black faces." One of the most explosive issues was affirmative action promotion—or selective certification, as it was called. Again the view from the mayor's office was of a recalcitrant chief: "Brush hated that [selective certification] with a passion, and he threatened to resign a number of times."

It is difficult to know whether Chief Brush was as hostile to blacks as his critics believe. His intransigence was not limited to racial matters. As has already been suggested, he was, apparently by nature, a fiercely independent chief whose primary concerns were corruption and low morale. Even his critics concede that he was effective on both these counts, and surely his success in raising police morale was directly related to his independence from political pressure.

It is, therefore, not at all surprising that his resignation was brought on by the mayor's insistence on overriding the chief on a disciplinary matter involving police harassment. From the perspective of the mayor's office, the chief was unwilling to deal with complaints. "When West went out to Mt. Zion Church and people complained, he wanted to be able to go back to Brush and get satisfaction." Conversely, the chief no doubt felt that discipline was an internal matter and that to yield to outside pressures would be to undercut his own officers. Similarly, his hostility to selective certification of minority officers was shared by the rank-and-file police officers. The police guild poured a relatively large amount of money into an unsuccessful court test of the selective certification program.

The record of Brush's successor, Goodfellow, is rather mixed on racial matters—a case of more show than go. Clearly though, he was on better terms with the black community. As one of the mayor's aides put it: "He had been going to the Black Pioneer's picnic for years." The black member of the City Council also believed that Goodfellow was more responsive on affirmative action as well as when questions were raised about police harassment.

There is, however, another view. By all accounts, Goodfellow does seem to have been an amiable man. As one council member put it, Goodfellow "was not uncomfortable with people as Chief Brush was." Goodfellow was, therefore, willing and able to reach out to the minority community. But this same council member, along with both white and black officers, expressed grave doubts about what had been accomplished during Goodfellow's stint as chief.

One of the presidents of the guild claimed that Goodfellow's watchword was: "Don't rock the boat."

The black folk are pressuring you: here are the stats that show you that we're doing a great job. And he'd look at the City Council and tell them the same thing. He'd tell the mayor the same thing. And the end result was he really wasn't doing anything, but it didn't look that bad on paper. He'd tell the feds the same thing . . . and he'd count everybody. It wouldn't matter whether they were janitors. The question was how does it look in the police department, and what they're asking really is how many minority officers do you have, and he just counted everyone including the janitors. It didn't look that bad. If it was a black female, you could take credit twice.

In short, Chief Goodfellow had a reputation for pleasing as many people as possible while doing very little. Perhaps his primary contribution was, then, to spread oil over troubled waters—at the cost of not tackling tough issues.[38]

Black police officers indirectly corroborated this view with an account of Goodfellow's covert resistance to the mayor's order that black officers be promoted. As they saw things, the chief finally complied, but only to the extent of promoting one black officer who was "culturally white" and had been passing as such. The black officers also complained about department practices for assigning black officers. Black officers were confined almost exclusively to the patrol division and thus were deprived of the kind of general knowledge and experience needed for promotion. When neither the mayor nor the chief responded to their grievance, the black officers organized and filed a formal complaint charging that the city was violating federal law by accepting funds from Washington while discriminating against black officers. Before this claim could be settled, the mayor's term ended, and his successor made an interim appointment in the police department.

What are we to make of the mayor's willingness to accept a chief of this sort? Surely it makes one wonder about the strength of the mayor's commitment to the perceived problems of the minority community. Perhaps as a result of his bad experiences with Brush, the mayor was more intent on a compliant chief than on a racially enlightened one—particularly if this chief was able to cool out the black community without making very many affirmative action waves among rank-and-file police officers.

Law and Justice Planning

The conflict between Mayor West and Chief Brush over Law Enforcement Assistance Administration (LEAA) funds once again had at least as much to do with power as with policy. Chief Brush, like many of his peers, was attracted by LEAA dollars but wary of the planners who dispersed those funds. The funds were, of course, an attractive target of opportunity—especially in an era when the private sector was responding to crime and civil disorder with a wide variety of increasingly prestigious high-tech, high-priced hardware. On the other hand, the funds came with strings attached in that they were supposed to be dispersed in accordance with a comprehensive plan.

Initially, the police got their way. Funds were provided virtually without restrictions—much of these grants going for better communications and more firepower. During this phase, Cedar City, with support from Chief Brush, was able to install a new communications system that made it easier for the public to contact the department and for the police to communicate with one another. LEAA money was also used for helicopters, which were much more controversial. The police defended them as effective tools of law enforcement: "To my knowledge, and during the time they were in use, there was never a robbery that was committed where the car was identified from the air that the suspect got away, once they were identified." Outsiders tended to be a good deal more skeptical. One City Council member put it this way: "The bells and whistles that the police convinced us were absolutely essential, like helicopters. . . . We knew they were expensive and that they were sometimes used to harass people in the central area—those whirlybirds flying over them at night." In any case, so long as the money came without strings attached, Chief Brush was supportive of LEAA projects.

As time passed, LEAA began to pose more questions about the necessity, even the desirability, of some of this equipment, and the law and justice planners began to take more initiative in developing programs. In Cedar City, the planners began with at least two strikes against them: they were not police officers, and they were located in the mayor's office and reported to him. Thus, the police had both professional and bureaucratic reasons for resisting the programs of the criminal justice planners. Since these programs were the work of planners without policing experience, how could they possibly know what had to be done?[39] Moreover, inasmuch as these funds were controlled by the mayor's office, the LEAA could be seen as an example of political interference.[40]

With the appointment of Goodfellow, relations between law and justice planners and the department improved to a considerable extent. Certainly, the chief was no longer an obstacle, and some management personnel were genuinely interested in utilizing LEAA funds effectively. Still, two different but related problems persisted. Reformers in the police department continued to be leary of the law and justice whiz kids, and other police managers were inclined to resist reforms of any kind.

Consider, in this perspective, the plight of a lower-level police manager with primary responsibility for one of the more elaborate LEAA pilot programs. This program was worked out between the police and the law and justice planners and was accepted by Mayor West and an interim chief of police appointed after Brush's departure.

> So we applied for the grant, and about two months later we were accepted. And at that time I went to the boss of CID, who was a major, and he said: "I'm not going to give you any bodies. I am not going to participate in this thing. It's being run by Law and Justice. Let them come up with the bodies." So there I sit. I'm a lieutenant and he says: "Screw you. You're not going to get any help here. I don't care what you do, but I am not giving you any bodies. They're so goddamned smart. Let them run it." So I went into my office and looked out the window and smoked my pipe, and I thought: "This is a great step for my career development. This may be the end of the road right here."

While the difficulty was ironed out and the program went ahead, there was reason to believe association with the law and justice whiz kids could be dangerous to one's career. Only a strong and committed chief could have effectively overcome the inertial bureaucratic resistance and the police mistrust of outsiders. Clearly, Charlie Goodfellow was no such chief.

During Mayor West's term in office, the Cedar City Police Department did make some significant strides toward reform. Chief Brush was able to consolidate the corruption purge; during Goodfellow's term, the department became more attentive to complaints from the black and Asian communities; department training standards and educational attainments improved; LEAA funding was also used to modernize department communications and to try out some policy schemes to enhance police crime control capabilities. But the foregoing analysis suggests at least two qualifications about the reforms accomplished under Mayor West's administration.

Such reforms as did develop were largely indirect consequences of power struggles between Mayor West and Chief Brush. And for the most part, the reforms were half-hearted and ephemeral. Only the post-payoff clean-up was systematically carried out, and it was imposed from outside as the result of a significant realignment of Cedar City politics. There were no firm indications that either Mayor West or Chief Brush was interested in pushing reform much beyond clearing out corruption. Chief Brush was unresponsive to the grievances of minorities and seemed otherwise content to preside over a largely traditional department—albeit one that was better trained and better equipped, due in large part to LEAA funding. Mayor West, once he finally got a compliant chief, was apparently willing to settle for ineffectual gestures to minorities. Going easy on gambling and after-hours clubs in the black and Asian neighborhoods was, for example, probably more meaningful to entrepreneurs than to the minority communities in general. There is no reason to fault West on the LEAA program, but it is also clear that the choice of Charlie Goodfellow as chief hardly indicates a commitment to substantial reform of any sort.

It would, however, be wrong to conclude that what happened during the West interlude is irrelevant to this inquiry into the forces and directions of police reform. At the very least, the course of the conflict between Mayor West and the police department establishes the marginal significance of street crime. Chief Brush and the police guild cultivated public images suggesting that crime control was a priority issue, but what really seemed to count was asserting police independence and improving the wages and working conditions of police officers. More fundamentally, it is during West's term in office that we get our first glimpse of the shifting balance in urban politics toward minorities—a shift that, as I see it, is the major driving force behind reform. That shift and its impact on the police department becomes much clearer in the period after West left office.

The Politics of Police Reform

The election of 1977 began a prolonged period of accommodation between the police department and the mayor's office.

Phillip Mercer, the new mayor, was a liberal who, incidentally, was one of the two media people put under surveillance by Chief Brush's police intelligence unit. Mayor Mercer once again reached outside the department, choosing a veteran big-city police executive, Richard Tracy, who was associated with the reform-minded Police Foundation. By all accounts, Mayor Mercer, who was not really a hands-on executive, gave Chief Tracy a good deal of leeway in running the department.

Tracy turned out to be an assertive chief with a good deal of staying power. Both his supporters and his critics agree that one of his strongest traits was his political savvy. For rank-and-file officers, this was, of course, a weakness, while for others it was seen as an important requirement for the job. Here is the view of a well-placed outsider: "I went to the opening of the new precinct and . . . watched Dick handle the City Council people, the city people that came in, and the mayor—almost the whole flow. And he's sharp. He's really an aware, savvy person." In contrast, there was a strong tendency among rank-and-file officers to see his accommodation with Mayor Mercer as compromising the integrity of the department.

That initial accommodation had distinct, albeit incipient, overtones of community policing. Virtually all of the rank-and-file objections to Tracy stemmed from his efforts to improve the effectiveness and the acceptability of police within the black community. These efforts were seen by the disaffected officers as indicative of political interference in internal department affairs and as a threat to impartial law enforcement. The accommodation, however, worked both ways. Mayor Mercer had no particular interest in interferring in the running of the department, so long as Chief Tracy worked within the boundaries of the mayor's political mandate. So the chief received strong support from the mayor and was effective in his relationship with both the media and the City Council. Chief Tracy even earned a certain grudging respect, but not much affection, from his officers.

Racial Tensions

While there is good reason to think of Mayor West's two terms as a period of largely symbolic gains for blacks, his successor seems to have made more headway. One index of the change that has taken place is to be found in the number of blacks

TABLE 3.2
Sworn Officers: Comparison of Blacks to Total Officers

Year	Chief	Total Sworn	Total Black	Percent Black
1969	Cheatham	1,098	12	1
1970	Brush	1,211	25	2
1974	Goodfellow	1,082	22	2
1977	Goodfellow	1,029	24	2
1980	Tracy	1,047	38	4
1982	Tracy	1,023	40	4

Sources: Barbara Hayler, "Police Patrol Activity and the Definition of Public Order," Ph.D. dissertation, University of Washington, Seattle, 1984, p. 74; Cedar City Police Department Annual Reports, Cedar City Police Department; Equal Opportunity Officer; and Cedar City Office of Affirmative Action.

working as sworn officers in the Cedar City Police Department. Table 3.2 indicates that the percentage of black officers remained largely stable during Mayor West's two administrations, 1970 to 1977, but increased substantially during the Mercer–Tracy era.

There are no comparable data on the important issue of minority mobility within the department. The attitudes of black and white officers on promotion and disciplinary policies suggest, however, that minorities made considerable progress under Mayor Mercer and Chief Tracy. As one well-placed officer put it: "I think that Tracy is totally political. I don't think any of his decisions are based on what's good for the department. His decisions are based on politics, on what he's been told that he will do by community pressure." Not surprisingly, blacks put a different spin on Tracy's racial responsiveness. According to the black City Council member cited earlier, Tracy did "magnificently" on affirmative action hiring and promotion. He also feels that rank-and-file police officers became more respectful of the minority communities. "They are basically sensitive in how they speak to you, so the atmosphere of everything has changed and smoothed down." Black police officers feel the same way. As one highly placed black officer put it: "There has been a tremendous change with Mercer and particularly since Chief Tracy."

The rank and file deny that they are standing in the way of increasing the numbers of minority and women police officers. Indeed, there is even some willingness to acknowledge the importance of minority representation as a way to promote good police work.

> What you get if you don't discriminate is a department that is going to be representative of the community at large, and candidly it's a real asset. If you're to deal with people whether they're a racial minority or whatever, it's a real asset to have some kind of identification other than a blue uniform there. It was an asset for me as a white officer dealing with blacks to have another black officer there. It lends a degree of legitimacy to what you're doing.

There are, however, strenuous objections to "a special class that would get special protection on the basis of sex or race." The strongest complaint is about affirmative action promotion, that is, selective certification, which permits, indeed encourages, promotion of minority or female officers who have lower test scores than white officers who are being passed over. To white officers, selective certification compromises quality police work and is also inequitable. "There was no question that they [blacks] had been discriminated against, but . . . the ones who had been discriminated against were long gone." In other words, the direct beneficiaries of selective certification had not themselves suffered discrimination, and so the guild fought selective certification unsuccessfully in the courts. Rank-and-file officers may have subsequently become resigned but certainly not content. A former guild president probably spoke for most rank-and-file officers: "Affirmative action has taken a strong hold in the police department. . . . That is the chief underlying cause of resentment and poor morale among the police department today. Hands down, that's the chief problem."

With respect to discipline, the most celebrated case involved some off-duty police officers who fired shots from their service revolvers late at night in the black residential area. Chief Tracy dismissed these officers, and even those among the rank and file who were in sympathy with firm discipline felt that the chief was too harsh in this case.

> A lot of police officers found themselves in hot water when Tracy became chief, but I always tried to put myself in his

place. And I can think of no situation where I disagreed with what the chief did, with the exception of Thorson [one of the officers discharged]. . . . There were circumstances in that case that led me to believe that he was suffering from true stress—two gunfights within a period of a year in which he killed assailants. He had a twelve-year-old daughter who died during the middle of the night at home unexpectedly. [He was a] tremendously hard worker, and the man was suffering from stress. The police department should have recognized that and didn't. I thought in that case the man should have had a second opportunity.

This seems to have been the view of the moderate rank-and-file officers and is interesting on at least two counts. In the first place, concern is expressed for only one of the discharged officers. Secondly, the chief and the rank and file clearly interpreted the two gunfights and the death in different ways. For the rank and file, these stressful events were a source of empathy, whereas the chief no doubt saw them as adding to the case against the officer.

More militant officers took issue with the disciplinary practices of Chief Tracy pretty much across the board. It seems quite clear that the officers all got the message that Tracy and Mayor Mercer were responsive, too responsive in their judgment, to minorities in general and to blacks in particular. These rank-and-file dissatisfactions seem to be a good indicator of a significant transformation of the police department's approach to racial problems.

The picture that emerges from this account is of a police department that responded, albeit slowly, to the increasing electoral importance of black voters and perhaps to a more open political environment more generally. Perhaps the results were best characterized by a black City Council member. As he saw it, while there was "no love affair between the police and the black community, there is not the enmity that existed."

Police Resources

Other rank-and-file complaints against Tracy concerned his personnel practices. The rank and file singled out a tendency to privilege the bureaucracy and "fringe" operations such as community relations while marginalizing street officers, who were in the front lines of the fight against crime.

I am not saying that community relations is a bad thing, but it should be minimally staffed rather than maximally staffed. In order for us to do our job properly, we have to have enough warm bodies out on the street. . . . Public relations or police relations don't mean more bodies out on the street, doesn't mean more protection for the citizens of Cedar City.

Even stronger were the objections to one-person patrol cars, which, it was charged, jeopardized safety and effectiveness. "I am not as aggressive when I work by myself, and I am not as willing to take chances. Whereas the police officer who is working with a partner is much more aggressive and much more willing to get into an investigation and much more willing to follow through and solve problems." The case against Tracy's personnel practice was, thus, couched in terms of departmental effectiveness and public safety.

But this restiveness among the rank and file can also be interpreted as resistance to the professional policing style at the heart of Tracy's reforms. The dissatisfaction with one-person patrol cars, for example, may have had as much to do with boredom as with danger. As one sergeant put it: "I think the one-man patrol car is probably in the best interests of the community that we serve. Probably not in the best interest of our membership, though." More generally, it was charged that Tracy was taking the department away from real police officers.[41]

If you look at the management of the CCPD at the present time, you'll find that a lot of those people spent very little time in . . . patrol. Quite often they were the police officers who were not the achievers when they worked out on the streets in a patrol car. They were very good when it came to promotional tests, but they were not good police officers.

One reason for their test proficiency, according to this line of thought, is that they were such poor street officers that they were relegated to positions "where all [you] had to do is sit there and study. . . . If you can spend eight hours a day studying for the next examination, your chances of passing are a hell of a lot better."

Not all of Tracy's critics were inclined to attribute his management practices to ignorance of what it is like to work the streets. The more moderate critics simply acknowledged a kind of natural division these days between the values and interests of police managers and those of rank-and-file officers. "I think the police chief has become, probably necessarily so, more of an administrator, and the city government's changed. . . . Now we have to answer to the office of management and budget, et cetera, and the chief does." This officer, a sergeant, drew a line between himself and lieutenants, who "are more involved in budgets and the money problems of the department itself. . . . As a sergeant, my concern is that I get the job done for other people. I don't care how much it costs. That's not a concern of mine. When I have to start worrying about how much it costs, then I guess I'm a manager or an administrator." But regardless of whether Chief Tracy's critics rage against the unacceptable or acquiesce in the inevitable, the underlying point is a growth of practices that are clearly at odds with traditional policing and thus provide circumstantial evidence of the development of a more professional department.

Chief Tracy had a very strong impact on the Cedar City Police Department. Working closely with Mayor Mercer, Tracy was not just a tough-minded administrator who was prepared to discipline the rank and file. Through his hiring and disciplinary policies, he also made the department more responsive to Cedar City's minority communities. The result was a positive image among Cedar City's moderation-oriented civic elite:

> I think he knows the police science. I think he knows the dimensions of the crime problem today in very realistic terms. I think he's a good administrator. There's a lot of police that don't like him but they respect him. I don't think anyone is going to say he is not a good police officer. . . . He's firm, fast. He doesn't delay. I think he's a good administrator. Dick's smart enough to select people who will be loyal to him and he reads people well enough to know people, competent people who won't be loyal—that will do the job but won't give him 100 percent loyalty. So I would say that Dick selected the right people that he feels comfortable with.

It must also be said, however, that Tracy was a good deal more successful with the downtown elite than with the small-business people in Crystal Valley who, as revealed in Chapter 2, were distinctly more sympathetic to the chief's law-and-order critics in the guild.

Within the department he was a very controversial figure who evoked unrelenting hostility from some officers. The most hostile critics questioned not just his values but his administrative capabilities as well. When this criticism was probed, however, the trail generally led back to promotional policies and to Tracy's inclination to turn the department over to administrators rather than to real police officers. A more moderate critic, who himself became a lower-echelon police manager, offers a more nuanced perspective. "I think that there is a perception within the department and certainly outside that Chief Tracy is more progressive, more open, more flexible, but in practice, at my level, running that operation, I really didn't perceive it as such. . . . It still filters down, and each layer maybe skims a little of it off." In other words, Tracy, like his predecessors, had problems coping with the inertial forces of bureaucratic resistance.

Tracy was also very reluctant to embrace community policing. While he was clearly responsive to the legitimate concerns of the black community, it was only after this research was completed that he set up a serious pilot project in community policing. It was one thing to direct the department along responsive lines and quite another to give up bureaucratic control to the extent required by community policing. Still, under pressure from a mayor who was dependent on the black community, Tracy did reshape the department in ways that made it more suitable for the responsibilities of community policing. He also was willing to undertake a serious test of community policing, although it is unclear in Cedar City, as it is elsewhere in the country, whether these experimental projects will become a prominent part of mainstream policing.

Four generalizations emerge clearly from this account of the policy and politics of policing in Cedar City between 1964 and 1983.

1. External political forces were the principal source of policy changes for the Cedar City Police Department: the exposure of the payoff system, the increasing influence of the black and Asian communities, and, to a lesser extent, the flow of LEAA money account for most of the shifts in policy.
2. While there were significant variations in police policy, the department did display a formidable capacity to resist and divert these external forces—although there was a modest reform constituency within the department.
3. Street crime was not an important determinant of police policy: the politicization of street crime did not impinge on department policymaking, nor was control of street crime a matter of intrinsic importance to police managers or rank-and-file officers.
4. Policy change did not develop in a punitive direction. On the contrary, the department became increasingly responsive to more progressive values.

So much for description. Let us now turn to the more difficult task of explaining these generalizations and to figuring out whether they are peculiar to Cedar City or reflect broader trends in policing and public policy.

Left to their own devices, police departments, like other agencies, tend to respond primarily to the inertial forces of past practice. In Cedar City, the key to change was, of course, the exposure of the payoff system, which temporarily weakened the department's defenses against reform. But the more enduring source of change was the empowerment of minority communities—based initially on a coalition among white liberals, Asians, and blacks. Of course, inasmuch as white flight increases the numerical strength of minorities in Cedar City and in other urban areas, police policy will be less dependent on the support, not to speak of the leadership, of white liberals. While there is no way to predict that minorities, left to their own devices, will continue along the progressive road toward community policing, the record to date in cities like Houston and Oakland is promising.[42]

Nevertheless, police departments have been and will continue to be resistant to change. Like ships at sea, police departments do not change direction easily. Moreover, it is difficult to distinguish the appearance of change from the substance of change—one of the lessons of West's two terms. Certainly the available data show no signs that Brush's crime-fighting image was turned into operative policy or that Goodfellow's department was genuinely responsive on racial matters.

In one important respect departments have become more resistant to change. The successful organizational efforts and legislative lobbying of rank-and-file officers have afforded them considerable control over their workplace. To police managers, the increasing and contractually mandated influence of the rank and file over a variety of organizational issues is disquieting. Of course, rank-and-file officers see these changes as a step in the right direction. But whatever value is attached to the consolidation of rank-and-file power, it enhances the capacity to resist reform.

The low salience of control of street crime as an issue in police policy processes is a reflection of two separate but related factors. On the one hand, other issues are simply more important, and, on the other, police tend to believe that there is not much that can be done that they are not already doing to control the spread of street crime.

Rank-and-file and managerial reactions to the LEAA are indicative of the strength of the policy status quo with respect to street crime. To the rank and file, LEAA funds were remembered almost exclusively as a source of funding for career advancement. As one police officer put it, "The average police officers here really don't know what LEAA did." Police managers were more aware of the variety of opportunities provided by the LEAA but tended to be quite selective in taking advantage of them. There seems to have been a willingness to add hardware, but considerable internal resistance to genuine policy innovation.

> There were a number of programs that were instituted but when federal funds dried up, so did the programs. . . . The old-school chiefs . . . . take money and they take personnel and equipment. . . . In many cases there was a lot of good and a lot of bad came out of it. When I say bad, it was because programs were funded hastily. Some were not thought out. Some were adopted in terms of long-term potential but the planning was very short range.

Whatever the final judgment on this issue, there is ample evidence in Cedar City and elsewhere of substantial bureaucratic resistance to the serious and systematic rethinking of crime-fighting methods that the LEAA was supposed to generate.[43]

This is not to say that rank-and-file officers or managers are not concerned about controlling street crime. But for police, as for other professions and occupations, bread-and-butter issues take precedence over ideology. Just as important is the broad-scale skepticism about what can be done to improve the crime-fighting capabilities of the police. By and large, the police believe that they already know how to catch criminals and certainly do not need any assistance from amateurs whose plans often challenge accepted dogma and may lead to unwelcome changes in comfortable routines. The police acknowledge that the fight against street crime is being lost but only because of the policies of the criminal courts—including both restrictions on the police and permissive sentencing.

The objections to permissive sentencing and constitutional restrictions do not, however, seem to have led Cedar City police in punitive directions. Under Chief Tracy, in particular, the department showed a commitment to restraint in the use of force and a willingness to pursue a variety of community crime programs that enlist the cooperation of citizens for property identification and block watches. There was, of course, considerable rank-and-file resistance, but an increasingly well-educated and well-trained rank and file seem likely to become more receptive to reform and particularly to community policing that allows street officers to exercise considerable initiative. Moreover, the political climate in Cedar City and elsewhere has been conducive to these sorts of changes.

It would, however, be easy to exaggerate the gulf and overlook the common bonds between reform-oriented and traditional police officers. Clearly, the professional version of police reform, probably the dominant mode of policing in the United States, has a punitive edge much like traditional policing. The emphasis on arrest entails a contextualization more than a repudiation of punitive values. The importance of force in policing and of incarceration in sentencing are taken for granted by such reformers They are, however, more inclined to reject expressive violence and to deploy it instrumentally instead. As for those committed to community policing, they will put more emphasis on informal dispute resolution and on mobilizing the support of citizens. Still, there is no reason to believe that they will be any less committed to punitive sentencing for those whose behavior does warrant arrest and charging. Certainly, there is no articulation of structural criminological views.[44] In the final analysis, then, both kinds of reformers as well as those who may still be committed to traditional policing operate well within the boundaries of volitional criminology.

4

Policy, Politics, and the Criminal Courts

The criminal courts are anchored in a contradiction that has significant policy implications. On the one hand, criminal courts are set up as autonomous agents of legal values and, more particularly, of adversarial justice and due process protections. These values are incorporated into institutional processes; they are intrinsic to the professional training of judges, prosecutors, and defense counsel; and they are at the heart of rule of law ideology. Generally speaking, these legal values tend to distance the criminal courts from the pressures and policies associated with the politicization of street crime.

On the other hand, there are powerful forces that work at cross purposes to legal autonomy and due process values. The authority of the criminal courts is, in the first place, directly dependent on continuing electoral scrutiny—thus compromising the ideal of legal autonomy. There are also organizational concerns related to managing case loads, maximizing predictability, and enhancing efficiency. These concerns lead toward bureaucratic and away from adversarial practices.[1] Even in strictly legal terms, due process values are not unchallenged, because, as Herbert Packer taught us, criminal process is grounded in the polarities of the crime control and due process models.[2] Finally, prosecutors and judges have their own personal values and preferences, which, as we shall see, play a very important role in their decisions.

These competing forces were at work in the Park County criminal courts, and this chapter traces the policy accommodations worked out by prosecutors and judges. With respect to prosecutors, our path will run through the machine-style law and order bravado of Dana Phillips (1964–1970), to the professional reforms and rehabilitative criminology initiated during the first term of his successor, Whitney Steele (1971–1974), and finally to the moderately punitive policies adopted during Steele's second term (1975–1978) and carried on by a Steele deputy who succeeded him. While it is more difficult to provide a systematic summary of judicial developments, suffice it to say that the courts also got caught up in the shift from rehabilitative to moderately punitive policies.

In might seem at first glance that the politicization of street crime provides the best explanation for these policy trends. It is, after all, during the period of heightened politicization (1975–1978) that sentencing takes a punitive turn with increasing reliance on incarceration. But a careful reading of the Park County findings casts considerable doubt on this interpretation. In the first place, the quantitative data presented in this chapter reveal that neither of the politicization variables—crime reporting or the crime rate—is very helpful in explaining the patterns of policy change. Second, the interview data considered here reinforce the findings already discussed in Chapter 2—namely, that judges and prosecutors, even in the 1975–1978 period, were pretty well insulated from the politicization of street crime. Third, the moderately punitive policies adopted in Park County—what has come to be called the "justice model"—are probably more accurately seen as a middle-of-the-road alternative to the punitive hard line. Finally, this policy shift was at least as much a reflection of personal criminological preferences as a response to the politics of law and order.

This introductory section looks in more detail at the competing pressures impinging on the criminal courts and at the accommodating devices developed by prosecutors and judges. It is in this context that the consensual attractions of the justice model emerge clearly.

Legal Values

While Packer identifies the criminal courts with due process values and the police with crime control values,[3] his more fundamental point is that the two sets of values taken together define the legitimate polarities of criminal process. "The two models merely afford a convenient way to talk about the operation of a process whose day-to-day functioning involves a constant series of minute adjustments between the competing demands of the two value systems and whose normative future likewise involves a series of resolutions of the tensions between competing claims."[4] To put it another way, the crime control and due process models reflect the polarities on which liberal legal authority is constructed. Governance, according to this mode of thinking, must accommodate the authority of the state to the rights of individual citizens.

If we then extrapolate from Packer's formulation to the prosecutors and judges, who are the subjects of this inquiry, we are urged to think of them primarily as autonomous agents of a liberal legalism divided only by their respective emphases on crime control and due process values. The idea that the essential policy choice for judges and prosecutors entails an accommodation of crime control and due process values rests on some firm ground. Certainly, one of the problems posed for judges and prosecutors is how to reconcile the "obstacle course" of due process protections with the speed, finality, and efficiency that are at the heart of the "assembly-line conveyor belt" of crime control.[5] But this is really the lawyer's-eye view of policymaking.[6]

Criminology and Legality

Insofar as criminal-process professionals think about crime control, they are as much concerned with sentencing policy as with the process considerations identified by Packer. Regardless of whether defendants are afforded their full complement of due process protections or are hustled through the criminal courts with maximum efficiency, the decision about what to do with those adjudged guilty remains.

Do we lock them up and throw away the key? Do we, instead, try to rehabilitate them—and, if so, through prison programs and indeterminate sentencing or through probation? And what about deterrence: punishment in measured doses aimed at modifying behavior or inducing a sense of individual responsibility in criminals as well as in others who might be tempted by crime? These can be seen, criminologically speaking, as crime control measures, but they do not necessarily promote the values that Packer associates with the crime control model.

Prosecutors and judges must work their way through this policy thicket, and their legal values do not offer much guidance. In addition to striking a balance between Packer's polarities, they must face up to the criminological implications of their decisions. No doubt, judges and prosecutors, like the rest of us, come to criminological problems with a variety of preconceptions. Unlike us, they have an opportunity to learn from their everyday experiences in criminal process. This learning seems to loom large in the policy process, but it is under constant pressure from the problems posed by electoral accountability.

Policy, Politics, and Law

The most troubling tension in the lives of judges and, to a lesser extent, prosecutors stems from their relationships with the public—through the electoral process and through media coverage of criminal process. Insofar as judges and prosecutors are responsive to the public, their capacity to formulate criminological policy and to maintain their legal independence is subjected to extraneous influences.

Packer simply ignores the pressures of political accountability—in all likelihood because he sees both the common ground and competing values of the two models as consonant with the broader political culture. "We are positing, not a criminal process that operates in any kind of society at all, but rather one that operates within the framework of contemporary American society. This leaves plenty of room for polarization, but it does require some limits."[7] In fact, the professional understandings and accommodations that are acceptable within the criminal process community are not necessarily in harmony with public values. The public debate tends to be substantially more polarized than the debate among legal professionals. The legal values and criminological wisdom that define common ground among professionals and allow them to compose their differences are often viewed with suspicion and even contempt by the general public—particularly by a public aroused about crime.[8]

The research findings that follow suggest that the primary response to this dilemma is to separate politics from law and policy as much as possible. That is to say, various stratagems are developed for transforming election campaigns and media coverage into symbolic activities that have as little as possible to do with operative policy.[9]

Park County judges and prosecutors thus preserved a significant measure of autonomy for dealing with the overwhelming majority of their cases by giving up much of their autonomy in those prosecutions that were inescapably politicized because of the notoriety of the participants or of the circumstances. But the charges strongly influenced by political calculations were something of a sideshow. In this and other ways, public attention was diverted from the vast bulk of cases that were dealt with according to sheltered routines. These routines reflected the values and interests of the criminal court community and were, therefore, more responsive to the professionals' criminological visions and to their personal political aspirations than to public concerns about street crime.[10]

What are the implications of this tendency to split cases into two categories? At first glance, it would seem that the two tracks undermine accountability by distancing the public from criminal process. To some extent, this is true. After all, the public is encouraged to think of exceptional crimes and exceptional punishments as the norm. Also, professionals are free to deal with the preponderance of their caseload without public scrutiny. Finally, prosecutors and judges are using their partial political insulation to advance their own version of criminological wisdom, to enhance organizational efficiency, and to promote their own careers quite independently of the legal forms that provide justification for the partial autonomy of criminal process.

More broadly, however, it is clear that criminal court professionals are constrained by the prevailing ethos and by institutional limitations, and do not, therefore, lose touch with the public. The result is something of a mixed picture: a striking measure of autonomy that is deployed in the service of essentially conventional principles and practices. The attractions of the justice model are best understood as a response to the underlying tension between partial autonomy and "contextual" accountability.

The Consensual Attractions of the Justice Model

In recent years, criminal courts in the United States have increasingly reconciled their process and policy dilemmas through recourse to the so-called justice model. It is rooted in a variety of principles including social equity,[11] formal justice,[12] and deterrence.[13] Taken together, this troika presents a powerful challenge to rehabilitation and to treatment.

At its most practical, the justice model promises crime reduction through deterrence insofar as punishment is in direct proportion to the seriousness of the crime and insofar as it is swift and certain. Clearly, these principles are altogether incompatible with the treatment model, which calls for "punishment" that fits the criminal rather than the crime.

But the advantages of the justice model over the treatment model can be expressed in moral as well as pragmatic terms. Rehabilitation puts several cherished values at risk. There is reason to believe that rehabilitation tends to work against minority and poor defendants. Who, after all, is going to look like the best bet for a successful probation program? Will it be the minority youth without a supportive family and with meager job skills? Or will it be the middle-class white with, say, a couple of years of college? Probation opportunities may, in short, be less readily available to the lower strata of the society. Second, for those who are given prison sentences, rehabilitation means indeterminate sentences—with actual time served dependent on progress toward rehabilitation as determined unilaterally by the parole board. Finally, rehabilitative sentences are not proportional to the harm done. Indeed, punishment may be withheld for a time or entirely in order to promote rehabilitation.

In stressing punishment to fit the crime rather than the criminal, the justice model makes a strong claim for advancing both social equity and just deserts. And in stressing determinate sentencing, the deterrence model promises to be less arbitrary and more humane—removing a good deal of uncertainty from prisoners' lives and making them less beholden to the whims of the prison bureaucracy and the parole board.[14]

The justice model, therefore, provides a neat package that is responsive through deterrence to crime control concerns and through equity to due process concerns. Politically, it has attractions for both the moderate left and the moderate right. Certainly that seems to have been the case in Park County, and this chapter traces the emergence of the justice model out of the criminological and political concerns of the prosecutor's office. Although in

Park County, as elsewhere, judges had serious reservations about the restrictions imposed on judicial discretion by the justice model, it had some appeal for them too as a constructive response to a significant dilemma.

Patterns of Policy Change

The purposes served by the quantitative data available on the criminal courts are much the same as they were for the police—that is, they trace the course of policy and identify explanatory variables. As with the police, regression analysis indicated that neither crime reporting nor the crime rate was very useful for explaining variations in policy, thus providing still more evidence of the modest role played by the politicization of street crime in Cedar City. Again paralleling the police findings, the regression analysis suggested that changes in the leadership of the prosecutor's office might be helpful in explaining policy outcomes.[15] This is hardly surprising given the control that prosecutors exercise over the flow and disposition of cases in the criminal courts.[16]

Policy Indicators

The quantitative indicators of policy change include charging practices, sentencing severity, and conviction and dismissal rates.[17] These indicators provide a systematic overview of each stage of the dispositional process: charging by the prosecutor, bargaining between the prosecutor and defense counsel, and sentencing. Moreover, variations in the severity of these dispositional practices also give a good sense of the responsiveness of the Park County criminal courts to the punitive values associated with the politicization of street crime.

Analysis of charging practices was confined to what were deemed to be politically salient crimes—namely, homicide, sexual assault, robbery, and burglary.[18] In general, crimes may be charged in the first degree or in lesser degrees of severity. These data thus reveal annual changes in charging practices by the prosecutor's office along a continuum from high end (aggressive) to low end (conservative) filing.

The impact of charging practices may be reinforced or attenu-

TABLE 4.1
Filing Rates for Criminal Charges by Prosecutor

Criminal Offense	Phillips		Steele	
	Percent	Number	Percent	Number
Homicide				
First-degree murder	17	59	32	133
Negligent homicide	42	150	32	133
All homicide	100	357	100	411
Sexual assault				
Rape	8	23	35	277
Attempted rape	1	2	12	91
Carnal knowledge	29	81	20	154
Indecent liberties	62	175	34	263
All sexual assault	100	281	100	785
Robbery				
Robbery	24	574	22	1,288
Attempted robbery	2	38	4	259
All robbery	100	2,386	100	5,759
Burglary				
First-degree burglary	2	22	5	185
Second-degree burglary	93	1,337	91	3,184
All burglary	100	1,442	100	3,483

Note: All percentages are column percentages within classes of crimes (e.g., of all homicide charges filed by Phillips, 17 percent were first-degree murder and 42 percent were negligent homicide). Not all subcategories add up to 100 percent because not all classes of crime were included.

ated by what happens at final disposition. A high rate of dismissals would, for example, tend to erode the crime control implications of aggressive charging practices. Similarly, a high conviction rate, frequently presented by prosecutors as evidence of effective crime control, is suspect when it is combined with conservative charging. Accordingly, data are included on conviction and dismissal rates—calculated as percentages of the total number of dispositions each year.

Finally, there is the question of severity of sentence. Under the indeterminate sentencing practices during the period of this study, it was the parole board rather than the judges who decided how much time would actually be served. Accordingly, the

TABLE 4.2
Disposition Rates by Prosecutor

	Phillips		Steele	
	Percent	Number	Percent	Number
All convictions	84	6,947	75	15,821
No time	51	3,563	56	8,820
Jail time	22	1,543	28	4,498
Prison time	27	1,841	16	2,503
Dismissals	11	942	20	4,252
All dispositions	100	8,227	100	21,139

Note: All percentages are column percentages. For each prosecutor, conviction rates are equal to the mean of the annual ratios of convictions to total cases disposed. Dismissal rates represent the mean of the annual ratios of dismissals to total cases disposed.

focus was shifted to probationary sentencings—as measured by the proportion of sentences each year that required no incarceration beyond time served prior to conviction—and on the proportion of jail as opposed to prison sentences.

Explaining Policy Change

As has already been suggested, changes in leadership in the prosecutor's office seem to account best for the variations in policy. There was during the period of this research only one major change in leadership—that is, when the machine-style prosecutor, Dana Phillips (1964–1970), was replaced by the reformer, Whitney Steele (1971–1978). Tables 4.1 and 4.2 reveal that virtually all the policy indicators showed significant changes after Steele took office. Steele, however, introduced two distinctly different sets of reforms—one, rehabilitative in character, during his 1971–1974 term and the other, more punitive, during his 1975–1978 term. It was, in other words, during Steele's second term that the justice model was introduced. The contrasting policies utilized during Steele's two term emerge clearly in Tables 4.3 and 4.4.

Generally speaking, filing data, presented in Table 4.1, indicate that Phillips filed more conservatively while Steele was more inclined to be aggressive. That is to say, Phillips was less likely to file at the high end than was Steele. This is particularly true of

TABLE 4.3
Filing Rates for Criminal Charges by Prosecutorial Term

	Phillips		Steele 1st Term		Steele 2nd Term	
	Percent	Number	Percent	Number	Percent	Number
Homicide						
First-degree murder	17	59	27	65	40	68
Negligent homicide	42	150	33	79	32	54
All homicide	100	357	100	242	100	169
Sexual assault						
Rape	8	23	38	116	34	161
Attempted rape	1	2	4	12	9	79
Carnal knowledge	30	81	15	44	23	110
Indecent liberties	62	175	43	131	27	132
All sexual assault	100	281	100	303	100	482
Robbery						
Robbery	24	574	21	671	24	617
Attempted robbery	2	38	3	81	7	178
All robbery	100	2,386	100	3,158	100	2,601
Burglary						
First-degree burglary	2	22	4	71	6	114
Second-degree burglary	93	1,337	91	1,461	92	1,723
All burglary	100	1,442	100	1,606	100	1,877

Note: All percentages are column percentages within classes of crimes (e.g., of all homicide charges filed by Phillips, 17 percent were first-degree murder and 42 percent were negligent homicide). Not all subcategories add up to 100 percent because not all classes of crime were included.

homicide and sexual assault, with Steele more likely to charge first-degree murder and rape while Phillips tended to settle for the lesser charges of negligent homicide and indecent liberties or carnal knowledge. In fact, the number of first-degree murder charges filed by Phillips ranged from a low of 4 in 1964 to a high of 16 in 1969, while those figures for Steele ranged from 8 in 1972 to 28 in 1974. The number of rape charges filed during Phillips's tenure ranged from 1 in 1968 to 9 in 1970. With Steele as prosecuting attorney, the lowest number of rape charges filed was 25 in 1972, while the highest number was 65 in 1975. With respect to robbery and burglary, filing practices are virtually indistinguish-

TABLE 4.4
Disposition Rates by Prosecutorial Term

| | Phillips | | Steele | | | |
| | | | 1st Term | | 2nd Term | |
	Percent	Number	Percent	Number	Percent	Number
All convictions	84	6,947	79	8,029	71	7,792
No time	51	3,563	62	5,136	47	3,684
Jail time	22	1,543	22	1,800	35	2,698
Prison time	27	1,841	13	1,093	18	1,410
Dismissals	11	942	16	1,620	24	2,632
All dispositions	100	8,227	100	10,197	100	10,942

Note: All percentages are column percentages. For each prosecutor, conviction rates are equal to the mean of the annual ratios of convictions to total cases disposed. Dismissal rates represent the mean of the annual ratios of dismissals to total cases disposed.

able, although Steele was somewhat more aggressive on first-degree burglary charges.

Table 4.2 presents a second measure of change, severity of sentences. Once again differences appear between Phillips and Steele, but here the differences are reversed, with Phillips taking the tougher stand—that is, being less likely to grant probation and more likely to impose prison time. Thus, when Phillips and Steele are compared, their statistical profiles turn out to be reverse images. Phillips was permissive when it came to charging but tough with respect to sentencing. Steele, in contrast, tended to charge at the high end but to sentence more permissively.

The picture is further refined by the data in Table 4.3 and Table 4.4, which distinguish between Steele's terms. Table 4.3 indicates increased high-end filings in the second term. The only exceptions are negligent homicide and rape. The percentage of first-degree murder charges rose from 27 percent to 40 percent; attempted rape rose from 4 percent to 16 percent; first-degree burglary went from 4 percent to 6 percent; and robbery rose from 21 percent to 24 percent. Conversely the percentage of indecent liberties, the lowest sexual assault charge, fell from 43 percent to 27 percent.

Table 4.4 reveals a parallel hardening of sentencing practices between Steele's first and second terms. Probationary sentences drop off from 62 percent during the first term to 47 percent during the second term. Note, however, the undercurrent of moderation in this increased incarceration. For the most part, convicts were sent to jail—with the rate rising from 22 percent to 35 percent—although imprisonment also increased somewhat. This moderately punitive trend is suggestive of the means and ends of the justice model.

There is an anomalous quality to these findings. On the one hand, it is clear, and hardly surprising by this point, that the leadership variable does a good job of explaining variations in filing and sentencing practices, while the politicization variables, crime rate and crime reporting, do not. On the other hand, there is a rough consonance between the hardening of policy during Steele's second term and the heightened politicization of street crime in Cedar City in the 1975–1978 period.

First, let us compare Phillips's and Steele's filing and sentencing practices, which point in different directions. Phillips was less aggressive in charging, but those convicted during the Phillips administration were more likely to be incarcerated and more likely to do prison time. In contrast, Steele charged more aggressively but had a lower conviction and higher dismissal rate. On the basis of these data, it cannot be said with confidence that one office was substantially tougher on crime than the other.

There is no doubt, however, that Steele developed a harder line on crime during his second term in office. Charging practices were still more aggressive and, more significant, there was a sharp drop in probationary sentencing. Can this be explained as a response to the politics of law and order? The answer is yes and no according to interview data and library research presented in subsequent sections of this chapter. Steele's second-term election campaign did not promise or even allude to a tougher line on crime, but he did get a sense that his prospects for *higher office* might be enhanced by a more forceful anticrime image, especially insofar as it was possible to construct a broad and progressive coalition on a foundation provided by the justice model. At the same time, the principal architect of office policy, his chief criminal deputy, was becoming increasingly skeptical about rehabilitation. In short, the impact of politicization was contingent and idiosyncratic, altogether consistent with findings in previous chapters. Accordingly, it is understandable that the politicization variables were not very helpful in explaining policy change.

Prosecutors: The Triumph of Reform

In 1970 the real policy watershed for the Park County Prosecutor's Office was the Republican party primary. Once Whitney Steele, a young, politically ambitious reformer, had defeated Dana Phillips, the long-time incumbent, significant change was almost certain to follow. Steele's victory was in effect the symptom of a new local political climate—a movement from machine-style to reform politics. The Democrat, whom Steele narrowly defeated in a Tweedledum–Tweedledee general election, also presented himself as a moderate reformer.

The policy changes introduced by Steele are interesting not only in their own right but also because they demonstrate clearly the tenuous links between campaigning and policymaking. In one sense, the electorate got the reform for which it was ostensibly voting. Once Steele arrived, the taint of corruption departed, although it was never established that corruption had any impact on the prosecution of street crime or on the processing of criminal cases more generally. In retrospect, what stands out was the transformation of the office from an unabashed cog in the prosecutor's personal political machine into a genuine career option for competent attorneys. There is no reason to believe that the electorate had clear views on this professional matter. With respect to street crime, the relevant policy changes were at best vaguely foreshadowed by the election campaign. Phillips's crime control campaign was a textbook example of symbolic politics, and Steele's campaign, although promising firmness on crime, emphasized corruption.

The two Republicans in effect talked past one another in the all-important primary. Steele began as an underdog. Indeed, one of his advisers told the would-be candidate that he "didn't have a prayer" of defeating Phillips, even though there were some promising campaign cards to play.

He had this awesome political system. But Phillips was quite controversial even then. The early stuff about gambling and corruption had come out, and there were those issues that made Phillips vulnerable. But the dissatisfaction with Phillips among all but the conservative parts of the community was widespread. He had been there a long time. He was a very conservative prosecutor, a competent prosecutor. The perception was that the office was competent technically but that it had bad social policies.

There were also problems with the civil division of the office, which engendered support for Steele within the legal community but did not generate a campaign issue.

> The civil division was perceived to be a disaster, poor quality. . . . He used the civil division as part of his method of maintaining power. . . . And the bar, particularly the civil bar, saw the need for reform, but it's hard to turn that into a political issue, and as I recall there wasn't much talk about that.

The obvious choice was, therefore, to campaign as a reformer, to talk corruption rather than crime.

Phillips, for his part, had an established reputation as a defender of law and order and predictably chose to campaign on crime. He sought to direct attention away from the payoff scandal, but the strategy did not work, and Steele won handily. Clearly the electorate felt that it was time for a change. It is less clear that the public appreciated exactly what was at stake in terms of reform or of crime.

The Stakes of Reform

Phillips's approach to his office was frankly and overtly political. The deputies were viewed as campaign workers and, perhaps to a lesser extent, as campaign contributors. As one senior official put it:

> You had to work in his campaign. You had to join the Young Republican Club. You had to do all kinds of things. I mean it was a requirement of the job. I mean you campaigned for him. And when he campaigned, I made speeches all the time. I used to go to coffee clubs and church bingo meetings and all kinds of things. They would be set up for me, and I would go

in and give a speech about how good Mr. Phillips was and why you should reelect him. That was part of my job, and if you didn't want to do it, you could just hit the road—every single deputy. . . . When I went to work for him, he said: "Look, this is a political office. You want to work for me, you work for me twenty-four hours a day. I want you to work on my campaign. Donate as much money as you can to it, because when I don't have a job, you don't have a job."

Most people accepted this arrangement. But the resentment of an attorney who began his career working in Phillips's unsuccessful campaign against Steele was probably not atypical.

I can still remember going out doorbelling: "Hi, I'm here for Dana Phillips." And they'd slam the door and say, "We're going to throw that crook out of office." You know, at the time that you're brand new, you just do it. . . . I can remember office meetings with the whole office being exhorted to pitch in for the election effort.

When occasionally someone protested or, as in the case of a woman who went on to high state judicial office, simply refused, Phillips "just somehow would get rid of them." That there was good reason to be leery of mixing law and politics in this blatant fashion was illustrated by a local attorney who complained that he had received electioneering calls from Phillips's deputies, even though he then had a case pending with the prosecutor's office.[19] In any event, this was clearly not a setting that encouraged deputies to take the initiative or to contribute to policy. Inasmuch as one of the attributes of professionalism is autonomy, Phillips's office did not really provide professional training. Instead, this was an office that stressed the technical expertise meant to introduce attorneys to the operative standards of criminal justice and to sharpen their trial skills. After the two or three years that it took to achieve these modest objectives, it was expected that the deputies would go elsewhere. "When you went to work for the boss, you were supposed to quit in three years, and the boss told you that when you went to work for him. 'Three years is all I want. . . . And in three years, I expect you to quit this office and get a job out there somewhere, and if you can't get a job, I will get one for you.' And he did." There was an obvious disadvantage to operating in this fashion. The office had to depend heavily on inexperienced attorneys and would tend to lose deputies at just the point when the learning curve had leveled off.

While the policy was, in certain respects, self-defeating, it also served some important purposes—albeit political rather than legal purposes. To put the best face on it, Phillips saw his office as a kind of proving ground for future legal and political leaders, and in fact a surprising number of prominent lawyers and politicians served their apprenticeship under Phillips's tutelage. With this objective, rapid cycling of attorneys through the office promised to multiply the benefits. But providing training and, in some cases, jobs for potential community leaders also served Phillips's personal political purposes, because it meant well-placed supporters whom he might reasonably call upon at election time. Still, it is probably better, once again, to think of three-year "terms" as a Phillips idiosyncrasy rather than as a necessary corollary of a machine-style prosecutor's office. After all, it was no doubt much easier to operate a centralized office with young and inexperienced attorneys. Well-trained veteran prosecutors would want more responsibility and would bridle at Phillips's preemptory approach to his staff.

The office style was radically altered during the Steele administration, and the professionalism he introduced continued under his successor, who had served as chief civil deputy under Steele. Among other changes, deputies were no longer expected to leave after a few years—that is, just when they became truly productive. This effort to lengthen terms of service was a significant success. Between 1971 and 1978, the first and last years of the Steele administration, the average length of service increased from seventeen to forty-three months.[20] Indeed, several of the top leaders interviewed for this project in 1983 had actually begun their service under Phillips almost twenty years earlier. They all made it clear that this would have been unthinkable had Phillips remained in charge.

The point was not that they looked back with distaste or disrespect to their work in Phillips's office. On the contrary, they tended to believe that they were well trained by senior lawyers who knew the ins and outs of criminal practice:

[The chief criminal deputy] was an absolutely superb lawyer. He knew everything. He had been there for a long time . . . and he could answer any question you asked him. . . . He was a superb technician, was also a superb bargainer and very highly respected by the defense bar. He was tough, but his integrity was never in question, nor his fairness, nor anything else.

Even Phillips's opponents recognized that he ran a "competent" office. Indeed, all of the respondents viewed their years under Phillips as productive and worthwhile. Moreover, they tended to feel that many of the changes that took place could be attributed to the increased volume of cases, an ever larger number of attorneys, and better financing by Park County. In short, they felt that even had Phillips remained in office, he would not have been able to continue his very personal style of management.

Nonetheless, the fact remains that Steele created a setting in which attorneys were encouraged to think of themselves as professional, career-minded prosecutors. There seem to have been a number of aspects to this transformation. The office ceased being run in a partisan fashion. Not only were deputies no longer required to work in political campaigns, but such campaigning was frowned upon. Moreover, because of the larger staff, a managerial hierarchy was established that provided increasingly responsible and better paid steps up through the administration. Steele was also adept at initiating programs that, whatever their crime control capabilities, were effective in getting the County Council to fund the prosecutor's office more generously. Finally, there was a willingness to reward initiative and to try new things. This last change is directly relevant to the crime issue to which we now turn. In any event, through improved working conditions, better salaries, and a career ladder, Steele's legacy was job satisfaction for the long haul.

Campaigning on Crime

While Steele campaigned on reform, Phillips campaigned on crime. In retrospect, this element of the election concealed at least as much as it revealed. There is good reason to believe that Phillips was not so hard-nosed a prosecutor as he wanted the public to believe. Steele, for his part, adopted a treatment, or rehabilitative, approach once in office, but he did not really articulate this position during the campaign.[21] Recall also that the quantitative data indicate that Steele introduced significant but somewhat contradictory policy changes during his first term and then reversed his field in the second term. This policy reversal was only indirectly linked to Steele's reelection campaign. To begin sorting this out, it is necessary to take a hard look at the records of Phillips and Steele.

Phillips clearly and unequivocally presented himself to the electorate as a safe-streets candidate, pledged to protect the citizenry from civil disorder and from conventional crime. He underscored the high conviction rate of his office, alluded to a "plan against civil disorder," reminded the voters of his determination to imprison those convicted of violent crimes, reassured parents that he had taken steps to protect children from "morals offenders", proclaimed his leadership in fighting "the destructive forces in our community," and so on. Indeed, of the sixteen points in the campaign ad from which the above examples were culled, only four were not direct appeals to a law and order constituency.[22]

Phillips also proudly reminded voters of the support he received from like-minded groups—including the big labor organizations, several of the local police guilds, and the Cedar City fire fighters. Conversely, he sought to portray Steele as inexperienced and too liberal to take the tough measures required to deal effectively with crime.[23] But Phillips's tough talk was to a significant degree symbolic rather than real.

The available data lend some superficial credence to Phillips's stance. As he saw it, his trump card in the election was a high conviction rate. Witness the following campaign claim:

> While the number of Superior Court criminal filings has doubled, Dana Phillips has maintained a conviction rate by plea and trial of 90% or higher year-after-year. . . . Phillips was the first prosecutor in the state to require that all Superior Court cases be reviewed, discussed, and planned in detail with a chief deputy prior to trial, thus assuring a consistently high rate of conviction.[24]

Some of the data from this research are consistent with Phillips's hard-line image. Table 4.4 reveals that after his defeat, probationary sentencing increased sharply, from 51 percent under Phillips to 62 percent during Steele's first term. Similarly, fewer convicts were sentenced to prison time, 13 percent during Steele's first term, compared to 27 percent under Phillips. But on both counts, there is less here than meets the eye.

Consider first the sentencing data. During the Phillips years, 51 percent of the convictions resulted in probationary sentences, and 27 percent in prison time. Even if we assume that these figures represent a relatively hard line, they are not consistent with Phillips's uncompromising campaign promises. Surely, the electorate would have been surprised to learn that more than half of those convicted by Phillips's office were given probation. But these numbers provide only one reason for a revisionist view of the Phillips administration.

Consider also one senior deputy's description of sentencing practices during the Phillips years. "He was fairly easy on first offenders who were disadvantaged. Like if you were from the Central Area. You didn't have a high school education. You're black. You're out burglarizing somebody, he was pretty easy the first time. You'd get probation and hopefully be required to get your GED and try to do it right." It appears, in short, that there was a kind of ad hoc treatment component to Phillips's policies, which were not so hard-nosed as he wished the electorate to believe.

As to the conviction rate, there is good reason to believe that it was a most misleading indicator of crime control values. In part, the conviction rate was high because of Phillips's conservative filing practices. Both the quantitative data and the interviews indicated that "Phillips was extremely conservative as to what got filed. Unless it was a lead-pipe winner, he didn't get into it," is the way one attorney in Phillips's office put it.

Another important factor to keep in mind was the role played by the preliminary hearing, a procedure discontinued by Steele. As explained by one of the leading members of the defense bar, the preliminary hearing provided another opportunity for screening out questionable cases and maintaining a high conviction rate.

It's like going to a preview of a movie. They don't have to tell you the whole plot and put on all the actors and actresses, but they have to do enough to show their hand and demonstrate probable cause to a judge. The beauty of the system was that after the hearing, the matter would be postponed for one or two weeks, and during that one or two weeks you could really do some effective plea bargaining.

Both the defense and prosecution, in other words, had a fairly clear idea after the preliminary hearing about their chances of winning—much better than after the discovery procedures that were introduced by Steele when he took office: "There's nothing as good as seeing the whites of their eyes. You could see the complaining witness and what he or she looked like and how they handled themselves." The preliminary hearing was thus the prelude to a meeting between the defense counsel and the chief criminal deputy, who would "kick the thing around . . . and a decision would be made: do you bind it over to the Superior Court, keeping it as a felony, or do you reduce it from the felony or grand larceny to the misdemeanor or petty larceny?"

Consider the implications. One cost of keeping a close watch on the office batting average was that many cases were simply not filed. When in doubt, do not prosecute at all. Second, the preliminary hearing could often provide defense counsel with the ammunition necessary to strike a hard bargain. Nor was the defense bar unaware of the prosecutor's preoccupation with his conviction rate and of the pressure on trial deputies not to lose cases. Clearly it was a setting conducive to frequent charge reductions. In sum, Phillips presented a facade of toughness: a high conviction rate and a commitment to heavy sentences in the well-publicized cases. There was, however, a soft core to Phillips's policies: the cases that were never filed, the willingness to bargain once preliminary hearings had cast doubt on the strength of the cases, and the partial acceptance of treatment.

But how was Phillips able to conceal the true character of his policy? In one sense the answer is obvious. What goes on in the prosecutor's office goes on behind closed doors. Nor was there reason for any of the participants to reveal just how ill-clothed the emperor really was, since the system served them all quite well—in the fashion well known to all students of criminal process. The prosecutor gets a high conviction record, the defense counsel can wheel and deal, and the court's docket moves smoothly.

Moreover, had a challenger come along with a proposal for change, it would not have been easy to make a case against Phillips. There was no way, short of systematic social science research, to get a clear picture of prosecutorial practices. And even in the unlikely event that a candidate had been armed with social science evidence, it is difficult to see how such evidence could have played a significant role in an election campaign. Research findings are not easy to present to the electorate in a compelling or even a readily comprehensible fashion and would not, therefore, have been terribly useful.

For his part, Phillips could provide the electorate with accessible and quite credible evidence of a firm commitment to law and order. It turns out that there were notable exceptions to Phillips's conservative filing practices. He was consistently hard on vehicular homicide, as the figures for negligent homicide presented in Table 4.3 suggest. He was also willing to take chances on prosecutions of high-profile crimes, according to one of his principal assistants: "Other than a first-degree murder case or a very notorious criminal case like involving someone in political life or something like that, . . . 98 percent of the felony cases there were initiated by being filed in one of the district courts." Given the data in Table 4.3 on first-degree murder, it would seem that even here Phillips filed rather conservatively. In any case, there was general agreement among respondents that those cases likely to catch the public's eye were treated differently. They did not go through the preliminary hearing process, and the office was less amenable to bargaining. So there were actually two quite different policies. When in the spotlight, the office would live up to its hard-line image—filing the risky cases, fighting the good fight. But the more conventional cases—involving the vast majority of crimes and criminals—were pleaded out in traditional ways.

Although Steele was able to defeat Phillips, it was not because he exposed the gap between the incumbent's tough talk and his operative policy. Indeed, Steele never really engaged on crime control issues, and Phillips foundered, not because the electorate saw through or rejected his crime control posturing, but because the payoff scandal made his office suspect and turned the voters toward reform.

Nonetheless, shortly after assuming power, the Steele administration did make some significant changes in the way it handled criminal cases, self-consciously rejecting Phillips's "very law and order, very rigid" policies, as the new chief criminal deputy put it. He acknowledged that these changes were, in some measure, stylistic rather than substantive:

> I would explain why I was doing things to the defense attorneys. . . . You know: "This guy's going to prison because of this." George Myers, who was my predecessor, was a different sort of person, and he just did it and was widely resented for it because he seemed to be arbitrary. At least I'd tell people why. And that produced debates and discussions. . . . I respected their intellects, and we would debate these issues. . . . And so it was like we'd have a continual series of seminars.

But this was only part of the story: Phillips's conservative filing practices were abandoned because they were seen as misleading window dressing. More fundamentally, at the outset of Steele's first term, the office moved toward a treatment model.

The treatment, or rehabilitative, approach was consistent with Whitney Steele's political values, although not really with his campaign platform. As this same chief criminal deputy put it: "Whit at that point was quite liberal. I mean he saw crime as a social problem—bought into, as I did, crime as a disease. You could identify causes and prescribe cures and accomplish something." This change was reflected in the shift to probationary sentences revealed in Table 4.4, and it was not altogether welcome within the office. To at least one holdover deputy prosecutor, it appeared that the new chief criminal deputy "was inclined to give away the store"—that he was too responsive to special pleading by defense attorneys about the life circumstances of their clients. The chief criminal deputy's own retrospective view was not altogether different:

> The first reform of the office was to implement the rehabilitative ideal. When we got there, the chief did all of the plea bargaining, so I was able to affect the dispositions in a high number of cases just by one person's decisions. I started to use the powers of bargaining to coerce people into treatment and that sort of thing as opposed to prison. We individualized a lot more beyond the crime to social causes and that sort of thing.

But to what extent did this principled commitment to treatment really alter the quality of justice in the prosecutor's office? Here the record is not entirely clear, and it is important to keep things in perspective.

Recall that there seems to have been a good amount of wheeling and dealing in Phillips's office and that Phillips did not turn a blind eye to treatment-based arguments. Moreover, the impression that I got from defense counsel with whom I spoke was that it was possible to adapt to the new philosophy without altering to any appreciable degree the service provided to their clients. It stands to reason that defense attorneys would be savvy enough to figure out the game and obliging enough to play it: if Steele wants to hold a seminar on the possibilities and limits of the treatment model, we'll provide the raw material and the appropriate rationale. Chances are these same attorneys would have been just as adaptable to the kinds of evidentiary considerations that threatened Phillips's batting average. Accordingly, the dramatic changes in the quality of justice implied by the shift from punishment to treatment may have never materialized—and such changes as did occur were reversed in Steele's second term.

From Treatment to Deterrence

The quantitative data reveal markedly punitive trends during Steele's second term, beginning in 1975. Charging practices became somewhat more aggressive. According to Table 4.3, the percentage of first-degree murder charges rose from 27 percent to 40 percent. Although rape charges dropped slightly, attempted rape charges rose from 4 percent to 16 percent, and there was a clear tendency to move away from the low-end charge of indecent liberties. High-end charges with respect to burglary and robbery also went up somewhat. The trend is still clearer in sentencing. According to Table 4.4, probationary sentencing declined sharply from 62 percent to 47 percent—although it should be noted that the shift toward incarceration was toward jail time rather than prison time. The rate of imprisonment increased from 13 percent to 18 percent—still well below the Phillips mean of 27 percent. How can this be explained?

The 1974 election is not much help in explaining Steele's retreat from treatment. On the contrary, one could say that Steele's victory was a vote of confidence for the policies followed during his first term. Steele was cast by his opponent as a liberal who was soft on crime. Either the challenger was under the misapprehension that Steele was vulnerable on law and order grounds, or perhaps there was no other issue available. In any event, Steele was attacked for allowing plea bargaining and for being soft on violent crime.[25] The police guild gave some credibility to these charges by endorsing the challenger. But this was to no avail. Against the same Democratic opponent, whom he had only narrowly defeated in 1970, Steele won handily in 1974—perhaps in part because of a small contribution received by the challenger from gambling interests.[26] Nonetheless, during the second term, Steele adopted policies much closer to those advocated by his opponent than to his own campaign position.

The seeds of change were sown during the campaign, when Steele discovered that the progressive constituents with whom he felt considerable rapport were becoming increasingly restive about crime. As one of his key aids put it when asked about public pressure:

> Oh yeah, those Hillside coffee hours. . . . The public wasn't buying rehabilitation on either effectiveness or justice grounds. . . . They rejected it before the system did. I think that's what law and order is about—leniency. They perceived it as leniency, and he was great at that—at listening to people. What I remember him saying is that these are not reactionaries. These are not Goldwater people. They are people like me and to the left of me—liberal lawyers who are saying you've got to do something about people who break into my house, "the liberal who's been mugged."

These public concerns made Steele receptive to an alternative approach to processing cases. And although the election was behind him, the electoral process was still directly relevant, because those who knew Steele were agreed that he was politically ambitious and had his eye on the governor's office.

Within the office, there was also increasing dissatisfaction with the treatment model. Among the holdover deputies, there was, of course, the dual concern that the new administration was "giving away the store," and that treatment just did not work. As one senior deputy put it: "The rehabilitative model was recognized as a fiasco, since we see the same people come back and back and violate probation." But even the architect of the treatment policy had become disenchanted by the start of the second term. He was uncomfortable with the power that the treatment model vested in him as the final arbiter of plea bargaining decisions:

> I became convinced that it's beyond present human competence. We simply aren't able to do it. And also there's this power thing. I mean there I sat, little ol' Billy Dorffler from Cleveland Heights, and people came to me like supplicants. They'd sit outside my office in chairs like at a dentist's office . . . and I'd sit there six, eight, ten, twelve times a day and decide the fate of a person. . . . At first you get into it and it's fun, the lawyers' game, debates, and making points about strengths and weaknesses, but power bothered me. Why should I have a decision that that guy should go to prison for life or five years. That's where the doubt started—in terms of power. It's wrong. I shouldn't have that power. It should be a collective decision.

Note the mixture of concerns—power and effectiveness. Clearly, each "mistake" reinforced his concerns about exercising too much power.

> I recommended the psychopath program for George Stowe, who had bashed a woman's head with a rock out in Beach Park and damn near killed her and raped her, and he escaped from [the hospital] and hung two teenagers in a tree. It was one of those cases that got a lot of press: "How come that guy wasn't in prison!" John Bender was the sentencing judge, and I remember talking to John and saying: "Damnit, I thought we were doing the right thing." And his reaction was that we did, with what we knew at the time. But two people died because of a decision that I made.

Accordingly, as Steele's second term began, both he and Dorffler were thinking about alternatives to the treatment model.

But not just any change would do. A dramatic switch to pure crime control would not have been satisfactory for either Steele or Dorffler. Both of them thought of themselves as progressive reformers, and a hard line on crime might have jeopardized Steele's ties to the moderate wing of the Republican party. "Whitney Steele is a Ripon Republican, and he saw the system as needing reform—but he was still very much into the liberal reforms of the sixties. So I'm sure a major factor was that we can do better, bring more humane policies, more enlightened policies." A law and order campaign at that juncture would, therefore, have been out of character and might have alienated the constituency on which he was counting to carry him to higher office.[27]

Accordingly, the "justice model," as it was rechristened, had just the right mix of the practical and the principled to make it an ideal vehicle for political moderates with second thoughts. Dorffler set to work developing plea bargaining guidelines for the prosecutor's office. These guidelines were based on the severity of the crime and the record of the offender. Henceforth, lawyers were not to be permitted to argue the rehabilitative potential of their clients. The prosecutor's office also spearheaded an effort to persuade the state legislature to replace its indeterminate sentences with determinate sentences, and the first bill to this effect was introduced in 1976.

Legislation clearly provided an opportunity to bring the issue to the public and perhaps to lay the foundation for a gubernatorial campaign for Steele. The legislative effort was, according to Dorffler, aided by proponents of the treatment model, who picked a particularly inauspicious time to try to carry indeterminate sentencing to its logical conclusion.

> They were proposing sentencing which . . . literally drew no distinctions between crimes. All crimes had one penalty— robbery, forgery, five-year maximum, with dangerous offender provisions designed to deal with the really nasty folks. . . . There it stood. You couldn't have built a better straw man. We said: "Whit, here's something to attack." The very first speech was the Police Officer of the Year Award. Steele was going to speak. It was perfect. Wham! It hit the front pages. We worked a real campaign for the hearts and minds of the public—speeches to the ACLU, to the State Corrections Association, making justice arguments to the ACLU, debating Al Waterman. He was begrudging, but there was a lot of support from the left for this.

In sum, in the period after the 1974 election, Steele's office seized the initiative politically and, at the same time, introduced a dramatic change in the way it processed cases. The political initiative was clearly successful in that it led to the subsequent adoption of determinate sentencing legislation. On the other hand, Steele got out of politics for personal reasons and, therefore, never tested the electoral power of the justice model.

For our purposes, the key point is that the change that took place was in no way foreshadowed by the 1974 election, which was not in any sense a referendum on treatment. Only after he was safely reelected did Steele alter the course of prosecutorial policy. It would therefore be a substantial oversimplification to attribute the tougher line taken in the second term to the politics of law and order at work. The actual picture is a good deal more complex.

The policy changes may not have been mandated by the election, but the changing climate of public opinion clearly influenced the punitive drift of the justice model. Steele brought this message from his campaign coffee hours. The influence of changing public attitudes in the mid-1970s is particularly clear with respect to crimes against women. In 1975 the state legislature passed a rape reform act that made it easier to prosecute rape. At about the same time, the Park County prosecutor's office designated rape a "high-impact" crime and created a sexual assault unit.[28] The data presented in Table 4.3 suggests that these reforms changed policy in the intended direction.[29]

While the introduction of the justice model had definite political overtones, the politicization of crime was not particularly insistent. Even at a time of heightened public concern about crime, the prosecutor's office was not really forced into reform. The justice model reflected Dorffler's personal disaffection with rehabilitation, Steele's nascent campaign strategy, and the moderate values of the office. The way in which the process of change could be managed and modulated suggests a significant measure of autonomy—albeit a politicized autonomy. But whatever label is applied, the justice model was introduced because it allowed policymakers in the prosecutor's office to reconcile their organizational priorities and their personal values with a modest politicization of crime.

Judges: The Politics of Independence

The parallels between judges and prosecutors are striking, although the quantitative data are less helpful for analyzing judicial politicization. Only the sentencing data are relevant to the judges, and sentencing is a joint enterprise involving judges and prosecutors working together with defense counsel according to generally accepted norms.[30] While there is no way to sort out responsibilities among the parties, the data suggest that, as between judges and prosecutors, sentencing practices were driven more by prosecutorial recommendations than by either independent judicial decisions or by changes in the political climate.[31] This inference is drawn from the close fit between changes in prosecutorial leadership and probationary sentences discussed in the previous section.[32]

Moreover, as is shown here, there was very little association between sentencing practices and the politicization of the Superior Court from 1964 through 1980. Judges, like prosecutors, seemed only indirectly linked to the political environment.

The Politicization of Crime

The reform climate that ran the Phillips machine off the rails and moved the police department in a progressive direction also had a significant impact on the superior courts. The initial judicial consequence of the good-government ethos was a sharp increase in the number of relatively liberal judges who were appointed by the new governor, a reform Republican. Between 1966 and 1970, there was a substantial changing of the guard, with fifteen of twenty-two incumbents leaving office. Although some of these new judges were elected, the more normal pattern was appointment by the governor to fill a vacancy and subsequent ratification by the voters. In 1969, for example, nine judges were added to the court, seven of them by appointment. Since the liberal Republican governor served three full terms in office, his influence continued well into the mid-seventies.

Working at cross-purposes to these liberal appointments were, of course, the conservative political forces that began to develop in the late 1960s. The relatively liberal superior court bench thus found itself in an increasingly uncongenial political setting. Until 1972 the judges were under little or no direct pressure. It is true that, in 1968, the crime issue was raised in three contested races for the superior court, but the strongest proponent of law and order in these judicial races was defeated by a candidate who argued on behalf of bolstering rehabilitation services as a way of reducing recidivism.[33]

In 1972 law and order pressures on the superior courts grew stronger. The most unequivocal sign of change was that there were *ten* contested elections, and crime was a major campaign issue. A number of candidates either took hard-line stands or allowed their endorsement by the Cedar City Police Officers Guild to speak for itself. Indeed, one former police officer, just out of law school, actually ran for a position on the Superior Court. The most outspoken law and order candidates were not successful, however, and at least one candidate unequivocally committed to rehabilitation was elected.

It is against this background that the 1976 elections take on special significance. There were a number of law and order aspects to the 1976 campaigns for the Superior Court. Eight races were contested, only two fewer than in 1972. Crime was a prominent issue in all but two. And in four races the lines were drawn clearly, with liberal incumbents being targeted by law and order groups. But it was the defeat of two sitting judges, previewed in Chapter 2, that was the most traumatic sign of politicization.

The defeated incumbents were both highly visible liberals. One of them was a widely respected jurist who had been on the bench for many years. The other was younger, with only a few years of judicial experience. He was something of a maverick who had been in charge of the state's prison reform program for the liberal Republican governor who appointed him. Both of them were outspoken about their commitment to rehabilitation and to defendants' rights. And both of them had been involved in highly publicized rulings that were challenged by the police.

Consequently, both of these liberals were targeted for defeat by a variety of organizations committed to law and order values—principally the city and county police officers associations and Crystal Valley hardliners. The President of the Cedar City Police Officers Guild condemned one of the targeted judges for "liberal sentencing practices and procedures" that led "to the return of convicted criminals to the streets."[34] The law and order advocates threw their support behind two conservative candidates. One of these conservatives, Judge Albert Williams, had been an attorney for the police department, and the other was a retired prosecutor who had also been a judge and was known for his tough sentencing—fifty years, with a twenty-five-year minimum, and a $40,000 fine to a heroin dealer was one reported example.[35]

All of this could be seen as a clear indication of the politicization of the criminal courts in general and of crime in particular. First, a liberal Republican governor moved the courts toward rehabilitation. Then, once the political climate changed, the superior court judges began—according to the data on probationary sentencing—to move away from probation and toward incarceration. Finally, two judges who resisted this new direction were defeated in their bids for reelection.

A closer look, however, suggests a more contingent process of politicization. As has already been suggested, neither of the two distinct breaks in probationary sentencing practices—in 1971 and 1975—fits well with the changes in judicial personnel just discussed.

Consider first the shift to probationary sentencing in 1971. The liberal Republican governor had already been in office for about six years without ascertainable influence on probationary sentencing. Why the sudden change in 1971? If the governor's appointments were actually responsible for turning the courts around, the changes should have appeared earlier and also developed more gradually.

As to the switch away from probation in 1975, this was the year *before* the crucial 1976 election. Of course, it could be argued that this election was more a symptom of a changing political climate than a source of altered judicial behavior. In other words, even without the 1976 elections, the liberal judges may have been well aware that the political climate was hardening and that they were in jeopardy. According to this way of thinking, the 1976 election worked to accelerate a process that was already under way. But this anticipatory version of direct politicization does not hold up under careful scrutiny. If proactive judicial prudence had really been the source of change, it would have begun earlier— say, in 1972 when an unprecedented ten superior court elections were contested.

The rejection of direct politicization is, however, based less on the quantitative data than on interviews. They suggest a more complex pattern of politicization—one generally consistent with shifts in the prosecutor's office. The judges were not so politically vulnerable as the 1976 election suggested. Indeed, a strong argument could be made that the judges were very well insulated and that these two campaigns were the exceptions that prove the rule. But that argument would miss the *sense* of vulnerability that seems to haunt judges and probably makes them more sensitive to changes in the political climate than they need be. Let us look now at that sense of vulnerability and the policy implications flowing from it.

Judicial Insulation

Generally speaking, the judges labored in obscurity, which provided a protective screen. They gained office through political connections and retained office through organizational endorsements and name familiarity. The public probably had very little understanding of their overall judicial records. They regularly ran unopposed for reelection and, on those occasions when they actually had opponents, the campaigns tended to be bland. Indeed, it was considered poor form to make sentencing into a campaign issue. The 1976 defeat of two sitting judges must be understood in this context.

Those persons appointed to the Superior Court bench were, as a rule, not very well known to the public but were likely to be reasonably prominent members of the legal community. Their prominence may have come from behind-the-scenes political activity. One judge explained that he "had been in general practice in Cedar City and had never been elected to an office, except as precinct committeeperson." Alternatively, they may simply have held positions that made them known among the professionals in the legal system. Another judge indicated that after "a couple of years in private practice with no notable success," he spent nine years in the prosecutor's office and about eight years in another appointed position, where "you meet every lawyer in town because you're down there signing orders and doing the divorce calendars and that sort of business, as well spending about half your time in juvenile court."

Decisions to file against sitting judges ordinarily seem to have been based on motives that were similarly divorced from the kind of policy issues that might concern the public. Typically, newly appointed judges were vulnerable to others who were better known. Consider the experience of one newly appointed judge who was immediately challenged for reelection. As he saw it, he was challenged by a well-known Republican who resented being passed over by a Republican governor for an obscure Democrat. Another judge who escaped challenge explained that no opponent filed against him because it was clear that he would get the endorsement of both political parties and the local labor movement: "Those are the things that people would have looked at, I think, in determining whether they wanted to run against me."

The campaigns themselves were usually lackluster affairs conducted primarily through appearances at district political caucuses and meetings of such organizations as the League of Women Voters and the Kiwanis Club:

> I can't tell you that I know that we contested about anything. . . . He's developed a set of speeches on George Washington, Abraham Lincoln, Thomas Jefferson, and I don't know who else, that I think are quite good speeches, with slides of him visiting the Washington Memorial and the Jefferson Memorial, and talking about Americana—and he's a Son of the American Revolution or something like that.

While the issue of criminal sentencing did regularly come up during these years, it was seldom met head on. One judge observed:

> They ask the same kinds of questions—the hot item then was law and order . . . but a lot of them were questions you simply couldn't answer. Ethically, you could not answer questions about what are you going to do in this case and what are you going to do in that case, and you explain that to them, and it's never completely satisfactory to them.

A liberal incumbent attributed his defeat in his postappointment election to the name familiarity of his opponent rather than to his views on sentencing, which did not really surface during the campaign.

He had been a state senator for many years in a district here in Cedar City. He had been Republican State Central Committee Chairman for I don't know how long, for years. He had run for lieutenant governor and he'd run for the Supreme Court in two successive elections. I'm not sure which came first, but they had all just occurred, just before the year he filed, or two years before he filed, against me. We were never in any kind of debate situation. The times were not many when he and I were at the same place at the same meeting. It was that two-minute "who am I" business.

In short, what usually counted was not policy or even demon-strated electoral success but endorsements, name familiarity, and perhaps some experience in the electoral game. Indeed, the de-feated incumbent just discussed was quickly reappointed to a vacancy by the governor, successfully stood in a contested elec-tion, and then ran unopposed for more than a decade. Similarly, the judge who knew "every lawyer in town" had not been filed against in his eight years on the bench.

The dominant pattern clearly was one of long-term tenure without serious challenge. Why was this so even during periods when the courts were suspect as bastions of permissive prac-tices? Indeed, how do we account for the general obscurity in which the judges seemed to labor? After all, judges did deal with sensitive issues in connection with sentencing and the admissi-bility of evidence. The simple explanation seems to be that sensi-tive cases were infrequent and isolated events and that it was relatively easy to avoid adverse fallout under even the worst of circumstances.

Judicial Prudence

The key to insulation and, therefore, to longevity seems to have been judicial prudence. In its most benign form, prudence has to do primarily with appearances. But prudence may some-times entail significant concessions to the political climate and, thus, a troubling retreat from principle. As will become appar-ent, there were a variety of judicial responses to this dilemma—including the unwillingness of the two defeated incumbents to make any compromises at all.

Among the most cautious judges, prudence may well have had a significant impact on their sentencing decisions. The quantitative data do not distinguish among judges, but it seems clear that at least some of them tailored their decisions to avoid controversy and criticism. As a retired member of the Superior Court bench remarked:

> I remember one judge, now deceased. It was a very special thing. If he won this next election, he would qualify for his pension. And he just wasn't about to make waves. I mean not only wasn't he about to make waves, he was going to make damn sure that he didn't offend anyone. And those Crystal Valley groups were the most vocal people at that time. And he was significantly impacted, and he hated himself for it and spoke very openly.

Another judge recalled his own reaction as well as those of his colleagues to the 1976 election.

> It was an intimidating experience for me in ways that I don't easily admit to. . . . I realized that I'm being more careful in the way I say things. I used to hope that I wasn't making a different decision on the merits. It was an erosive time. . . . It had its effect on me and I expect on other people.

The pressure was particularly heavy on those who had less than twelve years service, because they were not yet vested in the retirement system. Indeed, during the 1976 election itself, two or three of the liberal judges who were targets, albeit secondary targets, of the forces of law and order seem to have hardened their campaign positions—and perhaps subsequently their decisions.

Nonetheless, it does seem to have been possible to stay out of trouble without making real concessions. While a bad press could conceivably get one in trouble, it was relatively easy to avoid a bad press if reporters were treated with some care. The key was to stay out of the headlines and to be spared story leads that simplified complex decisions in a pejorative way. Apparently, this could be done by putting the press on notice. As one respondent put it:

I would call Wally or George and say: "I'm going to do something stupid tomorrow. You better come and see what it is." And they'd show up every damn time. And then I'd get an article, because I'd say in the courtroom what I thought the whole thing was about and reasons I was doing what I was doing. And that's what would come out in the newspaper. And it sold.

This judge acknowledged that the crime reporters have an impulse to sensationalize, but he felt that he could always get a fair representation of his views:

I always felt, and I'm pretty sure it happened every time, that if I laid out exactly what the pros and cons were, and the reasons why I was doing something, and the hopes and regrets that I had—be sure I'd covered the people that were involved and made all the files, except my private files, available and spoke slow enough so they could write the notes—what was printed did follow the thing you were saying.

Another judge roughly concurred:

You can have good press relations, and that helps. I'm sure it does. You can also learn to explain all the reasons or emphasize the reasons that you think will go down well. Or you can say things in a kind of inflammatory way. You can say to a motion to suppress: "I don't believe the policeman and I don't think he gave the warning at all." Or you can say: "The policeman's got the toughest job in town, and we all know that, and they are advocates of their cause and I think the officer (this happened eight months ago) is a busy person, and I think he honestly believes he did, but I'm afraid I'm not convinced. I'm afraid he didn't warn him."

Apparently these tactics worked. While these two judges did not feel that they were thereby immune from press criticism, they did consistently avoid electoral defeat and even electoral challenges. One of them retired undefeated and unopposed after seventeen years on the Superior Court, and the other was still serving at the time of this research and had not been opposed since the early 1970s.

If it is, therefore, so easy to remain in office without compromising principles, how are we to account for the defeat of two judges in the 1976 election? Perhaps they were more liberal than the others, but there is reason to believe that their defeat had more to do with appearances than with policy. According to one of the defeated incumbents, he and the judge who retired undefeated and unopposed after seventeen years "compared notes about our sentencing practices and found out that we were within 2 percent of each other—very, very close."

> John was perceived, I think to a considerable degree, as a conservative. I was perceived as very liberal. The fact is that we sentenced in very similar fashion. I mean in terms of what the sentence was. His style, personal style, is highly rigid. He is military in bearing. He is rigid appearing. He once said to me that he felt like when he put on the robe it was putting on the suit of a knight.

But it is also true that the two defeated incumbents refused to make any concessions to the hostile political climate. One was especially unwilling to maintain a low profile or to work with the press. On the contrary, he was willing, indeed eager, to speak out in a variety of forums on behalf of his liberal sentencing policies. The other defeated judge was characterized by a friend on the bench as follows:

> Bert never retreated from an argument, loved to debate, and was proud of his record—and maybe defensive about it sometimes. And I used to say—we were very, very good friends— "Gee, Bert, you really are taking on the issues. You're leaning into those issues. Are you sure you're not making a mistake?" God bless him, he went ahead and did it.

In short, neither judge was inclined to shy away from controversy.

To compound their political difficulties, these two judges played into the hands of their election opponents. They chose to make the campaign into something of a plebicite on the positions that they had been espousing publicly during their years in office. As one of them noted:

I think I had a better chance of winning if I had kept quiet. But that's not my way. I felt strongly about those issues, and I determined that I was going to take the risk because I believe in expressing my views, public education. And hopefully we've gotten somewhere. I don't regret it. Clearly, another course of action was available. A very prominent citizen in this town said to me just as the campaign was getting started. "Dave, if you just shut up and don't speak to the media on these issues, you will win on name familiarity. The bar will probably support you. If you choose to speak out on the issues, even if you speak out intelligently and well, you'll lose."

There was a clear contrast with two other liberal incumbents, who seem to have finessed these issues and retained their positions.

Then there was the anti-Semitism issue. According to one respondent, the two defeated incumbents might still have managed to squeak through if it had not been for anti-Semitism. "The people who run this town saw two Jews that they could get. And I know that's damn true." Anti-Semitism never surfaced as an issue, but both judges had obviously Jewish names, and one of them claimed that his campaign "had feedback from areas in the south part of the county that anti-Semitism was a factor."

In short, the political setting even during this period of politicization provided substantial opportunities for judicial independence. Judges generally labored in obscurity, and on those infrequent occasions when they dealt with sensitive cases or issues, the press was willing to transmit reasoned explanations for controversial judicial decisions. Only those judges who chose to make a public issue of their practices and policies seemed vulnerable, and even they might have been able to avoid defeat had they campaigned more prudently.

Finally, there is no reason to believe that judges were likely to be held to their campaign commitments—expressed or implied. Consider the record of Judge Williams, one of the successful conservatives in the 1976 election. His "campaign platform" was unequivocal in opposition to the treatment model, and he accepted the endorsement of hard-line law and order groups.[36] Once elected, he was a pleasant surprise to liberals and presumably a disappointment to his hard-line supporters. More specifically, he apparently had no qualms about granting probation. When asked during the course of this research whether he was breaking campaign commitments, his response was that the election was not fought over judicial practices but rather over the need for *legislative* action to limit judicial discretion. Absent such legislation, sentencing was a discretionary act. He therefore felt free to use probation on those occasions when it seemed appropriate. There was no indication that these apparent inconsistencies undermined his political base.

Despite what seems to be ample leeway, the Park County judges felt very strongly about maintaining the separation between policy and politics. There seemed to be a tacit agreement to reinforce this separation by conducting elections with as little reference to policy and "philosophic" matters as possible. Not surprisingly, the legal community was upset about the politicization of crime in the 1976 elections. After the elections, the bar association moved to formalize the tacit agreement by rewriting campaign guidelines to emphasize credentials rather than issues.

There were also strong feelings on the bench against the successful challengers—even against Judge Williams, who was otherwise highly respected. As one senior judge remarked: "Judge Williams, who got elected, came to me as a senior old man down in his court, and I said: 'Congratulations on it, but I don't like the fact that you earned it by violating a code of ethics.' 'What,' he says, 'was the code of ethics?' And I told him off. He's now still a judge, and every time I see him he knows what I am talking about." For his part, Judge Williams explained that he had conducted his campaign in terms of basic principles and was thus within accepted boundaries. Nonetheless, he and the other conservative were, at least initially, resented by their colleagues on the bench.

In part this strong reaction was based on the outcome: two sitting judges, one of them highly esteemed and both well liked, were defeated. But there was more to it than that. On both practical and principled grounds, sitting judges were decidedly ambivalent about electoral accountability.

Perceptions and Practices

There was, in the first place, an intensely practical side to the judges' concerns about independence. They were simply not comfortable with the career contingencies of the electoral process. Judicial appointments in the United States carry with them connotations of tenure until retirement or promotion to higher judicial office. Accordingly, the judges who were interviewed seemed to have a sense that they were entitled to retain their positions, given good behavior and reasonable competence. The defeat of two sitting judges following a campaign that raised substantial policy issues was threatening because it blurred a cherished distinction between law and politics and carried with it intimations of judicial mortality.

But there was also a principled side to this aversion to politics. While appreciating the values served by democratic accountability, campaign contacts with the public were also seen as potentially corrupting.

I think it's important that judges get out of their caves—we live in a cave, each one us lives in a cave—and go out and see where the folks are. That's not all bad. . . . But there are some unfortunate aspects about that, because they inevitably say: "Okay, how are you going to come out on this?" Where you feel that you can't answer it, you say so, but there's a kind of an erosion that takes place. You begin to say, "Well, it's okay to answer some of those questions." And afterwards you say: "Gee, I wonder if I didn't go too far."

And when one finally does succeed in gaining the endorsement of some organization or other: "What does that mean to them? Do they think that they've got me in their pockets?"

These tensions are resolved by falling back on a conception of independence that allows the judges to respond to the reality they experience. Both the conservative Judge Williams and one of his liberal counterparts expressed much this same point of view. Once on the bench, Williams discovered that even persons with "the most reprehensible records" could still "strike a note of sympathy." So while continuing to be impressed by the "repeated failure of probation" as an overall policy, he was willing to grant probation if he felt that there was "at least a chance of succeeding"—so long as the person was not a threat to the community.

During roughly this same period, liberals tended to move in the opposite direction. Sounding quite a bit like Prosecutor Dorffler, one such liberal expressed an increasing disenchantment with the rehabilitative model:

> There's been a distinct move toward punishment, and I guess I'm in there—I'm sure I'm in there. There were a lot of cases where I used to say, "Well, is jail necessary at all?" I used to sit and talk about: "Well, it's punishment enough in this case that you were arrested. You've never committed a crime before. You had to come to jail, be booked, blah, blah, blah." Some element of community work I always thought was fantastic, and then you find that that isn't supervised, and you can't be sure they're doing it. I think I have come to believe that punishment is a more appropriate element in sentencing than I used to. I pay less attention to all the sociological work-up and presentence reports than I did at first. All the talk about family abuse and all, it doesn't impress me as much as it used to, so I don't deny that I have moved to the right. And I think judges in general have done the same. I think I still am well over on the left of the group—quite confident of that.

Thus, for both liberals and conservatives, independence serves to protect discretionary expertise as much as, perhaps more than, the impersonal application of legal norms.

❦

The ostensible message of this chapter is the considerable independence of judges and prosecutors from electoral accountability. Electoral accountability was asserted only twice between 1964 and 1980, when Steele unseated Phillips in 1970 and when the two liberal judges were defeated in 1976. Note also that in 1970, it was not crime but corruption that was the key to electoral change. In the periods before and after these challenges, both the prosecutors and the judges were remarkably secure. For twenty-two years, Phillips presided over an essentially impregnable political machine; Steele served two terms and was succeeded by his chief civil deputy, who, at the time of this writing, had also served two terms—running unopposed for reelection. The judges, for their part, seldom had to face contested elections and ordinarily survived when they were opposed.

The essential question is what use prosecutors and judges make of their substantial policy autonomy, but two preliminary qualifications are in order. First, the freedom to pursue policy preferences in most cases seems to have been purchased at the price of responding to perceived public concerns in politically sensitive cases. The fate of the two judges who failed to heed warning signs suggests that it would be wrong to think of criminal-process professionals as free agents. Second, there are, no doubt, idiosyncratic factors that intrude into the policy process. Recall that Dorffler turned from rehabilitation at least in part because he was uncomfortable with the power that is integral to discretionary decision making. Needless to say, many criminal justice professionals are entirely comfortable with, indeed attracted by, power. Consider also the atypical determination of the two defeated judges to use the prominence of their judicial office for public advocacy of criminal justice reform—even at the risk of their positions. While it is therefore necessary to advance generalizations cautiously, it is possible to identify policy tendencies rooted in the political culture of criminal process.

At the core of this political culture is a kind of rough-and-ready version of Packer's two models. That is to say, prosecutors and judges tended to identify themselves as liberals or conservatives in a fashion suggestive of due process and crime control values, respectively. But the liberal/conservative frame of reference extends beyond Packer's bipolar abstractions of individual rights and public order to broader concerns with the haves and have-nots of American life. In other words, Packer's models provided our respondents with value-laden policy predispositions rather than with principles for deriving a nuanced legal response to the dilemmas of criminal process. In any event, given the tensions between liberal and conservative values, it might seem that there was little common ground on which to construct criminal court policy. But for several reasons, the criminal courts of Park County were very much a consensual enterprise—just as they are elsewhere.[37]

First, it is important to keep in mind the substantial common ground between liberals and conservatives—not only in terms of the legal values that preoccupy Packer but also, and more significantly, in terms of the mainstream understanding of crime and criminality in America. At first glance, there seems little on which to build consensus. Liberals are inclined to see criminals as victims of circumstances, while conservatives tend to view them as deficient human beings. But either way, there is a focus on the predatory nature of criminal acts and agreement that individuals must either be made to conform to society's norms or be excluded from it.[38] In other words, neither liberals nor conservatives call into question the norms and values of mainstream American society, and the individual offender remains very much the center of attraction—regardless of whether that attention is directed at punishment, rehabilitation, or deterrence.

Second, neither conservatives nor liberals were fully able to sustain their easy generalizations about crime and criminals when faced with the grim social and institutional realities of criminal process. Confronted with the complex personal and social predicaments of defendants, it became harder for conservatives to think of crime in terms of the abstractions of social rules and individual responsibility. Thus, Phillips and Williams turned to probation more regularly than their public images, or their own self-conceptions, would have suggested. But liberal presuppositions were under heavier pressure. Liberals tended, in the first place, to be hardened by regular exposure to recidivism and to the social and personal costs of predatory crime. It was also readily apparent that the rehabilitative resources available to prisons and to probations and parole offices were not even sufficient for adequate monitoring, much less for serious efforts at rehabilitation. Thus, liberals also found themselves increasingly on the lookout for good risks rather than thinking about rehabilitation as the norm.

Finally, for all their freedom from electoral accountability, judges and prosecutors were mindful of public moods—if ambivalent about responding to them. It seems inappropriate to them, given their legal status and political authority, to take their cues too readily from the public. They, therefore, developed strategies that put politically sensitive cases and routine policy on significantly different tracks, thus effectively misleading the public as to the real nature of criminal court policy. On the other hand, they believed in a kind of contextual accountability that afforded protection against losing touch with the basic values and changing priorities of the public that they served. Periodic elections and media exposure, in sum, provided constraints, even if they did not promote a continuing policy referendum or even an active and well-informed electorate.

We come up with something of a paradox. Although respondents learned from their day-to-day experiences that, in most instances of criminality, social and individual pathologies are inextricably intertwined, this insight tends to be repressed in practice. It is one thing to sense the social pathologies that are associated with crime and quite another to incorporate this insight into a coherent, policy-relevant approach to criminal process. Furthermore, to see crime as associated with structural problems puts prosecutors and judges at odds with the more conventional values of their constituents. Most fundamentally, structural insights lead to frustration: the individualizing mechanics of criminal process make it an ineffectual tool of social action.

As the futility of reform sinks in, there is a strong temptation to fall back on conceptions of crime and criminality that are compatible with the institutional forms and resources of criminal process. Even though the experiential evidence of criminal process makes it clear that crime cannot simply be thought of in volitional terms, it is equally clear that the institutions of criminal process are irredeemably biased in just that direction and altogether unsuited for structural responses to crime.

Under these circumstances, the attractions of the justice model are manifest. Determinate sentencing and just deserts are within the reach of criminal process—albeit problematically linked to legislatures, as we see in the concluding chapter. And the justice model has broad appeal across the political mainstream. It is, therefore, easy to see why the justice model took root in the Park County criminal courts as well as in other criminal courts around the country.

5

Politics, Criminology, and Crisis

This book has pursued two distinct but related themes. At its core it has been an inquiry into the political culture of criminal process: its objective has been to explore how society thinks about the nature, causes, and consequences of street crime; how these perceptions develop and change; and how they are politicized. Woven into this core has been a more narrowly criminological theme, an exploration of volitional and structural approaches to crime control. Linking these two themes has been an effort to understand how the political culture of criminal process influences crime control policy.

On most of these matters, the Cedar City findings are generally unequivocal, and they can be captured in three propositions. First, the politicization of criminological discourse tends to develop in and contribute to a punitive ethos. Second, the agencies of criminal process are reasonably well insulated from this punitive political climate, so the policy response to politicization is sluggish, unpredictable, and not necessarily punitive. There are, however, powerful constraints on the resultant discontinuities between ethos and policy. Both punitive and nonpunitive policies remain well within the bounds of volitional criminology, thus leading to the third proposition: structural interpretations of deviant behavior are pervasively and consistently marginalized in both political discourse and criminal process. One of the objectives of this concluding chapter is to summarize the evidence that provides the foundation for these three propositions.

But the research presented in this book raises another set of issues. All caveats and qualifications to the contrary notwithstanding, there has been an unprecedented politicization of criminal process since the mid-1960s. Traditionally, the agencies of criminal process have labored in welcome obscurity. Their insulation from external forces has meant that criminal process has responded primarily to internal needs in determining whom to prosecute and how to dispose of cases. From time to time, the veil has been lifted by a particularly newsworthy crime, a corruption scandal, or the efforts of an ambitious aspirant to the prosecutor's office. No doubt there have even been *brief* interludes of law and order anxiety, but nothing like the sustained politicization of the last two or three decades.

These interludes were once the exceptions that proved the rule. The relative autonomy of criminal process has been established by a plethora of research on the police, on plea bargaining, on criminal sentencing, and so on.[1] To a significant extent that insulation remains intact. Nonetheless, things have changed during the last twenty-five years. The message from Cedar City is that criminal-process professionals perceive themselves to be under continuing scrutiny. Second, a punitive discourse centering on criminal process has established a pervasive political presence. Finally, this discourse regularly calls into question the objectives, practices, and effectiveness of criminal process.

How is the increased political salience of criminal process to be explained? At the outset of this research, I was inclined to think of politicization as sporadic and ephemeral. I am now inclined to see politicization as a reflection of underlying social forces that are likely to continue into the foreseeable future. The explanations for the emergence and staying power of politicization offered here are extrapolations from my research rather than its manifest findings. The discussion is avowedly speculative and exploratory—pointing to a need for further research.

The scope of this speculation may seem to put a considerable, perhaps an inordinate, burden on the rather restricted research base provided by a single case study. Cedar City is, moreover, hardly "typical." Its urban problems are not *thought of* as intractable. Crime, racism, and corruption are considered to be temporary setbacks, not permanent blight. There is considerable optimism in the conviction that problems can be solved, social cleavages healed, and a sense of mutual respect and civility maintained. No doubt this distinguishes Cedar City from places like New York, where a number of highly publicized incidents, like the Central Park jogger and the Goetz cases, have symbolized and indeed fueled an ethos of impending "anomia"— that is, a fear, as Ralf Dahrendorf puts it, that law and order are breaking down and that predictability is fading from social life.[2]

There is, however, reason to believe that generalizations can be drawn, albeit cautiously, from the Cedar CIty research. The basic findings about politicization reported in this book are consistent with other research—in particular a thirty-year study of governmental responses to crime in ten U.S. cities.[3] It is also true that the policy directions taken by the Cedar City police and the Park County criminal courts parallel developments in other jurisdictions. Finally, all jurisdictions face comparable problems in striking a balance among legal, political, organizational, and criminological concerns. Thus, while specific outcomes may vary from time to time and place to place, the findings of this research do provide a defensible empirical base for identifying the relevant variables and for formulating plausible explanations of the sort offered in this chapter.

Criminology and Policy

In arguing that volitional criminology has been consistently privileged in the political and policy processes, I have tended to conceal a good many variations on the volitional theme. Volitional responses range from capital punishment at the punitive end to community-based policies favored by conscientious reformers seeking enlightened alternatives to the conservative hard line. Second, I have continually begged the question of what a structural crime control policy would look like. It is one thing to claim that crime is, in part, due to fundamental structural problems and quite another thing to specify structural responses that are within the reach of the institutions of criminal process. Recall, in that regard, the tendency of criminal-process professionals to repress structural insights precisely because they are beyond the institutional capabilities of the police and the criminal courts.

It is to these matters that I now turn—first at the level of principle. These principles will then be invoked in a concrete and critical assessment of actual policy trends.

Policy Principles

There are, of course, contrasting principles driving structural and volitional policies in divergent directions. The premise of structural criminology is that the sources of street crime are to be found in the pathologies of society. According to volitional criminology, street crime is attributable to individual shortcomings. Elliot Currie, who was our principal guide to structural criminology in Chapter 1, traces street crime to material inequality.[4] John Hagan and his associates broaden the argument somewhat in *Structural Criminology*, which, they argue, is "unique in its insistence that crime be understood and therefore studied in terms of power relations."[5] Either way, structural criminology emerges as something of a policy blind alley for criminal-process professionals.

This is not because the policy implications of structural criminology are unclear. William Julius Wilson, among others, proposes an agenda for attenuating inequalities—particularly the extreme, hereditary inequalities of the underclass. His reform package includes "a comprehensive program of economic and social reform (highlighting macroeconomic policies to promote balanced economic growth and create a tight-labor-market situation, a nationally oriented labor-market strategy, a child support assurance program, a child care strategy, and a family allowance program)."[6] There are, of course, other policy approaches to the problems of structural inequities, but there are no insurmountable obstacles to developing a workable program.[7]

It is, however, difficult to ascertain a role for criminal-process professionals in promoting structural reform. The "liberal" criminal justice agenda, with its emphasis on rehabilitating offenders, might seem at first glance to have at least a structural bias.[8] But this is true only insofar as rehabilitation is combined with macroeconomic policies altering job opportunities. Even then, rehabilitation remains at its core unequivocally volitional (although not punitive), because it is directed at remedying individual pathology. In any case, macroeconomic policymaking is the province of national political leaders and cannot even be influenced, much less undertaken independently, by criminal-process professionals or, for that matter, by local political leaders.

The findings of structural criminology do nonetheless have

implications for criminal process—suggestive, in the first place, of the policy futility of volitional responses to crime. Volitional criminology assumes individuals responding to the rewards and punishments provided by criminal sanctions. The focus of structural criminology is, in contrast, on probabilities, on the tendency for structural burdens to increase the likelihood of criminal activity. Structural understandings also weaken the moral case for punishment. As I have written elsewhere:

> For those at the bottom of the society to achieve success through legitimate channels requires combinations of talent, determination, and good fortune far beyond what is demanded from those with more advantages. Rather than condemn as morally deficient people who are unable to rise above the obstacles of poverty, perhaps we would be better advised to marvel at those who are not overpowered by the burden they must bear.[9]

In short, volitional measures are likely to be meaningful only with respect to the exceptional few—those who for whatever reasons beat the structural odds. For the society as a whole, only policies that change those odds can be expected to work as crime control measures and to be defensible on moral grounds. This does not mean that punishment or incarceration are never effective or justified. Even if the origins of street crime were exclusively structural, a proposition that is not borne out by criminological research, it would still be appropriate to protect society from the dangers posed by violent criminals.

What then is the policy message of structural criminology? Most broadly, that message is to tailor the criminal sanction as much as possible to the circumstances of the criminal act. The outcome is likely to be a less punitive sentencing structure and a reduced rate of incarceration. This follows from the proposition that street crime is largely a function of social rather than individual pathology and from research revealing that a great deal of street crime is not violent. The case for cracking down on criminals is, accordingly, weakened. Structural criminology also points toward the desirability of avoiding criminal sanctions whenever possible, because they work on the hapless individual rather than on the structural forces that constrain available

choices. This means more dispute resolution and less law enforcement. Community-oriented programs of policing, dispute
resolution, and corrections all move in this direction. While not
in themselves structural responses, they do at least focus policy,
albeit symptomatically, on the society rather than the individual.

Policy Practices

In terms of these principles, the police and the criminal courts
in Cedar City have moved in distinctly different policy directions. The progressive tendencies identified in the Cedar City
Police Department—and even more apparent in a number of
other American cities[10]—are suggestive of an upstream struggle
against the punitive current of public opinion. Conversely, the
tougher sentencing practices of the Park County criminal courts
and the overcrowded jails and prisons in Park County and elsewhere suggest that the criminal courts have gone with the punitive flow.

At the heart of the changes in sentencing practices is the
justice model rooted in determinate sentencing—fitting the sentence to the crime instead of to the criminal.[11] Both pragmatic
and moral cases can be made on behalf of determinate sentencing. Nonetheless, determinate sentencing is rooted in volitional
premises and has had, in practice, a distinctly punitive edge.

Fairness provides the moral grounding for determinate sentencing. In the abstract, justice is, after all, symbolized by the
blindfold, which is to assure that the law takes account of the
criminal act rather than of the person who commits it. More
concretely, determinate sentencing is based on the assumption
that discretionary alternatives tend to work against those at the
margins of society who are poorer risks for probation and parole
programs. Better, then, so the argument goes, to mete out punishment strictly in proportion to the offence rather than allow
judges to match sentences to the particularities of individual
offenders. This was certainly the primary attraction of the justice
model to Park County Prosecutor Dorffler. The justice model also
draws upon deterrence theory and research to underscore the
crime control potential of predictable sentences. Advocates of
determinate sentencing might acknowledge that it is, strictly
speaking, punitive—but not gratuitously so. After all, deterrence

theory stresses predictability rather than severity—moderate punishment in measured doses. And the Park County data do indeed indicate that under Dorffler's justice plan there was more incarceration, but short-term in local jails rather than long-term in state prisons.

This dual defense of the justice model is, however, suspect on a number of counts. In the first place, research does not reveal the substantial disparities that are at the core of the justice case for determinate sentencing.[12] Nor have researchers been able to demonstrate systematic race or class bias.[13] Admittedly, this is contested terrain. Structural criminologist John Hagan and his associates argue that these research findings are flawed by a failure to consider class and race in relational, and thus genuinely structural, terms. According to this way of thinking, the true impact of race on sentencing, for example, becomes apparent only insofar as it is measured in ways that distinguish interracial crimes that the state takes seriously from intraracial crimes that are treated in a "paternalistic" way. Hagan and others also argue that unemployment, with its connotations of disempowerment, may be a more important determinant of sentencing than class status, as such.[14]

But even assuming inequities in traditional practices, determinate sentencing may well be a step in the wrong direction, at least as measured by structural understandings of street crime. As a practical matter, determinate sentencing has resulted in higher rates of incarceration, sometimes accompanied by increased severity, without always reducing disparity.[15] More fundamentally, determinant sentencing incorporates into criminal process the pernicious influence of social, economic, and political inequality. This is because acts driven by inequalities and deprivations become the sole determinant of sentencing. As David Greenberg and Drew Humphries observe in their critique of the justice model:

> One need not deny individual responsibility . . . to see that, in placing my culpability and the punishment I should receive at the center of attention, other topics are pushed to the periphery: the dynamics of the capitalist economy; the manner in which it allocates benefits and injuries among classes, races, and sexes—and in so doing generates the structural condi-

tions to which members of the society respond when they violate the law; and the way class interests are represented in or excluded from the law. All these are neglected in favor of an abstract moral preoccupation with the conduct of the individual offender.[16]

The structurally sensitive alternative would be reforms that take account of underlying inequalities and deploy discretion in a compensatory fashion. In turning a blind eye to these inequalities, determinate sentencing acquiesces in the disease rather than providing even the symptomatic treatment that is within the reach of criminal process.

Community policing, in contrast, has a kind of quasi-structural bias. It refocuses energies from punishing criminals to enlisting the community in support of law enforcement and order maintenance.[17] The objective is to bring a consensual social order to neighborhoods that are suffering from, or threatened by, the forces of anomie.

There are two basic strategies associated with these efforts to transform policing from a confrontive to a collective enterprise. The first calls upon the police to develop a better understanding of and rapport with citizens.[18] Only then will police be able to curb the expressive violence that so antagonizes people. Moreover, if the police are to minimize recourse to the criminal sanction and to engage in genuine dispute resolution, rather than in the imposition of order from above, it is imperative that they become sensitive to local cultural norms. The second strategy is to make the police into neighborhood problem solvers.[19] In this problem-oriented form, the communitarian approach calls upon the police to act as go-betweens with city agencies, landlords, merchants, and others who are contributing to community frustrations. These interventions, it is expected, will enable the police to gain the confidence of citizens and also contribute to a sense of well-being and thus to community-building. Taken together, these two elements of police–community reconciliation are expected both to reduce crime and to promote solidarity—in short, to facilitate construction of a stable and beneficent social order.

This is a tall order, and there is good reason for skepticism about the prospects for community policing.[20] At this point, however, the issue is not whether it will work but why this basically nonpunitive, conciliatory form of policing has become the principal vehicle of reform.

There is, to be sure, a traditional justification for community policing—namely that a cooperative community will provide the police with the information they need to catch criminals. Insofar as it is thus directed at more effective crime control, community policing is clearly volitional, ultimately linked to punishment and consistent with the prevailing political ethos.

But punishment is clearly a minor theme in community policing, which seeks to maximize mediation and minimize coercion. Indeed, if police working in minority communities do truly become accountable agents of a consensual social order, then community policing will also have attenuated structural inequality. Marginalized citizens will have an effective voice in determining neighborhood norms and in invoking the power of the police. So, while not a truly structural response to crime, community policing does blur the distinction between volitional and structural responses. As such, it seems to be in some tension with the punitive political climate.

We are left with a puzzling picture. The currents of reform seem to be pushing the police and the criminal courts in distinctly different directions. The criminal courts are becoming more punitive, while the move toward community policing suggests a moderating element in police practices. Of course, we must be careful not to exaggerate what is happening. These are, after all, trends rather than accomplished transformations. Both determinate sentencing and community policing are in their experimental stages. We do not know how widespread they will become or what forms they will finally take.

Nonetheless, the divergence between the police and the criminal courts is surprising in a number of ways that warrant explanation. How is it, in the first place, that the same political ethos can be driving policy in ostensibly different directions? More specifically, why is it that the due process–oriented and well-insulated criminal courts have become more punitive while the traditionally punitive police, who are directly accountable to the mayor, are moving in the opposite direction? Indeed, what are we to make of the quasi-structural tendencies of police reform?

They seem to suggest that politicization does not necessarily privilege volitional criminology. From a different perspective, what requires explanation is the coexistence of currents of policy moderation and a continuing politicization of street crimes. To get at these explanations it is necessary to return to the primary theme of this book—that is, to the forces driving America's understanding of and response to street crime.

The Symbolic Politics of Street Crime

To inquire into the forces that promote and sustain the politicization of street crime in the United States is to refocus attention from the findings of this case study to speculative inferences that put those findings into the broader context of American politics and culture. To that end, I offer some general propositions and provide the suggestive evidence from which they are derived. These interpretations are, however, best seen in heuristic terms—that is, as a way of conveying the importance of the questions rather than of providing definitive answers to them.

The first proposition is that in order to understand the forces driving the politicization of street crime it is necessary to look well beyond street crime, or even crime generally, to the structural dislocations of the American society. It might seem that this proposition is derived directly from structural criminology, but that is not the case. My concern is not with criminology—that is, with crime and criminals—but with politics and, in particular, with the political utility of crime and criminals as symbolic enemies.

To begin with, political leaders have clear incentives for reframing structural problems as matters of crime control, for declaring war on crime or, for that matter, on drugs rather than on poverty, unemployment, homelessness, educational deprivations, or other structural sources of deviant behavior. Waging serious structural warfare requires expenditures of political and economic capital that political leaders are reluctant to make. It is, moreover, a relatively easy matter to politicize street crime or illicit drugs because of the public's willingness, indeed eagerness, to dwell on these matters. Finally, the public has a politically reassuring predilection to think about street crime in volitional or punitive terms, which empower the law enforcement agencies of the state.

To politicize crime is, in short, to divert attention from structural reforms, which are costly and divisive, to volitional responses, which are much less costly and encourage society to close its ranks against deviants. Here lies the true political significance of street crime and illicit drugs. They are symbolic enemies that can be deployed in support of political authority, as Murray Edelman and Stuart Hall, have argued. Edelman puts it this way: "The appeal of an emphasis upon the pathologies of criminals and the utility of punishing them lies partly in what it negates: the tracing of crime to pathological social conditions."[21] My own understanding of the power of these symbols is that they are deeply rooted in America's individualistic culture, which *increasingly* generates the kinds of insecurities that promote a yearning for scapegoats and synergistically supplies the volitional understandings that make these scapegoats credible.

But, irrespective of the precise source of street crime's symbolic significance, the broader conclusion is that the politicization of street crime is not an ephemeral episode associated with increases in criminal activity or in illicit drug use. Instead, it is a product of economic, social, and cultural forces that contribute to widespread insecurity among Americans. Rather than address the causes of these insecurities, the state cultivates the insecurities and focuses them on scapegoats. That, in a nutshell, is what the symbolic politics of street crime entails.

Politicization and Culture

Street crime, according to this way of thinking, is a powerful condensation symbol, which can under some circumstances be readily and safely politicized by enterprising political aspirants, as well as by established elites who wish to ward off threats to the political order. This assertion raises three different questions: Why is street crime such a compelling symbol? In what sense does street crime provide a safe mode of politicization? What are the right circumstances for successful politicization?

A plausible answer to all three questions can be derived from America's individualistic values, which have their advantages but also their perils. On the positive side, these values are said to generate a kind of self-perpetuating cycle of benefits, including freedom, opportunity, and reward. Individualism becomes a source of energy that is fulfilling for the individual and contributes to the well-being of the society.[22] But these benefits are purchased at considerable cost. The inequality that Elliot Currie and other structuralists see as the primary cause of street crime is one such cost.[23] Another is the endemic insecurity that is inherent in a competitive and mobile society—"fear of falling" is the way Barbara Ehrenreich puts it.[24]

It is not easy to live with a more-or-less constant fear of falling. To express such concerns is, however, to admit personal weakness and, indeed, subversive tendencies. Only a wimp would quaver at the invigorating challenge of a free and competitive society. Only a subversive would question the values that are responsible for the imposing wealth and opportunities provided by American society. So we are, more or less, forced to suffer in silence. And what of the latent guilt that is likely to be engendered by the inequalities of a competitive society? Does it not stand to reason that bottling up anxieties will eventually engender a good deal of free-floating anger and occasion a search for scapegoats against whom to discharge this anger and through whom to maintain the hollow illusion of control?[25]

My argument is that street criminals, conceived of as predatory strangers, are among those scapegoats—along with others who threaten to subvert the social order: communists, welfare cheaters, and drug addicts. Here are people we are entitled to hate—but only so long as we think of them as victimizers rather than victims.

This line of thought makes the American public's perverse fascination with violent crime fully comprehensible. As I have written elsewhere: "Culturally speaking, it is altogether fair to say that our problem is not too much crime but too little. Even though crime exists . . . in what the public chooses to think of as epidemic proportions, we still feel compelled to invent it."[26] Television news thrives on violent crime, as do television drama, popular fiction, and film. To cite examples would belabor the obvious, but the point is that street crime as a spectator sport provides a way of sublimating the anger, anxiety, and guilt generated by American social life.

But in what sense does the compelling imagery of street crime provide a "safe" symbol for politicization? While some argue that television violence poses a threat to social order, George Gerbner and Larry Gross have demonstrated just the opposite in research conducted a number of years ago.[27] To understand why this is so, it is necessary to explore our fascination with the ostensibly horrifying world of violence, drugs, and crime. What is crucial here is the stylized form in which we enjoy our vicarious adventures in the illicit and brutal. We are drawn to these gruesome crimes because the predator who commits them becomes the deserving target of our pent-up anger. These predatory acts are, however, only a prelude. What really signifies is the denouement, society's act of retribution, which discharges our anger. "Just deserts" are our favorite part, to paraphrase a typically telling Doonesbury cartoon. Seldom does popular culture deprive us of this gratification—be it through legal channels or by vigilantes who take the law into their own hands.[28]

This scenario reinforces the status quo and in this sense becomes a compelling symbol for safe politicization. Clearly the message is volitional. Individuals must either behave responsibly or else take the consequences. An alternative scenario that symbolized criminals as victims and emphasized social pathologies would, of course, be much more of a challenge to the status quo and, thus, unwelcome to political leaders who are not interested in taking the risks associated with structural reform. The crux is not, however, that the state somehow imposes retributive scenarios on American popular culture but rather that retribution expresses a collective yearning. The public then carries these retributive expectations from the world of drama to the real and infinitely more complex and intractable world of criminal process. Here, these expectations are frequently frustrated by criminals who somehow manage to escape their just deserts. It is these frustrations that become the raw material of politicization.

We are left with the third question posed what are the right conditions for successful politicization? Here we get into the most elusive and controvertible aspects of this intrinsically speculative venture. My position rests on the premise that there are long-term trends in contemporary American society that promote politicization—that there has been something special about the last twenty or thirty years that transcends street crime but is somehow connected to it in the public mind.

The most proximate and plausible explanation has to do with a decline in public order—or perhaps with the public's reduced tolerance for disorder.[29] Law and *order* is, after all, the catch phrase that characterizes the politicization of street crime. And the Gallup Poll has regularly combined the issues of "crime," "lawlessness," "law enforcement," "juvenile delinquency," and "immorality" in reporting findings to the open-ended question: "What do think is the most important issue facing the country today?"[30] The last thirty years have also been an era of unprecedented challenges to conventional values and to established social hierarchies—including most notably the antiwar movement of the late 1960s and early 1970s and the continuing campaigns of minorities and women.

In simple material terms, too, there seems to be a nagging, if subconscious, sense that the present and the future no longer look brighter than the past. Throughout most strata of the society, the American Dream seems increasingly elusive. Richard Sennett and Jonathan Cobb, for example, writing with reference to deindustrialization, note that white "ethnic workers are now coming to grips with their true position in American capitalism: they are powerless in the hands of the economic and political forces controlling the cities."[31] While plenty of new jobs are being created, they are disproportionately in retail trade and in the service sector more generally, which are "much the worst paying industry groups."[32] Barbara Ehrenreich's "fear of falling" identifies comparable insecurities among middle-class professionals in the 1980s. "For the first time in postwar America, a middle-level income no longer guaranteed what we have come to think of as a middle-class lifestyle. But the big news was that the 'middle class,' or more precisely, the middle range of income, was becoming more sparsely inhabited."[33] That is to say, a polarization has been occurring within the middle class as within the society more generally and, increasingly, families cannot do without double incomes if they are to maintain their places within the class structure.[34]

Christopher Lasch alerts us to the emotional costs of these precarious cricumstances, which are at work throughout the society, poisoning interpersonal as well as interclass relationships. "Today almost everyone lives in a dangerous world from which there is little escape."[35] Lasch reinterprets America's apparent hedonism as an intensifying struggle for survival in a culture that measures worth in material terms. "This hedonism is a fraud; the pursuit of pleasure disguises a struggle for power.

Americans have not really become more sociable and cooperative . . . they have merely become more adept at exploiting the
conventions of interpersonal relations for their own benefit."[36] In
sum, while the society exhibits the trappings of affluence, it is
deeply afflicted. We are rather like ducks that seem to float
effortlessly on the surface, but are paddling like hell underneath.

Lillian Rubin comes to very similar conclusions in her reflections on the Goetz case. She argues that "the enormous rage this
case has let loose" transcends crime as such:

> It is related also to a set of contradictions that inhere in our
> society and in our lives—in a society that once seemed so open
> and that suddenly, inexplicably, closed down. . . . Both eco-
> nomically and socially, we feel ourselves at risk. The economic
> retrenchment of recent years threatens the affluence to which
> so many Americans have become accustomed, leaving us
> frightened and insecure, fearful of poverty, even as we live in
> the midst of plenty. The breakdown of social order, the emerg-
> ing understanding that there will never be enough police to
> enforce the law in a society where some significant number of
> people refuse to respect it, threatens the very basis of our daily
> lives and leaves us feeling hopelessly out of control.[37]

With so much seemingly at risk, it is understandable that many
in the American mainstream would be engaged in a "search for
order," to borrow Robert Wiebe's characterization of the Progressive era.[38] As a result, they rise eagerly to the bait set by politicians—scapegoating crime and criminals and joining in the crusade for law and order. There were scapegoats in the Progressive
era as well, but crime does not seem to have been either a major
or a pervasive theme. Moreover, for all of the drawbacks of
Progressive politics, they were infinitely more constructive than
the politics of street crime today.

There is another interesting twist to the political culture of
street crime. The symbolic forms that define the politicization of
street crime are more salient in national than in local politics.
Thus George Bush found it relatively easy to construct a successful presidential campaign around the image of a predatory black
street criminal. Once in office, he diverted attention from problems less amenable to symbolic typifications by launching a

"war" against illegal drugs—as well as by the related tactic of wrapping himself sanctimoniously in the American flag. It simply has been much easier to mobilize the public around the abstractions of law and order politics in the national arena than in the local arena, where the policy implications are more immediate and comprehensible.

National politicians also have strong incentives to politicize street crime. For them it provides a unifying theme and thus a valence issue.[39] While victimization is experienced differentially according to class, race, gender, and geography, the *threat* it poses to property and person evokes comparable fears throughout the society. National political leaders can, therefore, deploy the fear of crime to unify the public against the criminal. This is, of course, all part of the process of diverting attention from structural problems, for which the government has responsibility but inadequate will, to individual failings, for which outrage and denunciation are ordinarily sufficient responses.

At the local level, where the direct responsibility for criminal process lies, the picture is significantly different, with the incentives running against politicization. First of all, local political leaders and criminal process professionals must to some extent answer for a failure to control crime. Since street crime poses insoluble policy problems, politicization gives rise to expectations that cannot be met. Secondly, the politicization of street crime in urban areas tends to exacerbate social divisions because racial minorities are disproportionately represented in arrest, conviction, and incarceration rates. Insofar as these minorities have a political voice, politicization is divisive. Finally, politicization of street crime is also likely to have an adverse impact on the local business climate. In short, politicization at the local level tends to impose burdens, while at the national level it is likely to confer benefits.

But the public also participates in the national bias of politicization by tending to be more responsive to the distant symbols evoked by a presidential candidate than to the same symbols evoked by a local politician. For successful politicization of street crime, it is necessary to construct a threat that is as frightening as possible and a victimizer who is without redeeming social value. To this end, we are presented with the stereotypical criminal who becomes the symbol of our jeopardy. As I have written elsewhere: "We learn how to identify criminals who are portrayed as predatory strangers. We are led to think of criminals as persons fundamentally different in character (and appearance) from law-abiding members of society; criminals are unknown predators awaiting their opportunity to attack persons and property."[40] But the real world bears relatively little resemblance to this imagined world of predatory strangers. Consequently, the more concrete knowledge we have about street crime and street criminals, the less likely it is that we will be beguiled by the media. Conversely, the less we know, the easier it will be to project our fantasies into the policy arena.

Consider the attractions of punitive policies, which, it follows from this way of thinking, vary directly with social distance. Punishment entails pointing the finger of blame at someone else—a relatively easy thing to do when the culprit is the stereo-typical predatory stranger. Perhaps this helps explain why "the rural hunting culture" has tended to be the most punitive element of the society.[41] Conversely, one of the reasons that blacks have been both more victimized yet seemingly less punitive may well be that they better understand and therefore identify with those who commit crimes.[42] A great many of these crimes, including some of the most frightening, are committed by acquaintances—not by strangers.[43] Most fundamentally, despite their multiplicity of problems, our urban areas are seldom, if ever, the sites of Hobbesian wars of each against all, as they are routinely portrayed.

It follows that familiarity with the local scene may undermine the credibility of the symbolic images that provide the raw material for successful politicization. At the same time, these images retain their suasive power and can therefore be successfully evoked by national leaders making vague allusions to a general breakdown of law and order. Accordingly, national politics are more likely to be dominated by predatory and punitive images and by high-intensity politicization, while local politics have been more amenable to moderation.

Cedar City in Context

The Cedar City findings are consistent with the symbolic and contingent interpretation of politicization developed here. Chapter 2 demonstrates that politicization was more closely associated with social turmoil in a declining neighborhood than with the crime rate or with victimization. Whites in that declining neighborhood, though no more victimized than blacks in an adjacent neighborhood, were much more responsive to the politics of law and order. At the same time, the contingent character of politicization at the local level was borne out by the modest success of efforts to campaign on crime. Overtly successful politicization of street crime in Cedar City was confined to only about four years (1975–1978) of the seventeen years (1964–1980) covered in this research.

But this is not the whole story. In Chapter 3 we learned that police officers perceived a much more enduring change in their circumstances, a kind of continuing scrutiny that was unheard-of prior to the 1960s. Judges and prosecutors experienced a similar sense of exposure according to data presented in Chapter 4. In short, while the direct impact of the politicization on street crime was modest, the ethos of criminal process was markedly changed. Moreover, there were a variety of idiosyncratic factors inhibiting politicization in Cedar City—including, most notably, the payoff scandal and a strong tradition of political civility.[44]

But what would happen if local turmoil were to become sufficiently intense in Cedar City or elsewhere so that conditions more closely resembled the imagined worlds of media violence? As things reached that stage, the forces of moderation would be increasingly weakened. Even if people continued at some level to be sensitive to the structural causes of street crime, their fear and anger could take over. And while political leaders might continue to have a stake in moderation, it is altogether possible that the moderate center simply would not hold.

From this perspective, we would do well to ponder both the "quiet rage" of Bernhardt Goetz and the extraordinary way in which many New Yorkers seemed to identify with him. Perhaps this is, as Lillian Rubin declares, "a time of madness," when "we cannot tolerate the knowledge of our own powerlessness, so we defend against it with our rage."[45]

> In our own time, it is the Goetz case that embodies our most compelling social concerns. . . . We worry about crime in our streets, on our subways and buses, in our homes. And because

young black men between the ages of fifteen and twenty-four commit a disproportionate number of those crimes, when we fill in the outlines of the phrase "crime in the streets," we tend to color it black. When, therefore, a lone white man shoots down four blacks youths on a New York subway, our first national response is a celebration—our first and, tragically, also our last.[46]

Bernhardt Goetz differs from the norm only in the sense that he chose to act out his fantasies rather than to sublimate them in the imagined world of violence or in the "political spectacle."[47]

How this will play out is anyone's guess and certainly an issue warranting careful attention and systematic research. Since the Goetz case, there have been a variety of other outrages of similar proportions that have victimized both blacks and whites. Still, as late as the 1989 mayoral election, moderation continued to win the day—although it might well be argued that for a rather inept white Republican to come as close to victory as did Rudolph Giuliani is a sign of serious racial polarization.

If the center does not hold, what kind of polarization is likely to develop? Insofar as law and order populism is anchored in the broader anxieties of white Americans and insofar as they associate blacks with criminal violence and with the breakdown of law and order more generally, it is difficult to imagine a stable, multiracial law and order constituency. On the other hand, the opposition of blacks to the politics of law and order can hardly be taken for granted. In a sense blacks are a natural constituency for law and order politics, as James Q. Wilson has long argued. As middle-class blacks in particular become sufficiently influential to put aside their fears of the police, they might well be willing to make common cause with the forces of law and order.

Politicization and Policy

The policy implications of politicization add a further note of uncertainty. Certainly, it would be mistake to take the rhetoric of politicization at face value. What you see is by no means what you get. The politicization of crime is frequently a symbolic exercise without serious policy intentions—particularly at the national level. In addition, the federal government is without significant jurisdiction over street crime and has only modest capabilities for influencing local crime control policy. Finally, local agencies are well insulated from, and generally resistant to, the pressures of politicization as well as to direct federal policy initiatives. For all of these reasons, which we must examine with some care, the impact of politicization on operative policy, punitive or otherwise, is likely to be distinctly attenuated.

Still, it is important to explore the significant, albeit indirect, part played by the politicization of street crime in the policy reforms that were summarized above. Three broad generalizations emerge from this analysis. The odds are strongly against structural reform. The national government has structural capabilities but few incentives to act structurally. At the local level, there is more inclination to seek structural solutions, but there are virtually no capabilities to do so. As for volitional policies, two further generalizations may be inferred from the dynamics of politicization. The predominance of predatory symbols tends to drive national policy in an unequivocally punitive direction. In contrast, the relatively moderate local political climate provides more resistance to, but by no means immunity from, punitive policy initiatives.

The Symbolic Character of National Policy

National political leaders tend to be distanced from the real world of criminal process, as are their most influential constituents. With crime as an abstraction and the consoling message of the myth of crime and punishment at their disposal, there is simply no motivation to face up to the costs of structural responses. On the contrary, the myth of crime and punishment provides a formula for a symbolic campaign, which diverts attention from structural problems and unifies the fearful and anxious majority against the predatory minority that "chooses" to threaten law and order.

Conservatives have taken the lead in exploiting that formula, but it remains to be seen whether liberals will face up to structural problems. William Julius Wilson seems mildly optimistic because he believes that a well-planned "program of economic reform designed to promote full employment and balanced economic growth" is an economic necessity that will benefit the underclass as well.[48] But given budgetary pressures and a restive electorate, it seems at least as likely that liberals would aim their policy proposals at the middle and lower-middle strata of the society. The result would be a kind of 80 percent solution that would leave the lowest quintile of the society, and certainly the underclass, languishing unless and until the economic and social costs of inequality become too threatening to ignore. At that point, structural alternatives might well be put on the political agenda, but there is no way to predict whether the policy responses would be repression to reinforce inequality or transformation to reduce it.

In the meantime, national political leaders will probably continue to be associated with punitive policies. But these punitive policies, although redolent with the rhetoric of assertive social action, may amount to little more than symbolic engagements. From this perspective, President Bush's largely punitive but modestly funded war on drugs is entirely consistent with past practice and with what might be expected—a question of speaking loudly and carrying a small stick. Thus, critics complain both that the program is predominantly punitive with very little support for drug prevention and that even taken on its own terms the funding is grossly inadequate for supply-side programs in distressed urban areas.[49] The discontinuity between dramatic rhetoric and limited commitment of resources is a clear tip-off that a federal program is more about getting elected, reinforcing flagging political authority, or enhancing federal law enforcement prerogatives than about serious policymaking.

The Limited Reach of National Institutions

Even with the best intentions, however, the transmission lines from national to local institutions are not very dependable. Herbert Jacob, reflecting on his study of thirty years worth of crime policy in ten U.S. cities, concluded that cities were active but ineffectual and disorganized. They "did many little things while pretending to pursue a grand strategy. Often they believed their pretensions."[50]

This was also the essential lesson of research on the war against street crime, launched by the Crime Control and Safe Streets Act of 1968 and conducted by the Law Enforcement Assistance Administration during the 1970s. Efforts by the LEAA to develop a coherent anticrime program foundered, according to Malcolm Feeley and Austin Sarat, on the ad hoc quality of the legislative mandate and on conflicts between the state planning agencies that distributed funds and the well-entrenched local law enforcement officials.

> As organs of state government, [state planning agencies] must function within an established criminal justice system that is overwhelmingly local in structure, funding, and orientation. As dispensers of funds, they control less than 5 percent of the total criminal justice budget in any state and thus have no real clout especially with respect to larger agencies or in large cities, where the problems of crime are most apparent.[51]

The Cedar City findings reveal two additional obstacles to LEAA effectiveness. The struggle between the mayor's office and the chief of police may have been idiosyncratic, but the tensions between professional planners and professional police officials are inherent in programs of this sort.

In any case, the result was that LEAA funds were not, generally speaking, used as intended—that is, to launch programs that if successful would be supported locally. Instead, the programs served as targets of opportunity: write as much hardware as possible into the proposal, go through the motions of implementing programs, and then terminate them when the funds run out.[52] The LEAA, in short, became just another source of funds. The Cedar City police data presented in Chapter 3 suggest that the mayor and the City Council tended to use LEAA funds as an alternative to local funding rather than as a crime-fighting supplement.

While it would, therefore, be incorrect to think of national initiatives as the source of *extensive* policy change at the local level, reforms have been forthcoming in Cedar City and elsewhere. Moreover, LEAA pilot projects have in some cases provided models for policy change. Indeed, Malcolm Feeley argues, with respect to the criminal courts, that if reform is going to occur, it will "usually [be] initiated by outsiders—private foundations or LEAA."[53] Left to their own devices, the agencies of criminal process, Feeley tells us, may respond to crises but will otherwise stick with established policies and procedures: "The central obstacle to change in the courts is not the resistance to reform, but is, more fundamentally, the lack of interest in even thinking about change."[54] The police are probably more directly resistant to change—making outside pressures and incentives all that much more necessary.

Outside agencies can, then, originate innovative programs such as community policing and determinate sentencing. They may also promote and fund demonstration projects. But whether these programs will take root and, if so, what shape they will take is determined locally. The character, the direction, and the pace of reform is, in other words, primarily a function of local conditions that are complex and unpredictable.

Policy Moderation at the Local Level

Punitive pressures have not, of course, been absent from the local political scene, but so far their influence seems to have been episodic and largely indirect. In Cedar City the law and order coalition was, according to findings presented in Chapter 2, able to have a significant impact for only a brief period in the late 1970s. Generally speaking, the coalition was weak—largely confined to the police guild and to small-business persons in the declining neighborhoods of Crystal Valley. The forces of moderation were considerably stronger—spearheaded by downtown elites, who were concerned with the Cedar City image, and including an increasingly influential black community, where there was less fear of street criminals than of a police department unleashed in a war against street crime.

The moderation of the local political climate complements the predispositions of many frontline fighters. Daily immersion in the struggles of criminal process makes it difficult to ignore the structural correlates of street crime. The dead-end lives of the underclass are only too apparent to the police who arrest them, to the lawyers who prosecute and defend them, and to the judges who sentence them. For at least a couple of reasons, however, these structural understandings are unlikely to be incorporated into operative policy. It will be "obvious" to those who have internalized America's individualistic values that people who are sufficiently well motivated, whatever their race or social class, have alternatives to street crime and illegal drugs. Second, the cognitive dissonance stemming from the gap between structural insights and volitional institutions—that is, institutions that are without capabilities to pursue structural policies—leads toward repression of the structural insights.

Despite the ideological and institutional temptations to ignore structural insights, they seem to have maintained sufficient residual force to promote moderate reforms like those that have been adopted by the police and criminal courts in Cedar City, as well as elsewhere in the country. From this perspective there is more common ground than divergence in the shifts to progressive policing and to the justice model. Of course, progressive policing promotes discretion and informal dispute resolution, while the justice model emphasizes formal law enforcement and limits discretionary authority. But in political and social terms, the two reforms are driven by roughly the same social values and by parallel dissatisfactions with the criminal process.

The justice model was offered as an alternative to the inequities, ineffectiveness, and repressive tendencies of rehabilitation—the so-called treatment model, which relied on indeterminate sentencing:

> Rehabilitation was not merely a laudable goal that scientific research had unfortunately failed thus far to achieve, but something far more insidious—an ideology that explained crime in highly individualistic terms and legitimated the expansion of administrative powers used in practice to discriminate against disadvantaged groups to achieve covert organizational goals (such as alleviating court backlogs and repressing political opposition).[55]

Certainly, it was just these kinds of concerns that drove Park County Prosecutor Dorffler to adopt determinate sentencing. Recall also that in political terms Dorffler's boss saw the justice model as conducive to positioning himself as a progressive gubernatorial candidate. In sum, the justice model was an egalitarian, antistatist response to institutional shortcomings and to a moderate, but hardening, political climate.

Community policing is also rooted in a belief that traditional practices are ineffectual and inequitable—with minorities, and blacks in particular, being unfairly burdened by police violence and harassment. Accordingly, the goal of community policing is to effect a reconciliation between accountable departments and the communities they police. Crudely expressed, the moderation that characterizes community policing can be traced to two sources. Confrontational tactics have been rejected by many police officers, who believe that, in the long run, such tactics isolate the police and are self-defeating. Just as important, these tactics are no longer politically acceptable, given the increasing political influence of urban blacks, who have gained control of City Hall in some cases and are better represented throughout the hierarchies of the police and the criminal courts.

In sum, policy reforms at the local level have a distinctly egalitarian thrust and are intended to curb the state. They are derived from an appreciation of the institutional limitations of criminal process and, to some extent, from an awareness of the structural sources of street crime.

The Trap of Volitional Moderation

Whatever their motives, policymakers will be hard pressed to reach their benevolent, egalitarian, and antistatist objectives. The justice model has taken a clearly punitive tack, as evidenced by increased rates of incarceration. As for community policing, it may well turn punitive and it seems destined, in any case, to significantly extend the reach of the state. Moderate policies go wrong because they are unable to transcend their volitional premises. Both the justice model and community policing are limited to a symptomatic papering over of structural flaws. This leaves intact the underlying crises of crime and authority that fuel the politics of law and order and threaten policy moderation.

The situation is reasonably straightforward with respect to the justice model. Initially, there were indications, according to early research by David Greenberg and Drew Humphries, that the objectives of the justice model would simply be defeated by judges and prosecutors who were able to retain considerable sentencing discretion and by punitive sentencing guidelines.[56] More recently, it appears that discretionary practices have been brought under control in some states. On the other hand, the tendency of legislatures to thwart moderation by ratcheting up sentences has continued.[57]

This seems to suggest, although the evidence is meager and mixed, that legislators, like national politicians, are caught up in the symbols of social action—albeit with more policy bite. It seems plausible that state politics should be receptive to the punitive fantasies of the "rural hunting culture," although a persuasive New York State case study does not bear out that supposition.[58] In any case, moderation at the local level has tended to be overridden by state legislators, many of whom are distanced from the everyday realities of street crime and criminal process. But those same legislators who have found law and order values compelling in the abstract seem more willing to increase sentences than to provide the funds for prison construction and the other costs associated with punitive policies.[59] The results have been overworked officials and overcrowded facilities and a variety of coping strategies that mitigate, but are unlikely to neutralize, the punitive redirection of the justice model.

Community policing presents a more complex and uncertain picture. This response to growing concerns about street crime and illicit drugs is unquestionably the product of a conscientious search for alternatives to hard-line measures aimed at cracking down on criminals by unleashing the police, eliminating plea bargaining, increasing sentences, and the like. There is, moreover, at least a quasi-structural thrust to efforts to reconstruct and empower neighborhoods and to provide them with more responsive institutions for resolving disputes and voicing grievances. These days, community approaches to policing are increasingly seen as a promising way of curbing street crime and street violence while at the same time reconstructing shattered neighborhoods. I have myself in the past defended this approach on grounds of criminological effectiveness and social morality.[60]

But are these realistic goals? Wesley Skogan's reading of the research record leads him to be skeptical about street crime as a source of organizing energy in "the poorer, high crime areas" where "redistributive social and economic policies" are more likely to bring people together.[61] Of course, the incorporation of these structural claims is likely to expose rifts within the community and alienate the small-business persons who at least in Cedar City spearheaded the activism that ultimately led to the introduction of a community policing program. And if the police get caught in between the "insurgents" and the "preservation-ists," to use Skogan's terminology, their community-building mission is likely to be irredeemably compromised.[62]

And just exactly what is the connection between the order-maintenance function that is at the heart of community policing and the building of community? "What is missing from the dis-cussion of community policing as aggressive order mainte-nance," according to Stephen Mastrofski, a friendly critic, "is a delineation of the noncoercive tools of the trade."[63] Under prod-ding from an anxious and vindictive citizenry, community polic-ing could easily degenerate into the punitive styles associated with traditional policing.

But even in its nonpunitive form, with the tactics and strategy spelled out in some detail, there is a darker side to community policing and, indeed, to other community-oriented reforms. The ambivalent implications of communitarian criminology are ex-amined in an especially insightful way by Stanley Cohen, who draws heavily on the work of Michel Foucault. He characterizes the dangers of the process as a combination of "penetration and absorption."[64] On the one hand, police engage in community organization:

[They] provide neighborhood centres for potential delin-quents, organise all sorts of surveillance and early reporting schemes, take part in court watching programmes and con-duct crime prevention seminars in their homes. . . . Some projects call for collective surveillance and reporting (block clubs, neighborhood watch, radio-alert networks, tenant pa-trols, secret witness programmes) while others teach personal survival and protective techniques.[65]

At the same time, the police are "more actively 'reaching out,' by joining neighbourhood organizations, serving on local commit-tees, and helping in school and youth groups. . . . The system penetrates the space of the family, the school and the neighbour-hood."[66] What these schemes do, then, is blur the line between state and society—projecting state power into, and by way of, a community mobilized against criminal behavior and incipient criminality, such as graffiti, disorderly conduct, and the like. The goal is to "take back" the streets and the neighborhoods, not just from the predatory but from the unruly as well—on the assumption that there is an axiomatic developmental connection between disorder and crime.[67] And precisely because they appear to be humane and consensual, there is a tendency to deploy these community-oriented practices indiscriminately, to "thin the mesh and widen the net," as Cohen puts it.[68]

Even a critic like Cohen acknowledges the good intentions and occasionally beneficial consequences of communitarian approaches to crime control.[69] No doubt it is also possible to build in protections that will limit penetration and absorption and provide remedies for abuses. There will, however, also be pressures pushing communitarian criminology toward its intrusive extremes. This is because the structural sources of community disorganization, social cleavage, and street crime are out of reach.

In at least two ways, community criminology is profoundly unrealistic. The point, Cohen argues, is "to reproduce pre-urban systems of mutual responsibility, peacekeeping and good neighbourliness . . . the conditions of an eighteenth-century rural parish." But, he contends, "closed-circuit television, two-way radios, vigilante patrols, private security companies and police decoys hardly simulate life in a pre-industrial village."[70]

There is more common ground among the punitive, communitarian, and justice versions of volitional criminology than there seems to be initially. Simply put, although neither community nor justice reformers are motivated by punitive sentiments, their goal is to crack down on crime and criminals—with a focus on symptoms and without regard for the structural roots of street crime.

The essential difference is between what Foucault has characterized as discipline and punishment.[71] Communitarian practices lean in a disciplinary direction insofar as they mobilize the community not only against the criminal but against the kinds of disorderly behavior that are seen as the precursors of crime. The idea is, in the words of Diana Gordon, "coercive control by observation"[72]—continuing surveillance to encourage both obedience to the criminal law and conformity with the informal norms of the community. The war on drugs is moving in this same intrusive direction with its requirements for mandatory drug testing in the workplace.[73] And, indeed, the state has more generally acquired an imposing disciplinary technology for peering into our lives.[74] Conversely, the justice model is focused on after-the-fact punishment for discrete infractions of the criminal law, thus circumscribing the warrant of the state to intervene in the lives of its citizens. Determinate sentencing was, after all, at least partly a reaction to the therapeutic model of sentencing that gave the state access to the minds as well as the bodies of offenders.

The bottom line is, then, that within the boundaries of volitional criminology the available options are distinctly problematic. Only symptomatic relief is possible so long as the underlying structural issues are ignored, and criminal process is destined to oscillate between the harshness of punishment and the intrusiveness of discipline. Moreover, while disciplinary responses seem at first glance to be the lesser of the evils, this may not be so. Not only do disciplinary measures extend the reach of the state from the bodies to the minds of offenders; they also extend that reach beyond offenders to the members of the community, all of whom are potential offenders and therefore the more or less legitimate targets of preventive social control.

In a sense, these problematic alternatives develop directly out of the circumstances of contemporary life, with its reduced social space, greater interdependence, and more fragile and vulnerable institutions. Insofar as these problems are intrinsic to contemporary life, there is no escape from the choice between discipline and punishment.

But we contribute to social crisis and thus to our own insecurity so long as we ignore the message of structural criminology and turn our backs on the conditions that are producing anxiety and economic insecurity throughout the society and, more particularly, a hostile and hopeless underclass of the truly disadvantaged—that is, a portion of the society without a real stake in or a commitment to civility and mutuality.

Given this kind of threat from the bottom, which can only contribute to malaise elsewhere in the society, there is likely to be an increasingly irresistible temptation to engage in proactive practices that preempt rather than punish. But the mechanisms of anticipatory social control pose the ultimate threat to liberal democratic values, leading, therefore, toward the increasingly familiar paradox of destroying society in an attempt to save it. Without serious structural reform, underlying material deprivations and social conflicts will in the long run frustrate and defeat even the most ingenious forms of symptomatic relief.

Notes

1: Street Crime, Criminology, and the State

1. W. Lance Bennett, *Public Opinion in American Politics* (New York: Harcourt, Brace, Jovanovich, 1980), p. 397.

2. Murray Edelman, *Political Language: Words That Succeed and Policies That Fail* (New York: Academic Press, 1977).

3. See two books by Richard Quinney, *Critique of Legal Order: Crime Control in Capitalist Society* (Boston: Little, Brown and Company, 1974), and *Class, State and Crime*, 2d ed. (New York: Longman, 1980).

4. See Stuart A. Scheingold, *The Politics of Law and Order: Street Crime and Public Policy* (New York: Longman, 1984), and Stuart Hall, Chas Critcher, Tony Jefferson, John Clarke, and Brian Robert, *Policing the Crisis: Mugging, the State, and Law and Order* (London: Macmillan, 1978).

5. Ralf Dahrendorf, *Law and Order* (London: Stevens, 1985).

6. Scheingold, *Politics of Law and Order*, pp. 60–64.

7. See Elliot Currie, *Confronting Crime: An American Challenge* (New York: Pantheon, 1985), and Steven Box, *Recession, Crime and Punishment* (London: Macmillan, 1987).

8. Hall et al., *Policing the Crisis*.

9. Scheingold, *Politics of Law and Order*.

10. Douglas Hay, "Property, Authority and the Criminal Law," in Douglas Hay, Peter Linebaugh, and E. P. Thompson, eds., *Albion's Fatal Tree* (New York: Pantheon, 1975). See also Joseph R. Gusfield, *The Symbolic Crusade: Status Politics and the American Temperance Movement* (Urbana: University of Illinois Press, 1963).

11. Isaac Balbus, *The Dialects of Legal Repression: Black Rebels before the American Courts* (New Brunswick, N.J.: Transaction Books, 1982).

12. Christopher Jencks, "Genes and Crime," *New York Review of Books*, 12 February 1987, pp. 33–41.

13. Currie, *Confronting Crime*.

14. James Q. Wilson and Richard J. Herrnstein, *Crime and Human Nature: The Definitive Study of the Causes of Crime* (New York: Simon and Schuster, 1985).

15. Ibid., p. 43.

16. Ibid., p. 69.

193

17. James Q. Wilson, *Thinking about Crime* (New York: Vintage, 1977).

18. Wilson and Herrnstein, *Crime and Human Nature*, p. 315.

19. Ibid., p. 70.

20. Ibid., pp. 100–102.

21. Ibid., p. 70.

22. Currie, *Confronting Crime*, p. 146.

23. Ibid., p. 149.

24. Ibid., pp. 166–71.

25. Ibid., p. 178.

26. Ibid.

27. Ibid., p. 149.

28. Ibid., p. 147.

29. Wilson and Herrnstein, *Crime and Human Nature*, p. 447.

30. Currie, *Confronting Crime*, p. 168.

31. Ibid., pp. 149–51.

32. Ibid., p. 117; italics added.

33. Wilson and Herrnstein, *Crime and Human Nature*, p. 335; italics added.

34. Currie, *Confronting Crime*, pp. 23–24.

35. Ibid.

36. Wilson and Herrnstein, *Crime and Human Nature*, p. 480, and James Q. Wilson, *Thinking about Crime*, rev. ed. (New York: Vintage, 1985), pp. 17–18. Volitional criminology does not necessarily lead in punitive directions. Liberal interpretations of volitional criminology would tend to emphasize the rehabilitation of individual offenders or deterrence through increasing the benefits of law-abiding activity. The distinction between volitional and structural responses to crime is not, then, the stick versus the carrot but micro versus macro. Volitional criminology focuses on the individual, while structural criminology focuses on the foundations of society.

37. Wilson and Herrnstein, *Crime and Human Nature*, p. 491.

38. Ibid., p. 495.

39. Ibid., p. 490.

40. Currie, *Confronting Crime*, p. 171.

41. Ibid., p. 168.

42. Ibid., p. 277.

43. Ibid., p. 171.

44. Dahrendorf, *Law and Order*.

45. Hall et al., *Policing the Crisis*, p. 21.

46. Dahrendorf, *Law and Order*, p. 37.

47. Ibid., pp. 28–37.

48. Ibid., p. 26.

49. Ibid., p. 44.

50. Ibid., p. 160. For Dahrendorf, anomia is an inherently unstable condition, a transition point on the way from a democratic through an authoritarian toward a totalitarian polity. "Anomia cannot last. It is not just chaos, but also a vacuum which attracts the most brutal forces and powers. . . . My worry is that the road to Anomia will awaken Be-

hemouth as well as Leviathan, and that a new wave of totalitarianism will sweep the world" (ibid., p. 159).

51. Ibid., p. 107.

52. Ibid., p. 118. Dahrendorf's own criminology, while striking a balance between structure and volition, tilts clearly in the latter direction. "The dissipation of law and order by impunity and the resulting disorder and uncertainty, is the social problem of our own time, and may well continue to be that for many decades to come (ibid., p. 40).

53. Wesley Skogan, "Fear of Crime and Neighborhood Change," in Albert J. Reiss, Jr., and Michael Tonry, eds., Communities and Crime (Chicago: University of Chicago Press, 1986), p. 220.

54. Wesley G. Skogan and Michael G. Maxfield, Coping with Crime: Individual and Neighborhood Reactions (Beverly Hills, Calif.: Sage, 1981), p. 191. See also Fred Dubow, Edward McCabe, and Gail Kaplan, Reactions to Crime: A Review of the Literature (Washington, D.C.: National Institute of Law Enforcement and Criminal Justice, 1979), p. 66. It is not necessarily the case that taking "something" means carrying a gun—as opposed to some other weapon or potential weapon, or even a dog.

55. Dahrendorf, Law and Order, pp. 28–37.

56. John Clarke, Stuart Hall, Tony Jefferson, and Brian Roberts, "Sub Cultures, Cultures and Class," in Tony Bennett, Graham Martin, Colin Mercer, and Janet Woollacott, eds., Culture, Ideology and Social Process (London: Batsford Academic and Educational, 1985), pp. 67–68.

57. Clarke and his coauthors see post–World War II youth subcultures in England as a crisis of culture—neither a rite of passage nor, in themselves, a threat to authority and order. They argue that the hedonistic, self-expressive cast of these subcultures evidences a contradiction in contemporary capitalism. Traditional bourgeois culture with its "intricate emotional restraints and repressions, its regulated tempo of restraint and release, its commitment to the protestant 'ethic' of work, career, competitive achievement and possessive individualism . . ." was consistent with a period of capital accumulation, limited productivity, and modest disposable income. But all this changed after World War II. "Advanced capitalism now required not thrift but consumption; not sobriety but style; not postponed gratifications but immediate satisfactions of needs; not goods that last but things that are expendable; the 'swinging' rather than the sober life-style" (ibid., p. 75). From this perspective, youth subcultures are simply the cutting edge of a contradiction that puts pervasive pressure on traditional capitalist values.

58. Samuel Walker, Sense and Nonsense about Crime, 2d ed. (Pacific Grove, Calif.: Brooks/Cole, 1989), p. 4.

59. Arthur L. Stinchcombe, Rebecca Adams, Carol Heimer, Kim Lane Scheppele, Tom W. Smith, and D. Garth Taylor, Crime and Punishment: Changing Attitudes in America (San Francisco: Jossey-Bass, 1980), pp. 112, 117.

60. Ibid., p. 67.

61. Charles Silberman, Criminal Violence, Criminal Justice (New York: Random House, 1978), p. 116.

62. Gusfield, *Symbolic Crusade*, p. 17.

63. Lillian B. Rubin, *Quiet Rage: Bernie Goetz in a Time of Madness* (Berkeley: University of California Press, 1988), p. 262.

64. For an analysis of the cultural presence of the myth of crime and punishment, see Scheingold, *Politics of Law and Order*, pp. 59–77, from which this analysis is drawn.

65. Ibid., p. 60.

66. Ibid., pp. 65–74.

67. Cf. ibid., p. 71.

68. Stuart Hall and Phil Scraton, "Law, Class and Control," in Mike Fitzgerald, Gregor McLennan, and Jennie Pawson, eds., *Crime and Society: Readings in History and Theory* (London: Routledge & Kegan Paul, 1985), p. 479. See also Stuart Hall, "The Rise of the Representative/ Interventionist State, 1880s–1920s," in Gregor McLennan, David Held, and Stuart Hall, *State and Society in Contemporary Britain* (Cambridge, England: Polity Press, 1984), p. 11.

69. Hall and Scraton, "Law, Class and Control," p. 489.

70. Hall et al., *Policing the Crisis*, p. 150.

71. Malcolm M. Feeley and Austin D. Sarat, *The Policy Dilemma: Federal Crime Policy and the Law Enforcement Assistance Administration, 1968–1978* (Minneapolis: University of Minnesota Press, 1980). Cf. Quinney, *Critique of Legal Order*.

72. Herbert L. Packer, *The Limits of the Criminal Sanction* (Stanford: Stanford University Press, 1968), pp. 149–246. This discussion of Packer is taken directly from Stuart A. Scheingold and Lynne A. Gressett, "Policy, Politics, and the Criminal Courts," *American Bar Foundation Research Journal* (1987): 464–69.

73. Packer, *Limits of the Criminal Sanction*, p. 154.

74. Willard Gaylin, *Partial Justice: A Study of Bias in Sentencing* (New York: Vintage, 1975), pp. 51–52.

75. Stanley Cohen, "The Punitive City: Notes on the Dispersal of Social Control," *Contemporary Crises* 3 (1979): 343.

76. Ibid., p. 360. See also Stanley Cohen, *Visions of Social Control* (Cambridge, England: Polity Press, 1987).

2: The Politicization of Street Crime

1. Stuart A. Scheingold, *The Politics of Law and Order: Street Crime and Public Policy* (New York: Longman, 1984), pp. 43–45.

2. James Q. Wilson, *Thinking about Crime* (New York: Vintage, 1977), pp. 72–73. Wilson seems to drift from this position in the revised edition (1985) of *Thinking about Crime*.

3. Scheingold, *Politics of Law and Order*. See also Stuart Hall, Chas Critcher, Tony Jefferson, John Clarke, and Brian Roberts, *Policing the Crisis: Mugging, the State, and Law and Order* (London: Macmillan, 1978), and Lillian B. Rubin, *Quiet Rage: Bernie Goetz in a Time of Madness* (Berkeley: University of California Press, 1988).

4. Roger W. Cobb and Charles D. Elder, *Participation in American*

Politics: The Dynamics of Agenda-Building, 2d ed. (Baltimore: Johns Hopkins University Press, 1983), p. 14.

5. Ibid.

6. Murray Edelman, *Political Language: Words That Succeed and Policies That Fail* (New York: Academic Press, 1977).

7. John Kingdon, *Agendas, Alternatives, and Public Policy* (Boston: Little, Brown, 1984), p. 21. "The proposals that survive to the status of serious consideration meet several criteria, including their technical feasibility, their fit with dominant values and the current national mood, their budgetary workability, and the political support or opposition they might experience."

8. See also Cobb and Elder, *Participation in American Politics,* and Robert Eyestone, *From Social Issues to Public Policy* (New York: John Wiley, 1978).

9. Kingdon, *Agendas, Alternatives, and Public Policy,* p. 21.

10. Ibid., p. 165. "They hear from interest groups' leaders both in Washington and in the hustings; they read newspaper editorials; they give talks and listen to questions and comments at meetings; they see how public events are being covered in both general and specialized media; and they talk to party activists and other politicos who presumably have their ears to the ground. . . . And the national mood may, in some important respects, be an echo of events at the governmental level. . . . A president communicates his sense of national priorities to the nation, influencing the viewpoints relayed by the general public to their elected representatives."

11. Ibid., p. 63, 157.

12. Wesley G. Skogan and Michael G. Maxfield, *Coping with Crime: Individual and Neighborhood Reactions* (Beverly Hills, Calif.: Sage, 1981), p. 60.

13. George Gerbner and Larry Gross, "Living with Television: The Violence Profile," *Journal of Communications* 26 (1976); 173–97.

14. Skogan and Maxfield, *Coping with Crime,* pp. 157, 155.

15. Scheingold, *Politics of Law and Order,* pp. 75–88.

16. The original dataset was created using Statistical Package for the Social Sciences (SPSS), from which frequency tables were then generated. The yearly frequencies for dependent and independent variables were then read into the Time Series Processor (TSP) for the subsequent statistical analyses. See Lynne A. Gressett and Stuart A. Scheingold, "The Politics of Law and Order: Politicizing Amorphous Public Concerns," paper prepared for delivery at the 1984 Annual Meeting of the American Political Science Association, Washington, D.C., 30 August–2 September 1984.

17. Because of the extensiveness of the coding sheets and the sheer bulk of crime reporting, the sample was confined to two months of each year from 1964 to 1980. The months chosen were January and October. October was the month immediately preceding November elections, while January was arbitrarily chosen as a more "normal" month. Initially, it was thought that something might be learned about politicization by contrasting January, the "normal" month, with October, the

"election" month, but that did not prove to be a useful strategy. More generally, the guiding assumption was that two months would, in the first place, provide a substantial sampling. And while there may be no special magic in these two months, there was no reason to believe that the objective of looking at changes through time would be compromised so long as consistency was maintained from year to year.

18. *Cedar City Tribune*, 6 March 1964.

19. *Cedar City Sentinel*, 24 January 1964.

20. *Sunset District News*, 31 August 1967.

21. Coders were asked to read daily and Sunday newspapers in their entirety. They were instructed to content-code all newspaper articles about particular criminal incidents, crime or law and order as a public problem, or the criminal justice system and its components. All articles that contained references to crime within the United States were coded. The volume of articles eventually forced us to retain only a Sunday, Monday, Wednesday, and Friday sampling of the newspapers for each of the two months in the 1964–1980 period. A total of 7,138 individual articles was coded.

Punitive policies were those that were retributive in nature, or aimed at deterrence or at protecting society from criminals. Managerial polices were those justified as being more efficient, time-saving, or cost-cutting. Finally, due process policies reflected concerns with rehabilitation of offenders, protection of constitutional rights, or generalized benefits to the society as a whole (without being punitive).

These classifications are not mutually exclusive in that both national and local articles could be straight crime reporting or could advocate policy. Similarly, the articles could advocate policies that supported or challenged the status quo in ways that advanced punitive, due process, or managerial values.

22. These indicators only bring us closer to institutional politicization, because the coding scheme does not distinguish between local and national policy articles. The more direct evidence of institutional politicization is provided by the analysis of campaigning on crime.

23. In 1979 an initiative for mandatory five-year prison sentences for first-time, first-degree felony offenders failed to secure enough signatures to be put on the ballot.

24. From 1965 to 1980, support for capital punishment grew from 38 to 67 percent. Scheingold, *Politics of Law and Order*, p. 46.

25. Latency is consistent with available data from national opinion sampling. Gallup Poll data from the late 1960s to 1980 indicate that the salience of crime fluctuated widely on *open-ended questions* where respondents were asked to identify "the most important issue facing the country today." Conversely, *forced choice* questions from the Roper Center for roughly the same period reveal that "halting the rising crime rate" was consistently identified as the most important *domestic* policy problem on which "too little" money was spent. Scheingold, *Politics of Law and Order*, pp. 43–45. These findings indicate the kind of suggestibility that is compatible with street crime as a latent issue.

26. Summarized in Scheingold, *Politics of Law and Order*, pp. 38–49.

27. For the more discerning residents of Cedar City, national crime reporting would have been a relatively reliable indicator of the national crime rate (Pearson's $r = .448$). On the other hand, general impressions of the national crime rate drawn from total articles would have been misleading (Pearson's $r = -.252$).

28. Hall et al., *Policing the Crisis;* Edelman, *Political Language;* Joseph R. Gusfield, *The Symbolic Crusade: Status Politics and the American Temperance Movement* (Urbana: University of Illinois Press, 1963).

29. *Cedar City Sentinel,* 12 September 1970.

30. Wilson, *Thinking about Crime,* rev. ed., pp. 78–79.

31. *Cedar City Sentinel,* 16 December 1969.

32. *Cedar City Magazine,* July 1970, pp. 30–33.

33. See *Voters Pamphlet,* 1975.

34. *Cedar City Tribune,* 3 November 1975.

35. *Cedar City Sentinel,* 30 April 1969.

36. Ibid.

37. *Cedar City Tribune,* 27 March 1974.

38. Ibid., 15 September 1976.

39. *Cedar City Sentinel,* 30 April 1970.

40. Ibid., 20 February 1972.

41. *Cedar City Tribune,* 2 October 1975.

42. Ibid., 10 September 1969.

43. *Cedar City Sentinel,* 18 March 1969.

44. *Cedar City Tribune,* 16 July 1977.

45. Scheingold, *Politics of Law and Order,* p. 87.

46. Holly Jeanne Myers-Jones, "A Geographical Analysis of Political Opposition to Busing in [Cedar City]," M.A. thesis, University of Washington, Seattle, 1980, pp. 100–156.

47. See Herbert Jacob, *The Frustrations of Policy: Responses to Crime by American Cities* (Boston: Little, Brown, 1984); Herbert Jacob, Robert L. Lineberry, with Anne M. Heinz, Janice A. Beecher, Jack Moran, and Duanne H. Swank, *Governmental Re-Sponses to Crime: Crime on Urban Agendas* (Washington, D.C.: National Institute of Justice, 1982); and Anne Heinz, Herbert Jacob, and Robert L. Lineberry, eds., *Crime in City Politics* (New York: Longman, 1983).

48. Jacob, *Frustrations of Policy,* pp. 20–21. Jacob and Robert Lineberry, the other principal investigator, come to a different conclusion in an earlier publication: "Unquestionably, crime has been a key issue in local politics for many years. . . . During the 31-year period (1948–78) examined here, six clusters of local issues dominated urban elections in these cities. . . . The two most common issues seemed to be the amorphous and catchall categories of mayoral leadership and law and order. . . . Setting aside the common charge that the incumbent was somehow an inept local leader, it appears correct to say that crime was the most frequent single substantive issue in postwar local elections of these cities." Herbert Jacob and Robert Lineberry, "Crime, Politics, and the Cities," in Heinz, Jacob, and Lineberry, eds., *Crime in City Politics,* p. 3.

49. Ibid., p. 23.

3: Policy, Politics, and the Police

1. Stuart A. Scheingold, *The Politics of Law and Order: Street Crime and Public Policy* (New York: Longman, 1984), p. 140.

2. Jonathan Rubenstein, *City Police* (New York: Ballantine, 1973), p. 23.

3. Albert J. Reiss, *The Police and the Public* (New Haven: Yale University Press, 1971), p. 150.

4. James Q. Wilson: *Varieties of Police Behavior: The Management of Law and Order in Eight Communities* (New York: Atheneum, 1968), pp. 147–49. See also John A. Gardiner, *The Politics of Corruption: Organized Crime in an American City* (New York: Russell Sage Foundation, 1970).

5. Michael Lipsky, *Street-Level Bureaucracy: Dilemmas of the Individual in Public Service* (New York: Russell Sage Foundation, 1980).

6. Rubenstein, *City Police*, p. 152.

7. Wilson, *Varieties of Police Behavior*, pp. 257–71.

8. Scheingold, *Politics of Law and Order*, p. 108.

9. Ibid., pp. 139–40.

10. According to research conducted by the Police Executive Research Forum, there were dramatic increases in the educational levels of police officers during the 1970s and 1980s. Between 1960 and 1988, the proportion of police officers nationwide with no college education dropped from 80 percent to 34.8 percent. Conversely, the proportion with four or more years of college increased from 2.7 percent to 22.6 percent. David L. Carter, Allen D. Sapp, and Darrel W. Stephens, *The State of Police Education: Policy Direction for the 21st Century*, (Washington, D.C.: Police Executive Research Forum, 1989), p. 38. I am grateful to Dorothy Guyot for calling my attention to this research on the incidence and impact of higher education on American policing.

11. Richard A. Stauffenberger, ed., *Progress in Policing: Essays on Change* (Cambridge, Mass.: Ballinger, 1980). The Police Foundation, created by the Ford Foundation, promotes research directed at police reform.

12. Jerome H. Skolnick and David H. Bayley, *The New Blue Line: Police Innovation in Six American Cities* (New York: Free Press, 1986), chap. 8.

13. James Q. Wilson, *Thinking about Crime*, rev. ed. (New York: Vintage, 1985), p. 28.

14. George L. Kelling and Mark H. Moore, "From Political to Reform to Community: The Evolving Strategy of Police," in Jack R. Greene and Stephen D. Mastrofski, eds., *Community Policing: Rhetoric or Reality* (Westport, Conn.: Praeger, 1988), p. 21.

15. Ibid.

16. Herman Goldstein, *Problem-Oriented Policing* (Philadelphia: Temple University Press, 1990).

17. Charles E. Silberman, *Criminal Violence, Criminal Justice* (New York: Random House, 1978), pp. 204–5.

18. Wilson, *Thinking about Crime*, chap. 5.

19. William Ker Muir, Jr., *Police: Streetcorner Politicians* (Chicago: University of Chicago Press, 1977), p. 20.

20. Ibid., p. 20.
21. Ibid., p. 18.
22. Ibid., p. 26.
23. Ibid., p. 25.
24. Kelling and Moore, "From Political to Reform," p. 19.
25. Scheingold, *Politics of Law and Order*, pp. 133–37.
26. The most direct test of the politicization of crime hypothesis available in the Cedar City data is provided by the policy journalism indicator already used in Chapter 2. The assumption here is that articles that discuss policy alternatives reflect a policy debate and are, thus, suggestive of politicization. A similarly political rationale lies, in part, behind a consideration of the relationship between the crime rate and policy change. Insofar as street crime is a political priority, a rising crime rate might lead to increases in police funding and perhaps to pressure for a more aggressive arrest policy. Of course, the department on its own might well alter its arrest policy in response to a rising crime rate.

The regression analysis yielded high R^2 values, thus suggesting that the equation explained a substantial portion of the variance. On the other hand, the particular variables were for the most part not statistically significant. Moreover, the regression analysis made it difficult to test the leadership variable, which both the available literature and the interview data suggested would be important. Chief Cheatham, who provided the base for this dummy variable, was effectively excluded from the regression analysis. It also turned out that when the regression analysis was run without the leadership variable, its explanatory power dropped markedly. For details, see Stuart A. Scheingold and Lynne A. Gressett, "The Politics of Police Policy Making," unpublished paper presented at the 1985 annual meeting of the Law and Society Association, San Diego, Calif., 6–9 June 1985.
27. This analysis is based on a one-year lag of the four chiefs' terms. The assumption is that because of inertial forces, there will be relatively few policy changes made in the first year. There were also two interim chiefs between Cheatham and Brush and another interim chief between Goodfellow and Tracy. The two interim chiefs prior to Brush were in office sufficiently long so that 1970 is removed from the calculations.
28. What seemed to be the most revealing indicator of policy change, complaints about police misconduct, turn out to be too problematic to include in the analysis. It was hoped that these complaints would reveal shifts between traditional and progressive policing. The assumption was that traditional policing, with its emphasis on coercive and confrontational street tactics, would generate more complaints. But there were two problems with this indicator. Data were not available until 1969. Thus there were no figures for the early years of the study, which were the high point of traditional policing according to qualitative data to be presented in this chapter. Indeed, the failure to keep or at least to publish such data is suggestive of the closed world of traditional policing. Second, it may well be that these data are misleading in that people might be more likely to complain about police misbehavior to a department that is responsive than to one that is abusive. This interpretation is

consistent with the qualitative data to be presented in subsequent sections, because by other criteria the department became increasingly progressive, especially at the end of the 1970s and into the 1980s, but complaints tended to rise in those later years. Similarly, the one possible indicator of responsiveness, complaints sustained, tended to vary inversely with complaints. That is, the more complaints that were sustained, the fewer the complaints that were brought. For all of these reasons, the findings on complaints against the police have been relegated to this note.

29. Wilson distinguishes legalistic policing, which stresses arrests, from service and traditional—what he calls "watchman style"—policing, which emphasizes more informal ways of dealing with violations of the law. *Varieties of Police Behavior*, chaps. 5–7.

30. Note that the street crime indicator comprises murder, rape, robbery, and burglary, not UCR Part I crimes. The assumption here is that these "street crimes" were the primary sources of public concern.

31. Barbara Hayler, *"Police Patrol Activity and the Definition of Public Order,"* Ph.D. dissertation, University of Washington, Seattle, 1984), p. 75.

32. Much earlier, in the mid-1950s, the public had rejected a referendum that would have given the police a substantial increase in salary. This electoral experience gave the fledgling Police Guild considerable impetus. "I was a charter member. It was about 1953 or 1954. The wages were so low. We got tired of it. I think it was in 1955 or '56 they put a proposition on the ballot, and it was for raises for policemen, and it went down soundly to defeat. We already had the guild started then, and we were making minuscule headway. After Proposition 8 went down, our total wage increases was $5 per month. So that was when the guild really started to take off. Before then it was a kind of fraternal organization."

The connection between salary and the payoff system was apparently made explicit to incoming officers: "I had a young supervisor, a young sergeant that was involved in the corruption. He took us aside when we went to work for him. He took us all aside and he said: 'Here's what's happening in the police department as it relates to corruption. There's money available in bail bonds and chasing for attorneys, tow companies, prostitution. . . . You can get involved or you can stay out of it.' " There were, in effect, parallel police departments, with officers nominally free to avoid the corrupt department.

33. Brush did have a number of personal idiosyncrasies that made him a difficult person to get along with. One City Council member remembered him as "the chief with no eyelids, because he would sit and listen to you without blinking." Someone in the mayor's office described him as "extremely rigid, very insecure, and, I personally believe, a mentally unbalanced individual." Even his defenders in the police department found him a little hard to take. "W. C.—and I was one of his supporters—was a strange man, a strange man. But I felt that he was exactly what we needed at the time. We needed someone with integrity

at the time. [He] had it, whether you liked the man or not. He was cold; God, he was as cold as this desk." But these were minor peccadillos compared to his great strengths, so far as rank-and-file officers were concerned.

34. One of the clearer signs of how important mayoral prerogatives were to West was the way in which Goodfellow was chosen. He had been the mayor's primary pipeline into the department—the man who is said, for example, to have told Mayor West about some inappropriately heavy drinking by Chief Brush and his department cronies. The selection process further indicates that Mayor West's overriding goal was to establish tight control over the police department. An ostensibly independent selection committee was stacked in a way that predetermined the results of its search. The lone dissenter on the committee recalled: "When I accepted the job to find a new police chief, I was nicknamed Snow White, because I had the other political henchmen of West's who were on the committee. I was told that Charlie Goodfellow was going to be the next police chief. And I said, 'No way!' . . . and seven months later I was the only no vote in the group." Goodfellow's appointment was narrowly confirmed by the City Council after bitter hearings. The case against Goodfellow was that he had had an undistinguished career, that a number of better-qualified candidates had been passed over, including one black, and, more important, that he was completely beholden to the mayor. One member of the City Council who opposed the appointment was very worried that Chief Goodfellow in deciding "who the law was enforced for and against, would be influenced by the mayor."

35. *Cedar City Tribune*, 17 March 1974.

36. Ibid., 21 March 1974.

37. A willingness to grant favors to campaign contributors or to acknowledge neighborhood mores is not indicative of corruption in the police department, nor did any subsequently come to light. Mayor West, however, did withdraw from politics after his second term amid rumors concerning the letting of public works contracts.

38. Not surprisingly, the mayoral advisers who shared in the appointment of Chief Goodfellow were more favorably disposed toward him. Their defense is, however, almost as damning as the indictments by the black and white officers. As one of the mayor's closest advisers saw it, Chief Goodfellow was useful to the mayor. "Goodfellow at least handled public relations with the black community. If there was a problem, he would go there. You can really feel the tension with the black community relax. Allowed us to stop worrying about the police department. With Brush we never knew what was going to happen." But this same adviser doubted that Goodfellow had any significant impact on the department, and his views correspond to those of the other respondents. "[He] would tell us he was going to do one thing and tell the department he would 'keep the mayor off our backs.' I really don't think he cared about affirmative action. He disciplined some woman officer for sleeping with a *black* officer—not an officer. I just don't think he did very

much. He did what he had to to keep us happy. I don't think the department changed very much while he was there. The irony of it is that we got someone who was very loyal but he was ineffective."

39. Clearly, the planners contributed to their own problems in that they tended to be overly aggressive and insufficiently attentive to department sensibilities. A department manager who dealt directly with law and justice planners complained about one of the directors as follows: "Nick's problem was that . . . he was working out of the mayor's office and he had the mayor's ear. And the mayor's telling him on the one hand, 'Go, man, go!' And then he comes over to us and we're saying: 'No, wait a minute!' And he's saying: 'Hey, you wait a minute. I'm speaking for the man.' And we're just having to say: 'Sorry, that won't fly.'" A subsequent director of the Law and Justice Planning Office acknowledged that the planners bear a major share of the responsibility for what went wrong: "We made lots of mistakes and continued to make the same mistakes over and over because of an organizational ego. We sort of billed ourselves as the whiz kids. It's fairly easy to do in somebody else's arena—especially when in that profession not much attention has been paid to looking at data and trying to do some real problem solving. It is easy to come up with some good solutions." The challenge, as this administrator saw it, "one that we met on only a couple of occasions, was to make the management part of the change process itself—getting the police department to buy into an idea and actually implement it correctly and precisely as their own idea." The overall result, in his view, was that although "we caused a lot of change, we created a lot of friction in the process."

40. Brush's obsession with independence extended beyond politicians to other law enforcement agencies. At one point he resigned from the state's law and justice planning committee because he was as reluctant to cooperate with other police agencies as with the politicians and planners. According to one of the leading members of the City Council, Chief Brush resisted efforts to establish an integrated state criminal justice training institute and successfully held out for an autonomous local facility.

41. True to the values of traditional policing, only officers who were actually on the street were accorded real respect by many among the rank and file. A former president of the guild commented, "I think I'd lose a lot of the position, stature that I have in the department if I were to go up a career ladder." The obvious result was an abiding distrust of careerist officers who get off the streets as soon as possible.

42. Skolnick and Bayley, *New Blue Line,* chaps. 4, 6.

43. As Feeley and Sarat see it, the shortcomings of the LEAA can be traced, on the one hand, to the ad hoc quality of its legislative mandate and, on the other, to conflicts between the state planning agencies, through which funds were distributed, and well-entrenched local law enforcement officials. "As organs of state government, [state planning agencies] must function within an established criminal justice system that is overwhelmingly local in structure, funding, and orientation. As

dispensers of funds, they control less than 5 percent of the total criminal justice budget in any state and thus have no real clout, especially with respect to larger agencies or in large cities, where the problems of crime are most apparent." Malcolm M. Feeley and Austin D. Sarat, *The Policy Dilemma: Federal Crime Policy and the Law Enforcement Assistance Administration, 1968–1978* (Minneapolis: University of Minnesota Press, 1980), p. 146.

44. The one Police Foundation "progressive" who offers a structural analysis of crime is Anthony Bouza, who became prominent during his tenure as police commander in the South Bronx, otherwise known as Fort Apache. Later he became a controversial police chief in Minneapolis. But Bouza is considered a rather irresponsible maverick by other progressives. Moreover, despite his structural analysis of crime, his policies have a decidedly punitive ring to them. He sees no alternative to these hard-line policies, since structural corrections are far beyond the reach of police resources. Philip B. Taft, Jr., "Tony Bouza of Minneapolis: Is He a Reform Chief or a Flake?" *Police Magazine*, January 1982, pp. 19–28.

4: Policy, Politics, and the Criminal Courts

1. W. Boyd Littrell, *Bureaucratic Justice: Police, Prosecutors, and Plea Bargaining* (Beverly Hills, Calif.: Sage, 1979). Organizational forces were surely at work in the Park County criminal court system, but neither the quantitative data nor the interviews suggested that organizational imperatives were important determinants in policy change. This finding is at odds with James Eisenstein and Herbert Jacob's extensive study, *Felony Justice: An Organizational Analysis of Criminal Courts* (Boston: Little, Brown, 1977), in which organizational variables provided the best predictors of policy outcomes. They were, however, looking at changes within generally stable systems, whereas this project focused on major breaks in policy. The findings did reveal that charging practices were sensitive to variations in case load, but other factors—personal values, criminal court experiences, and the political setting—were more central to the choices made. Accordingly, the strictly organizational issues are not incorporated into this analysis. But see Stuart A. Scheingold and Lynne A. Gressett, "Policy, Politics and the Criminal Courts," *American Bar Foundation Research Journal* (1987): 473.

2. Herbert L. Packer, *The Limits of the Criminal Sanction* (Stanford: Stanford University Press, 1968), pp. 153–54.

3. Ibid., p. 173.

4. Ibid., p. 153.

5. Ibid., pp. 159, 163.

6. Packer's analysis is also nonempirical: it is rooted in case law, does not shed much light on the concrete circumstances facing prosecutors and judges, and avoids any effort to see how the competing policy pressures in criminal process are reconciled. Accordingly, Packer is best seen as a useful and an important starting point for a broader, empirical inquiry into the political culture of criminal process.

7. Ibid., p. 154–55.

8. Stuart A. Scheingold, *The Politics of Law and Order: Street Crime and Public Policy* (New York: Longman, 1984), pp. 65–68.

9. Murray Edelman, *The Symbolic Uses of Politics* (Champagne–Urbana: University of Illinois Press, 1967), p. 67.

10. On the role of values and interests in criminal court policy-making, see Scheingold, Politics of Law and Order, chap. 7.

11. American Friends Service Committee, *Struggle for Justice: A Report on Crime and Punishment in America* (New York: Hill & Wang, 1971).

12. Andrew von Hirsch, *Doing Justice: Report of the Committee for the Study of Incarceration* (New York: Hill & Wang, 1976).

13. James Q. Wilson, *Thinking about Crime*, rev. ed. (New York: Vintage Books, 1985), chap. 7.

14. Andrew von Hirsch, *Past or Future Crimes: Deservedness and Dangerousness in the Sentencing of Criminals* (New Brunswick, N.J.: Rutgers University Press, 1987), chap. 1.

15. Sentencing is a combined responsibility of prosecutors and judges. The judges' contribution will be considered in a subsequent section. Because of changes in recording practices, our data do not include Steele's last year (1978) or 1979 or 1980, when a new prosecutor, Griffin, was elected. There is, however, reason to believe that no significant changes were undertaken during those three years. Griffin had been one of Steele's two top lieutenants, and the other one, Dorffler, remained chief criminal deputy.

16. See Littrell, *Bureaucratic Justice*.

17. Data were not uniformly available for all of the years convered by this research. Thus, the data on filing practices run through 1975, on conviction and dismissal rates, through 1980, and on sentencing severity, through 1977.

18. Collecting data on filing practices presented some problems. The figures on criminal charges filed in the county court system are for cases where a charge is filed and the case is disposed of in the same calendar year. Thus cases have been omitted where a charge may have been filed in one year but the case was not resolved until a subsequent year. All data on filings and on sentencing come from the *Annual Reports of the Prosecuting Attorney of Park County*.

Over the time period of this study, as a result of new programs and procedures and a shift to computerized record-keeping, there were several changes in reporting practices of the prosecutor's office. The changes that most directly affected data collection resulted from the enactment of the new state criminal code on 1 July 1976, which altered the classification of several types of crimes. The annual report for 1976 separates charges filed under the old criminal code from those filed under the new code. As much as possible, the data have been grouped according to their original classifications (e.g., first-degree murder, manslaughter, negligent homicide). Crimes from the new and old criminal code classifications were, however, merged—for example, aggravated first-degree murder charges (new code) were counted in the first-degree murder charges (new and old codes). Every effort was made to preserve consistency across crime categories for our quantitative analysis.

19. *Cedar City Sentinel,* 28 June 1970. Phillips not only ran the office "as a political fiefdom," he also employed an intrusive administrative style and an autocratic leadership style. My respondents agreed that the deputy prosecutors had very little influence on decisions about which cases to prosecute and on the course of plea bargaining. "The trial deputies did not have a whole bunch of leeway. The assistant chief criminal deputy that I worked for told me basically what to do. I went to him and said: 'What can I do on this particular case as far as plea negotiations? Can we reduce it to a misdemeanor? What can we do?' And my assistant chief would tell me: 'No, we can't do that. Here's what we can do.' And he'd say: 'You can drop one count of this particular information and he can plead to the other count and our recommendation is going to be a, b, c, and d, and that's it.'" Phillips also tended to be tough on his subordinates. He personally called trial deputies on the carpet if, for example, they lost cases that he felt should have been won. He would also call deputies into his office occasionally to ask them questions about cases on which they were working—often quite penetrating questions, according to one respondent, who saw this as a way of conveying to deputies that they were under close scrutiny. "He was a very interesting person. He was a very, almost tyrannical, dictatorial individual. He ran a very tight office in which there was a great deal of centralized control." His preemptory style was not, perhaps, to be taken entirely seriously. "Over the time I was in the office, I was canned twice by the boss for insubordination. He was an Irishman and you could argue with him a little bit, but you were taking your life in your hands, or your job in your hands, when you did it. And if he didn't like you, he'd just say: 'Get out, you're fired.' That's it. But then normally cooler heads would prevail, and both times I wound up securing my job back again." There is a temptation to attribute this autocratic style to the patronage and corruption associated with the Phillips machine, but there is no evidence that Phillips's political objectives impinged on the prosecution of street crime. And had the office been larger, neither the centralized control organized by the chief criminal deputy nor Phillips's intrusive sorties would have been effective. While it may, therefore, be that the office style was simply an idiosyncratic reflection of Phillips's personality, it is not surprising that he would want to maintain effective control over the heart of his political machine.

20. Park County Office of the Prosecuting Attorney, *Annual Report,* 1978, p. 5.

21. *Cedar City Sentinel,* 2 June 1970.

22. Ibid., 9 September 1970.

23. *Cedar City Tribune,* 14 September 1970.

24. *Cedar City Sentinel,* 9 September 1970.

25. *Cedar City Tribune,* 4 November 1974.

26. Ibid., 12 October 1974.

27. Even during the 1970 general election, Steele resisted the considerable temptation to embrace the politics of law and order. Steele's opponent was a liberal Democrat who won his primary against a prominent black attorney by stressing the connection between law enforcement and social justice—promising an office "that attempts to bring about change in our society to accomplish social justice for all the people rather than . . . resists change" (*Suburban Press*, 6 May 1970). In the background was Phillips's failure to prosecute a police officer who had killed a young black man—this despite a 2-to-1 decision by a coroner's jury that the policy officer had used "criminal means." The case was a lightning rod for community sentiment, since the young black was shot running away from a post office where he allegedly had planted a bomb. Thus racial tension and law and order concerns were inextricably linked.

In any case, there was obviously an opportunity in the general election for Steele to stake out some law and order turf had he wished to do so. There was also an incentive to do so, because it was a close and hard-fought campaign, with Steele's final margin of victory so close that there was a recount. Finally, there was not much to be gained by continuing to hammer away at the corruption issue against an opponent who had not been tarred by the payoff brush.

Nonetheless the campaign was relatively moderate, with the two candidates so closely aligned that the more conservative of the city's two newspapers called it a "campaign of subtleties" (*Cedar City Tribune*, 1 November 1970). There is a somewhat paradoxical lesson to be drawn from this campaign. Although the campaign was misleading in important ways, the electorate did get what it was promised.

28. Wallace D. Loh, "The Impact of Common Law and Reform Rape Statutes on Prosecution: An Empirical Study," *Washington Law Review* 55 (1980): 550–52, 580–85. High-impact crimes, so designated because of their effects on victims and society, were not supposed to be filed at lesser charges simply to obtain guilty pleas.

29. Loh's research on the impact of rape reform statutes finds that charging practices did not change between Steele's first and second terms (Loh, "Impact," table 3, p. 602). There are no obvious ways to resolve this discrepancy. At the heart of the matter, however, are different ways of reconciling the categories of the old criminal code with those of the new code passed in the latter half of 1976. In addition, Loh's figures are derived from tracing individual cases through the records of the police, prosecutor, and the courts, while the data presented here came exclusively from the annual reports of the prosecutor's office. Finally, the two projects deal differently with the categories of statutory rape, which are not included here, and with indecent liberties, which Loh does not tabulate separately.

30. David Sudnow, "Normal Crimes: Sociological Features of the Penal Code in a Public Defender's Office," *Social Problems* 12, no. 255 (1965); James Eisenstein, Roy B. Flemming, and Peter Narduli, *The Contours of Justice: Communities and Their Courts* (Boston, Little, Brown, 1988), pp. 246–48; Douglas W. Maynard, "Defendant Attributes in Plea Bar-

gaining: Notes on the Modeling of Sentencing Decisions," *Social Problems* 29 (1982): 347; Littrell, *Bureaucratic Justice.*

31. For what it's worth, retained counsel who were interviewed warned against taking announced policy changes at face value. They were inclined to believe that they could ordinarily adapt to new policies without disadvantaging their clients. The public defender, in contrast, acknowledged that the bargaining position of his attorneys tended to wax and wane with changes in the policy climate. Given the favorable resource differential of retained counsel, it is reasonable to believe that they would be better insulated from the adverse impact of policy change than public defenders.

32. The interviews suggest that data on motions to suppress evidence would probably be the most sensitive indicator of politicization, but these are not available. It might also be true that sentencing following trials might be more independently derived, but these data are only available for some of the years of this study.

33. *Cedar City Sentinel*, 1 November 1968.

34. *Cedar City Tribune*, 31 August 1976.

35. *Cedar City Sentinel*, 8 September 1976.

36. *Cedar City Tribune*, 20 September 1976.

37. On criminal courts as communities, see Eisenstein, Flemming, and Narduli, *Contours of Justice.*

38. Scheingold, *Politics of Law and Order*, p. 4.

5: Politics, Criminology, and Crisis

1. See, for example, James Eisenstein, Roy B. Flemming, and Peter Narduli, *The Contours of Justice: Communities and Their Courts* (Boston: Little, Brown, 1988); James Eisenstein and Herbert Jacob, *Felony Justice: An Organizational Approach to Criminal Courts* (Boston: Little, Brown, 1977); W. Boyd Littrell, *Bureaucratic Justice: Police, Prosecutors, and Plea Bargaining* (Beverly Hills, Calif.: Sage, 1979); William K. Muir, Jr., *Police: Streetcorner Politicians* (Chicago: University of Chicago Press, 1977); Michael Lipsky, *Street-Level Bureaucracy: Dilemmas of the Individual in Public Service* (New York: Russell Sage Foundation, 1980); Albert J. Reiss, *The Police and the Public* (New Haven: Yale University Press, 1971).

2. Ralf Dahrendorf, *Law and Order* (London: Stevens, 1985), p. 117; Lillian B. Rubin, *Quiet Rage: Bernie Goetz in a Time of Madness* (Berkeley: University of California Press, 1988; See also columns on the "wilding" in Central Park by George Will, "Rape and Beatings, Just for Fun," *Seattle Times*, 30 April 1989, and by Richard Cohen, "The Perils of Urban Living," *Washington Post*, 21 May 1989.

3. Herbert Jacob, *The Frustration of Policy: Responses to Crime by American Cities* (Boston: Little, Brown, 1984). That research was primarily concerned with the failure to establish coherent policies for coping with crime and was, thus, exclusively focused on policy processes and programs. This project puts policy in the broader context of politicization and political culture. Despite these different perspectives, there is a

good deal of overlap in coverage. Significant discontinuity between politics and policy was a central theme of both studies.

4. Elliott Currie, *Confronting Crime: An American Challenge* (New York: Pantheon, 1985).

5. John Hagan, *Structural Criminology* (Cambridge, England: Polity Press, 1988), p. 2.

6. William Julius Wilson, *The Truly Disadvantaged: The Inner City, the Underclass and Public Policy* (Chicago: University of Chicago Press, 1987). For an incisive summary of this argument, see Samuel Walker, *Sense and Nonsense about Crime*, 2d ed. (Pacific Grove, Calif.: Brooks/Cole, 1989), pp. 259–63.

7. As long ago as 1980, Lester C. Thurow made an economic case for egalitarian reforms in *The Zero-Sum Society: Distribution and the Possibilities for Economic Change* (New York: Penguin, 1980), pp. 191–214.

8. Walker, *Sense and Nonsense*, pp. 199–266.

9. Stuart A. Scheingold, *The Politics of Law and Order: Street Crime and Public Policy* (New York: Longman, 1984), p. 27.

10. Jerome H. Skolnick and David H. Bayley, *The New Blue Line: Police Innovation in Six American Cities* (New York: Free Press, 1986).

11. The initial case for the justice model was made by the American Friends Service Committee, *Struggle for Justice: A Report on Crime and Punishment in America* (New York: Hill & Wang, 1971). In two subsequent books, Andrew von Hirsch became one of the leading advocates for the justice model: *Past or Future Crimes: Deservedness and Dangerousness in the Sentencing of Criminals* (New Brunswick, N.J.: Rutgers University Press, 1987), and *Doing Justice: Report of the Committee for the Study of Incarceration* (New York: Hill & Wang, 1976). See also Willard Gaylin, *Partial Justice: A Study of Sentencing Bias* (New York: Vintage, 1975). Cf. Stanley Cohen, *Visions of Control* (Cambridge, England: Polity Press, 1987), pp. 245–54.

12. For a summary of the relevant research, see Scheingold, *Politics of Law and Order*, pp. 163–64.

13. Stephen Klein, Joan Petersilia, and Susan Turner, "Race and Imprisonment Decisions in California," *Science* 247 (16 February 1990): 812–16. While this research is based on data collected after the implementation of the California determinant sentencing act, other researchers have come up with the same kind of results in more traditional settings. See, for example, Eisenstein and Jacob, *Felony Justice*, p. 284. Race tends to lose its explanatory power as the statistical analysis becomes more refined—that is, as an increasingly complete range of legally permissible variables, such as the seriousness of crime and criminal record, are incorporated into the analysis. But see Cassia Spohn, John Gruhl, and Susan Welch, "The Effect of Race on Sentencing: A Re-Examination of an Unsettled Question," *Law and Society Review* 16 (1981–1982): 83–85.

14. Hagan, *Structural Criminology*, pp. 7–11.

15. Malcolm M. Feeley, *Court Reform on Trial: Why Simple Solutions Fail* (New York: Basic Books, 1983), pp. 143–48. Given the relatively recent introduction of determinant sentencing and the diversity of programs,

generalizations may be premature. But as Feeley points out, restricting judicial discretion does "nothing to curb the discretionary authority of prosecutors and may even encourage plea bargaining" (ibid., p. 143). There is also evidence from California and elsewhere that moderate legislative programs, once in place, tend to become more punitive—presumably in response to a punitive political climate. See David F. Greenberg and Drew Humphries, "The Cooptation of Fixed Sentencing Reform," *Crime and Delinquency* 26 (April 1980): 220–21.

16. Greenberg and Humphries, "Cooptation of Fixed Sentencing," p. 216.

17. For an excellent overview and constructive critique of community policing, see the collection edited by Jack R. Greene and Stephen D. Mastrofski, *Community Policing: Rhetoric or Reality* (New York: Praeger, 1988).

18. Lee P. Brown, "Community Policing: A Practical Guide for Police Officials," *Police Chief*, August 1989, pp. 76–79.

19. Herman Goldstein, "Improving Policing: A Problem-Oriented Approach," *Crime and Delinquency* 25 (April 1979): 251–57.

20. See, for example, Peter K. Manning, "Community Policing as a Drama of Control"; Carl B. Klockars, "The Rhetoric of Community Policing"; and Stephen D. Mastrofski, "Community Policy as Reform: A Cautionary Tale," in Greene and Mastrofski, *Community Policing*.

21. Murray Edelman, *Constructing the Political Spectacle* (Chicago: University of Chicago Press, 1988), p. 27. See also Stuart Hall, Chas Critcher, Tony Jefferson, John Clarke, and Brian Roberts, *Policing the Crisis: Mugging, the State, and Law and Order* (London: Macmillan, 1978).

22. George Gilder is only one of the more recent to make this kind of argument. See his *Wealth and Poverty* (New York: Bantam Books, 1982).

23. Elliott Currie, *Confronting Crime: An American Challenge* (New York: Pantheon, 1985). See also Charles Silberman, *Criminal Violence, Criminal Justice* (New York: Random House, 1978), pp. 87–116.

24. Barbara Ehrenreich, *Fear of Falling: The Inner Life of the Middle Class* (New York: Pantheon, 1989).

25. Harold Lasswell, *World Politics and Personal Insecurity* (New York: McGraw-Hill, 1935).

26. Scheingold, *Politics of Law and Order*, p. 68.

27. George Gerbner and Larry Gross, "Living with Television: The Violence Profile," *Journal of Communications* 26 (Spring 1976): 173–97.

28. Andrew von Hirsch has quite correctly pointed out to me in private correspondence that the "just deserts" of popular culture tend to be vindictive and thus quite different from the genuinely desert-based calibrations of the justice model.

29. I am grateful to Jack Katz for calling my attention to this way of looking at things.

30. Scheingold, *Politics of Law and Order*, pp. 43–44.

31. Richard Sennett and Jonathan Cobb, *The Hidden Injuries of Class* (New York: Vintage, 1972), p. 17.

32. Emma Rothschild, "The Reagan Economic Legacy," *New York Review of Books*, 21 July 1988, p. 38.

33. Ehrenreich, *Fear of Falling*, p. 205.

34. Stephen Rose and David Fasenfest, *Family Incomes in the 1980s: New Pressures on Wives, Husbands, and Young Adults*, Working Paper No. 103 (Washington: Economic Policy Institute, 1988). Rose and Fasenfest report that overall in the United States, "40 percent have lost income since 1979, and another 20 percent maintained roughly stable incomes because wives have had to work harder in order to compensate for the falling wages of their husbands. The study also confirms that this is not simply a problem of older blue-collar workers in a few declining industries as is often alleged" (p. 13).

35. Christopher Lasch, *The Culture of Narcissism: American Life in an Age of Diminishing Expectations* (New York: Warner Books, 1979), pp. 129–30.

36. Ibid., pp. 127–28.

37. Rubin, *Quiet Rage*, pp. 238–39.

38. Robert H. Wiebe, *The Search for Order 1877–1920* (New York: Hill & Wang, 1967).

39. Herbert Jacob and Robert L. Lineberry, "Crime, Politics, and the Cities," in Anne Heinz, Herbert Jacob, and Robert L. Lineberry, eds., *Crime in City Politics* (New York: Longman, 1983), pp. 3–4.

40. Scheingold, *Politics of Law and Order*, p. 60.

41. Arthur Stinchcombe, Rebecca Adams, Carol A. Heimer, Kim Lane Scheppele, Tom W. Smith, and D. Garth Taylor, *Crime and Punishment—Changing Attitudes in America* (San Francisco: Jossey-Bass, 1980), p. 112.

42. Ibid., p. 67.

43. Vera Institute of Justice, *Felony Arrests: Their Prosecution and Disposition in New York City's Courts*, rev. ed. (New York: Longman, 1981), p. 19.

44. Even the payoff scandal itself was by and large finessed rather than confronted. See William Chambliss, *On the Take: From Petty Crooks to Presidents* (Bloomington: Indiana University Press, 1978), pp. 146–47.

45. Rubin, *Quiet Rage*, p. 239.

46. Ibid., p. 260.

47. Edelman, *Constructing the Political Spectacle*.

48. Wilson, *Truly Disadvantaged*, p. 122.

49. Richard L. Berke, in the *New York Times*, 6 September 1989.

50. Herbert Jacob, *Frustrations of Policy*, p. 165.

51. Malcolm M. Feeley and Austin D. Sarat, *The Policy Dilemma: Federal Crime Policy and the Law Enforcement Assistance Administration, 1968–1978* (Minneapolis: University of Minnesota Press, 1980), p. 146.

52. Malcolm M. Feeley, *Court Reform on Trial: Why Simple Solutions Fail* (New York: Basic Books, 1983), pp. 220–21.

53. Ibid., p. 200.

54. Ibid., p. 192.

55. Greenberg and Humphries, "Cooptation of Fixed Sentencing," p. 208.

56. Ibid., pp. 218–25. Greenberg and Humphries also point out that the egalitarian objectives of the original supporters of determinant sen-

tencing have been betrayed by a failure either to decriminalize minor offenses or to criminalize "serious capitalist offenses or . . . government repression" (p. 219).

57. Michael H. Tonry, *Sentencing Reform Impacts* (Washington, D.C.: National Institute of Justice, 1987). This review of the available data on the impact of determinate sentencing indicates some success in reducing disparity but a tendency toward increased severity. See also Samuel H. Pillsbury, "Understanding Penal Reform: The Dynamics of Change," *Journal of Criminal Law and Criminology* 80 (1989): 726–89, and David L. Fallen, *Sentencing Practice under the Sentencing Reform Act: Fiscal Year 1987* (Olympia, Wash.: Sentencing Guidelines Commission, undated).

58. James B. Jacobs and Laura Berkowitz, "Reflections on the Defeat of New York State's Prison Bond," in James B. Jacobs, *New Perspectives on Prisons and Imprisonment* (Ithaca, N.Y.: Cornell University Press, 1983), pp. 115–32.

59. Susan L. Rhodes, "State Policy-Makers and the 'Get Tough' Movement: The Politics of Prison Building and the Prison Overcrowding Crisis in California," paper prepared for presentation at the annual meeting of the Law and Society Association, 9–11 June 1989, Madison, Wis. See also Peter Lewis, "Justice Systems Facing Cash Crisis," *Seattle Times*, 4 April 1990.

60. Scheingold, *Politics of Law and Order*, chap. 8.

61. Wesley G. Skogan, "Community Organizations and Crime," in Michael Tonry and Norval Morris, eds., *Crime and Justice* (Chicago: University of Chicago Press, 1988), pp. 68–69.

62. Ibid.

63. Mastrofski, "Community Policing as Reform," p. 55.

64. Stanley Cohen, *Visions of Social Control: Crime, Punishment and Classification* (Cambridge, England: Polity Press, 1985), p. 83.

65. Ibid., p. 82.

66. Ibid., p. 83.

67. James Q. Wilson, *Thinking about Crime*, rev. ed. (New York: Vintage, 1985), pp. 75–89.

68. Stanley Cohen, "The Punitive City: Notes on the Dispersal of Social Control," *Contemporary Crises* 3 (1979): 346–50.

69. Ibid., p. 350.

70. Cohen, *Visions of Social Control*, p. 69.

71. The distinction between discipline and punishment is from Michel Foucault, *Discipline and Punish: The Birth of the Prison* (New York: Vintage, 1979).

72. Diana R. Gordon, *The Justice Juggernaut: Fighting Street Crime, Controlling Citizens* (New Brunswick, N.J.: Rutgers University Press, 1990), p. 7.

73. John Gilliom, "Rights and Discipline: Competing Modes of Social Control in Supreme Court Decisions on Employee Drug Testing," paper prepared for presentation at the annual meeting of the Law and Society Association, 9–11 June 1989, Madison, Wis.

74. Gordon, *Justice Juggernaut*, chap. 4.

Bibliography

American Friends Service Committee. *Struggle for Justice: A Report on Crime and Punishment in America*. New York: Hill & Wang, 1971.

Balbus, Isaac. *The Dialectics of Legal Repression: Black Rebels before the American Courts*. New Brunswick, N.J.: Transaction Books, 1982.

Bennett, W. L. *Public Opinion in American Politics*. New York: Harcourt, Brace, Jovanovich, 1980.

Berke, R. L. "No Change in Basics." *New York Times*, 6 September 1989.

Box, Steven. *Recession, Crime and Punishment*. London: Macmillan, 1987.

Brown, L. P. "Community Policing: A Practical Guide for Police Officials." *Police Chief*, August 1989, 72–82.

Carter, D. L., A. D. Sapp, and D. W. Stephens. *The State of Police Education: Policy Direction for the 21st Century*. Washington D.C.: Police Executive Research Forum, 1989.

Chambliss, W. J. *On the Take: From Petty Crooks to Presidents*. Bloomington: Indiana University Press, 1978.

Clarke, John, Stuart Hall, Tony Jefferson, and Brian Roberts. "Sub Cultures, Cultures and Class." In Tony Bennett, Graham Martin, Colin Mercer, and Janet Woollacott, eds., *Culture, Ideology and Social Process*. London: Batsford Academic and Educational, 1985.

Cobb, R. W., and C. D. Elder. *Participation in American Politics: The Dynamics of Agenda-Building*. 2d ed. Baltimore: Johns Hopkins University Press, 1983.

Cohen, Richard. "The Perils of Urban Living." *Washington Post*, 21 May 1989.

Cohen, Stanley. "The Punitive City: Notes on the Dispersal of Social Control." *Contemporary Crises* 3 (1979): 339–63.

———. *Visions of Social Control*. Cambridge, England: Polity Press, 1987.

Currie, Elliott. *Confronting Crime: An American Challenge*. New York: Pantheon, 1985.

Dahrendorf, Ralf. *Law and Order*. London: Stevens, 1985.

Dubow, Fred, Edward McCabe, and Gail Kaplan. *Reactions to Crime: A*

215

Review of the Literature. Washington D. C.: National Institute of Law Enforcement and Criminal Justice, 1979.

Edelman, Murray. *Constructing the Political Spectacle.* Chicago: University of Chicago Press, 1988.

———. *Political Language: Words That Succeed and Policies That Fail.* New York: Academic Press, 1977.

———. *The Symbolic Uses of Politics.* Champaign–Urbana: University of Illinois Press, 1967.

Ehrenreich, Barbara. *Fear of Falling: The Inner Life of the Middle Class.* New York: Pantheon, 1989.

Eisenstein, James, R. B. Flemming, and Peter Narduli. *The Contours of Justice: Communities and Their Courts.* Boston: Little, Brown, 1988.

Eisenstein, James, and Herbert Jacob. *Felony Justice: An Organizational Analysis of Criminal Courts.* Boston: Little, Brown, 1977.

Eyestone, Robert. *From Social Issues to Public Policy.* New York: John Wiley, 1978.

Fallen, D. L. *Sentencing Practice under the Sentencing Reform Act: Fiscal Year 1987.* Olympia, Wash.: Sentencing Guidelines Commission. Undated.

Feeley, M. M. *Court Reform on Trial: Why Simple Solutions Fail.* New York: Basic Books, 1983.

Feeley, M. M., and A. D. Sarat. *The Policy Dilemma: Federal Crime Policy and the Law Enforcement Assistance Administration, 1968–1978.* Minneapolis: University of Minnesota Press, 1980.

Fishman, Mark. "Crime Waves as Ideology." *Social Problems* 29 (1978): 31–43.

Foucault, Michel. *Discipline and Punish: The Birth of the Prison.* New York: Vintage, 1979.

Gardiner, J. A. *The Politics of Corruption: Organized Crime in an American City.* New York: Russell Sage Foundation, 1970.

Gaylin, Willard. *Partial Justice: A Study of Bias in Sentencing.* New York: Vintage, 1975.

Gerbner, George, and Larry Gross. "Living with Television: The Violence Profile." *Journal of Communications* 26 (1976): 173–97.

Gilder, George. *Wealth and Poverty.* New York: Bantam Books, 1982.

Gilliom, John. "Rights and Discipline: Competing Modes of Social Control in Supreme Court Decisions on Employee Drug Testing." Paper prepared for presentation at the annual meeting of the Law and Society Association, Madison, Wis., 9–11 June 1989.

Goldstein, Herman. *Problem-Oriented Policing.* Philadelphia: Temple University Press, 1990.

Gordon, Diana R. *The Justice Juggernaut: Fighting Street Crime, Controlling Citizens.* New Brunswick, N.J.: Rutgers University Press, 1990.

Greenberg, David F., and Drew Humphries. "The Cooptation of Fixed Sentencing Reform." *Crime and Delinquency* 26 (April 1980): 206–25.

Greene, Jack R., and Stephen D. Mastrofski, eds. *Community Policing: Rhetoric or Reality.* New York: Praeger, 1988.

Gressett, Lynne A., and Stuart A. Scheingold. "The Politics of Law and Order: Politicizing Amorphous Public Concerns." Paper prepared for delivery at the annual meeting of the American Political Science Association, Washington, D.C., 30 August–2 September 1984.

Gusfield, Joseph R. *The Symbolic Crusade: Status Politics and the American Temperance Movement.* Urbana: University of Illinois Press, 1963.

Hagan, John. *Structural Criminology.* Cambridge, England: Polity Press, 1988.

Hall, Stuart. "The Rise of the Representative/Interventionist State, 1880s–1920s." In Gregor McLennan, David Held, and Stuart Hall, *State and Society in Contemporary Britain.* Cambridge, England: Polity Press, 1984.

Hall, Stuart, Charles Critcher, Tony Jefferson, John Clarke, and Brian Roberts. *Policing the Crisis: Mugging, the State, and Law and Order.* London: Macmillan, 1978.

Hall, Stuart, and Phil Scraton. "Law, Class and Control." In Mike Fitzgerald, Gregory McLennan and Jennie Pawson, eds., *Crime and Society: Readings in History and Theory.* London: Routledge & Kegan Paul, 1985.

Hay, Douglas. "Property, Authority and the Criminal Law." In Douglas Hay, Peter Linebaugh, and E. P. Thompson, *Albion's Fatal Tree.* New York: Pantheon, 1975.

Hayler, Barbara. "Police Patrol Activity and the Definition of Public Order." Ph.D. dissertation, University of Washington, Seattle, 1984.

Heinz, Anne, Herbert Jacob, and Robert L. Lineberry, eds. *Crime in City Politics.* New York: Longman, 1983.

Jacob, Herbert. *The Frustrations of Policy: Responses to Crime by American Cities.* Boston: Little, Brown, 1984.

Jacob, Herbert, and Robert L. Lineberry. "Crime, Politics, and the Cities." In Anne Heinz, Herbert Jacob, and Robert L. Lineberry, eds., *Crime in City Politics.* New York: Longman, 1983.

Jacob, Herbert, Robert L. Lineberry, with Anne M. Heinz, Janice A. Beecher, Jack Moran, and Duanne H. Swank. *Governmental Re-Sponses to Crime: Crime on Urban Agendas.* Washington, D. C.: National Institute of Justice, 1982.

Jacobs, James B., and Laura Berkowitz. "Reflections on the Defeat of New York State's Prison Bond." In J. B. Jacobs, *New Perspectives on Prisons and Imprisonment.* Ithaca, N.Y.: Cornell University Press, 1983.

Jencks, Christopher. "Genes and Crime." *New York Review of Books,* 12 February 1987, 33–41.

Kelling, George L., and Mark H. Moore. "From Political to Reform to Community: The Evolving Strategy of Police." In Jack R. Greene and Stephen D. Mastrofski, eds., *Community Policing: Rhetoric or Reality.* New York: Praeger, 1988.

Kingdon, John. *Agendas, Alternatives, and Public Policy.* Boston: Little, Brown, 1984.

Klein, Stephen, Joan Petersilia, and Susan Turner. "Race and Imprisonment Decisions in California." *Science* 247 (16 February 1990): 812–16.

Klockars, Carl B. "The Rhetoric of Community Policing." In Jack R. Greene and Stephen D. Mastrofski, eds., *Community Policing: Rhetoric or Reality*. New York: Praeger, 1988.

Lasch, Christopher. *The Culture of Narcissism: American Life in an Age of Diminishing Expectations*. New York: Warner Books, 1979.

Lasswell, Harold. *World Politics and Personal Insecurity*. New York: McGraw-Hill, 1935.

Lewis, Peter. "Justice Systems Facing Cash Crisis." *Seattle Times*, 4 April 1990.

Lipsky, Michael. *Street-Level Bureaucracy: Dilemmas of the Individual in Public Service*. New York: Russell Sage Foundation, 1980.

Littrell, W. Boyd. *Bureaucratic Justice: Police, Prosecutors, and Plea Bargaining*. Beverly Hills, Calif.: Sage, 1979.

Loh, W. D. "The Impact of Common Law and Reform Rape Statutes on Prosecution: An Empirical Study." *Washington Law Review* 55 (1980): 543–652.

Manning, Peter K. "Community Policing as a Drama of Control." In Jack R. Greene and Stephen D. Mastrofski. *Community Policing: Rhetoric or Reality*. New York: Praeger, 1988.

Mastrofski, Stephen D. "Community Policing as Reform: A Cautionary Tale. In Jack R. Greene and Stephen D. Mastrofski, *Community Policing: Rhetoric or Reality*. New York: Praeger, 1988.

Maynard, Douglas W. "Defendant Attributes in Plea Bargaining: Notes on the Modeling of Sentencing Decisions." *Social Problems* 29 (1988): 347–60.

Muir, William K., Jr. *Police: Streetcorner Politicians*. Chicago: University of Chicago Press, 1977.

Myers-Jones, Holly J. "A Geographical Analysis of Political Opposition to Busing in [Cedar City]." M.A. thesis, University of Washington, Seattle, 1980.

Packer, Herbert L. *The Limits of the Criminal Sanction*. Stanford: Stanford University Press, 1968.

Pillsbury, Samuel H. "Understanding Penal Reform: The Dynamics of Change." *Journal of Criminal Law and Criminology* 80 (1989): 726–89.

Quinney, Richard. *Class, State and Crime*. 2d ed. New York: Longman, 1980.

———. *Critique of Legal Order: Crime Control in Capitalist Society*. Boston: Little, Brown, 1974.

Reiss, Albert J. *The Police and the Public*. New Haven: Yale University Press, 1971.

Rhodes, Susan L. "State Policy-Makers and the 'Get Tough' Movement: The Politics of Prison Building and the Prison Overcrowding Crisis in California." Paper prepared for presentation at the annual meeting of the Law and Society Association, Madison, Wis., 9–11 June 1989.

Rothschild, Emma. "The Reagan Economic Legacy." *New York Review of Books*, 21 July 1988, 33–41.

Rose, Stephen, and David Fasenfest. *Family Incomes in the 1980s: New Pressures on Wives, Husbands, and Young Adults*. Working Paper No. 103. Washington, D.C.: Economic Policy Institute, 1988.

Rubenstein, Jonathan. *City Police.* New York: Ballantine, 1973.

Rubin, Lillian B. *Quiet Rage: Bernie Goetz in a Time of Madness.* Berkeley: University of California Press, 1988.

Scheingold, Stuart A. *The Politics of Law and Order: Street Crime and Public Policy.* New York: Longman, 1984.

Scheingold, Stuart A., and Lynne A. Gressett. "Policy, Politics, and the Criminal Courts." *American Bar Foundation Research Journal* (1987): 461–505.

———. "The Politics of Police Policy Making." Paper prepared for delivery at the 1985 annual meeting of the Law and Society Association, San Diego, Calif., 6–9 June 1985.

Sennett, Richard, and Jonathan Cobb. *The Hidden Injuries of Class.* New York: Vintage, 1972.

Silberman, Charles. *Criminal Violence, Criminal Justice.* New York: Random House, 1978.

Skogan, Wesley G. "Community Organizations and Crime." In Michael Tonry and Norval Morris, eds., *Crime and Justice.* Chicago: University of Chicago Press, 1988.

———. "Fear of Crime and Neighborhood Change." In A. J. Reiss, Jr., and Michael Tonry, eds., *Communities and Crime.* Chicago: University of Chicago Press. 1986.

Skogan, Wesley G., and M. G. Maxfield. *Coping with Crime: Individual and Neighborhood Reactions.* Beverly Hills, Calif.: Sage, 1981.

Skolnick, Jerome H., and D. H. Bayley. *The New Blue Line: Police Innovation in Six American Cities.* New York: Free Press, 1986.

Spohn, Cassia, John Gruhl, and Susan Welch. "The Effect of Race on Sentencing: A Re-Examination of an Unsettled Question." *Law and Society Review* 16 (1981–1982): 83–85.

Stauffenberger, Richard A., ed. *Progress in Policing: Essays on Change.* Cambridge, Mass.: Ballinger, 1980.

Stinchcombe, Arthur L., Rebecca Adams, Carol A. Heimer, Kim L. Scheppele, T. W. Smith, and D. G. Taylor. *Crime and Punishment— Changing Attitudes in America.* San Francisco: Jossey-Bass, 1980.

Sudnow, David. "Normal Crimes: Sociological Features of the Penal Code in a Public Defender's Office." *Social Problems* 12, no. 255 (1965): 255–76.

Taft, Phillip B., Jr. "Tony Bouza of Minneapolis: Is He a Reform Chief or a Flake?" *Police Magazine,* January 1982, 19–28.

Thompson, E. P. *Albion's Fatal Tree.* New York: Pantheon, 1975.

Thurow, Lester C. *The Zero-Sum Society: Distribution and the Possibilities for Economic Change.* New York: Penguin Books, 1980.

Tonry, Michael H. *Sentencing Reform Impacts.* Washington, D.C.: National Institute of Justice, 1987.

Vera Institute of Justice. *Felony Arrests: Their Prosecution and Disposition in New York City's Courts.* Rev. ed. New York: Longman, 1981.

Von Hirsch, Andrew. *Doing Justice: Report of the Committee for the Study of Incarceration.* New York: Hill & Wang, 1976.

———. *Past or Future Crimes: Deservedness and Dangerousness in the Sentencing of Criminals.* New Brunswick, N.J.: Rutgers University Press, 1987.

Walker, Samuel. *Sense and Nonsense about Crime*. 2d ed. Pacific Grove, Calif.: Brooks/Cole, 1989.

Wiebe, Robert H. *The Search for Order, 1877–1920*. New York: Hill & Wang, 1967.

Will, George. "Rape and Beatings, Just for Fun." *Seattle Times*, 30 April 1989.

Wilson, James Q. *Thinking about Crime*. New York: Vintage, 1977.

———. *Thinking about Crime*. Rev. ed. New York: Vintage, 1985.

———. *Varieties of Police Behavior: The Management of Law and Order in Eight Communities*. New York: Atheneum, 1968.

Wilson, James Q., and Richard J. Herrnstein. *Crime and Human Nature: The Definitive Study of the Causes of Crime*. New York: Simon and Schuster, 1985.

Wilson, William J. *The Truly Disadvantaged: The Inner City, the Underclass and Public Policy*. Chicago: University of Chicago Press, 1987.

Index

Those names followed by a description of roles in parentheses are pseudonyms.